SCIENCE.
BAD.

JONATHAN HICKMAN
WRITER

NICK PITARRA
ARTIST

JORDIE BELLAIRE
COLORS

RUS WOOTON
LETTERS

WITH
RYAN BROWNE
ARTIST (CHAPTER 19)

IMAGE COMICS, INC.
Robert Kirkman – Chief Operating Officer
Erik Larsen – Chief Financial Officer
Todd McFarlane – President
Marc Silvestri – Chief Executive Officer
Jim Valentino – Vice-President
Eric Stephenson – Publisher
Ron Richards – Director of Business Development
Jennifer de Guzman – Director of Trade Book Sales
Kat Salazar – Director of PR & Marketing
Jeremy Sullivan – Director of Digital Sales
Emilio Bautista – Sales Assistant
Branwyn Bigglestone – Senior Accounts Manager
Emily Miller – Accounts Manager
Jessica Ambriz – Administrative Assistant
Tyler Shainline – Events Coordinator
David Brothers – Content Manager
Jonathan Chan – Production Manager
Drew Gill – Art Director
Meredith Wallace – Print Manager
Monica Garcia – Senior Production Artist
Jenna Savage – Production Artist
Addison Duke – Production Artist
Tricia Ramos – Production Assistant
IMAGECOMICS.COM

THE MANHATTAN PROJECTS, VOLUME 4
First Printing / May 2014 / ISBN: 978-1-60706-961-4

MP

THE MANHATTAN PROJECTS

4

IT'S WORSE THAN I THOUGHT

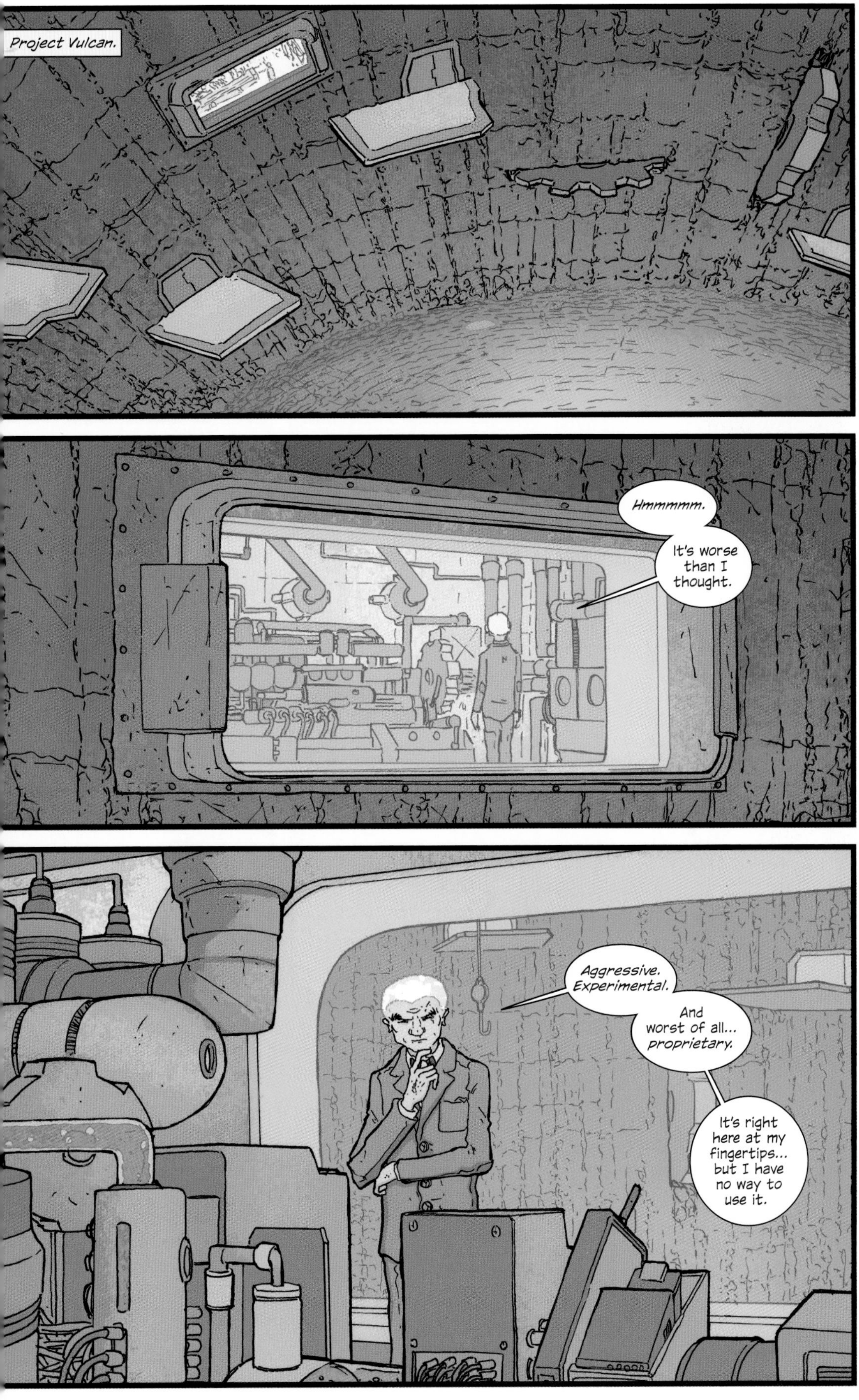

Project Vulcan.
Hmmmmm.
It's worse than I thought.
Aggressive. Experimental.
And worst of all... proprietary.
It's right here at my fingertips... but I have no way to use it.

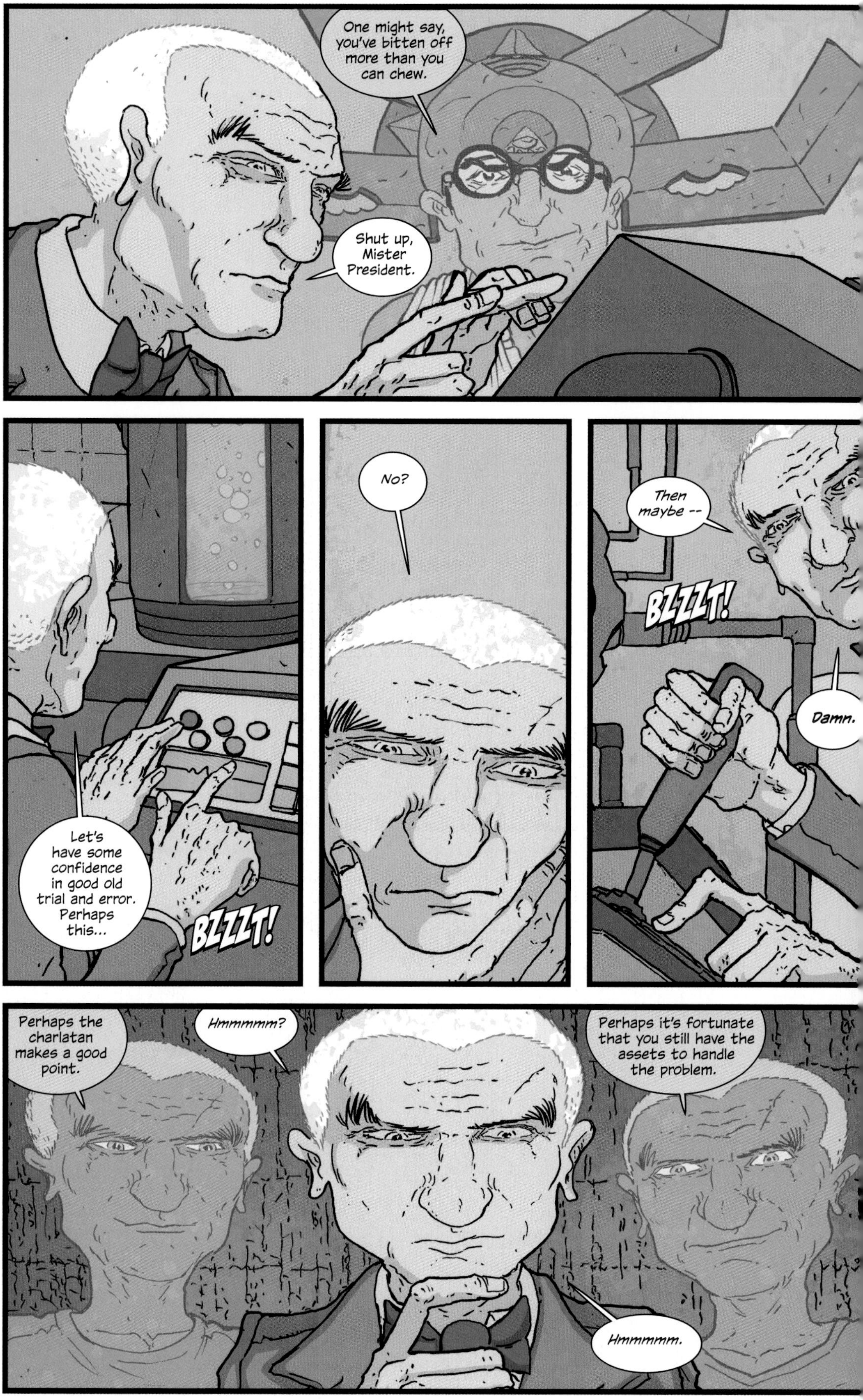
One might say, you've bitten off more than you can chew.
Shut up, Mister President.
Let's have some confidence in good old trial and error. Perhaps this...
BZZZT!
No?
Then maybe --
BZZZT!
Damn.
Perhaps the charlatan makes a good point.
Hmmmmm?
Perhaps it's fortunate that you still have the assets to handle the problem.
Hmmmmm.

"PROJECT VULCAN FED INTO PROJECT CHARON. IN RETROSPECT, IT WAS BORN FROM RUIN."

CLAVIS AUREA
THE RECORDED FEYNMAN | **VOL. 4**

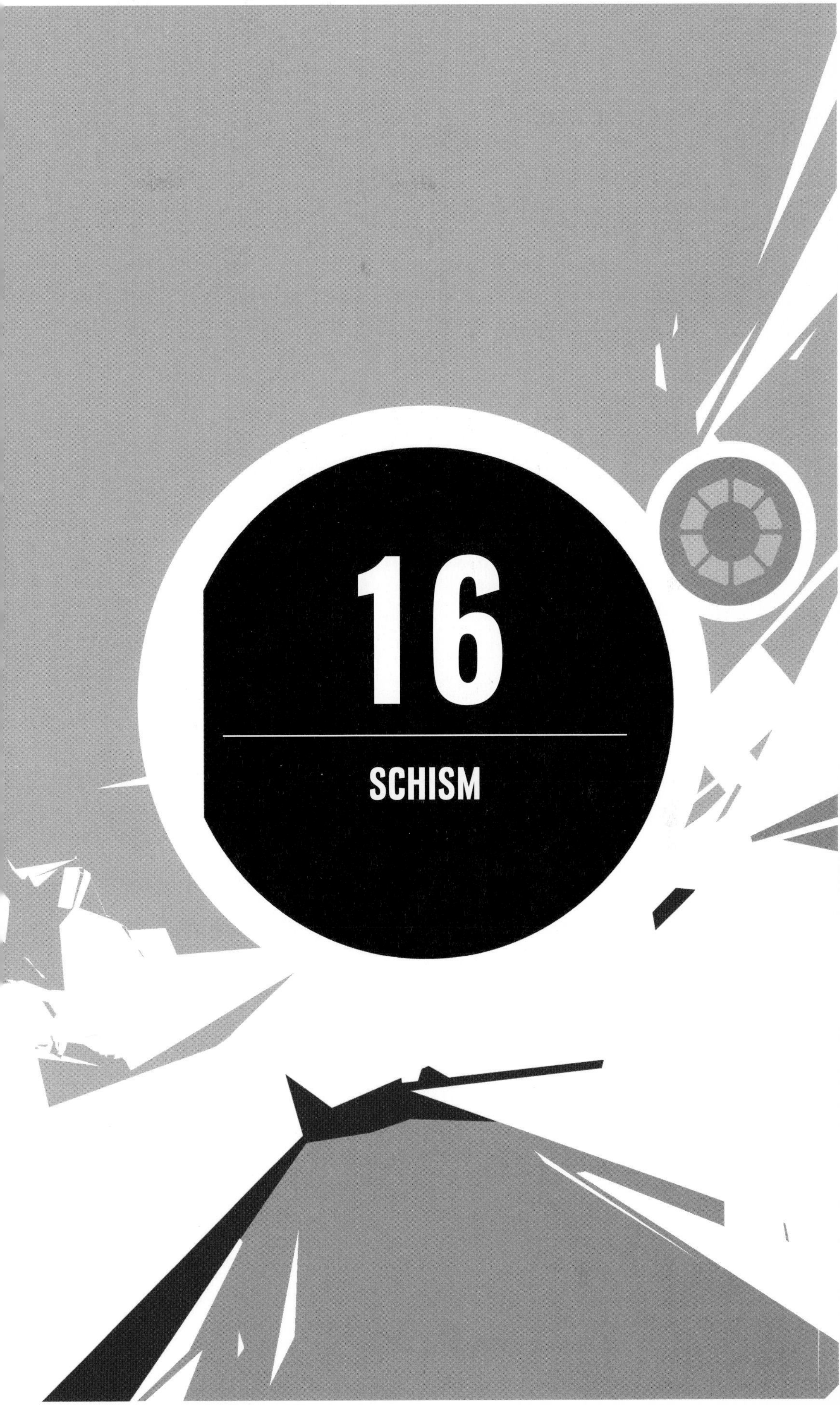

16

SCHISM

"PROJECT GAIA FED INTO PROJECT CHARON. IN RETROSPECT, IT WAS BORN FROM RUIN."

CLAVIS AUREA
THE RECORDED FEYNMAN | **VOL. 4**

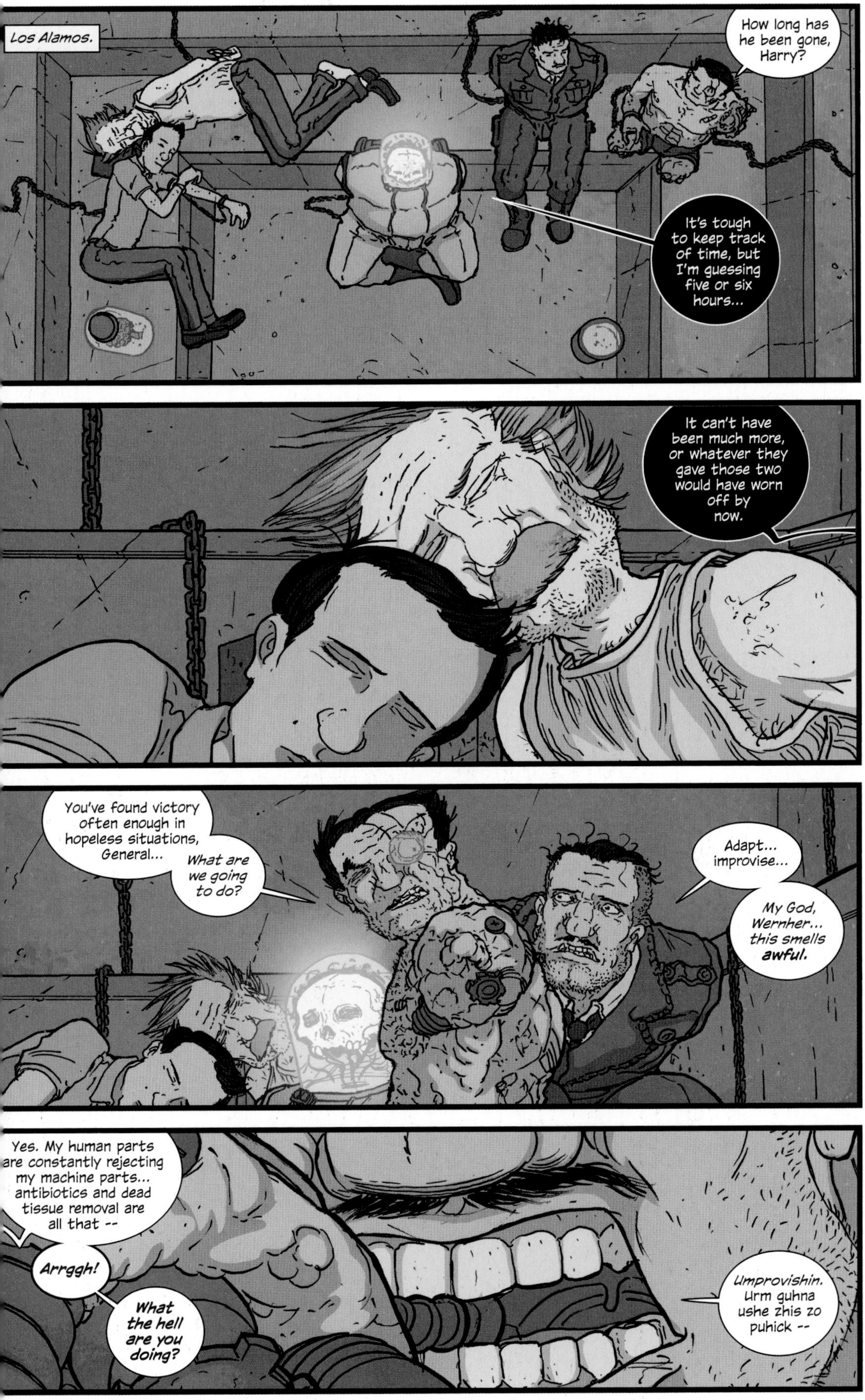
Los Alamos.
How long has he been gone, Harry?
It's tough to keep track of time, but I'm guessing five or six hours...
It can't have been much more, or whatever they gave those two would have worn off by now.
You've found victory often enough in hopeless situations, General...
What are we going to do?
Adapt... improvise...
My God, Wernher... this smells awful.
Yes. My human parts are constantly rejecting my machine parts... antibiotics and dead tissue removal are all that --
Arrggh!
What the hell are you doing?
Umprovishin. Urm guhna ushe zhis zo puhick --

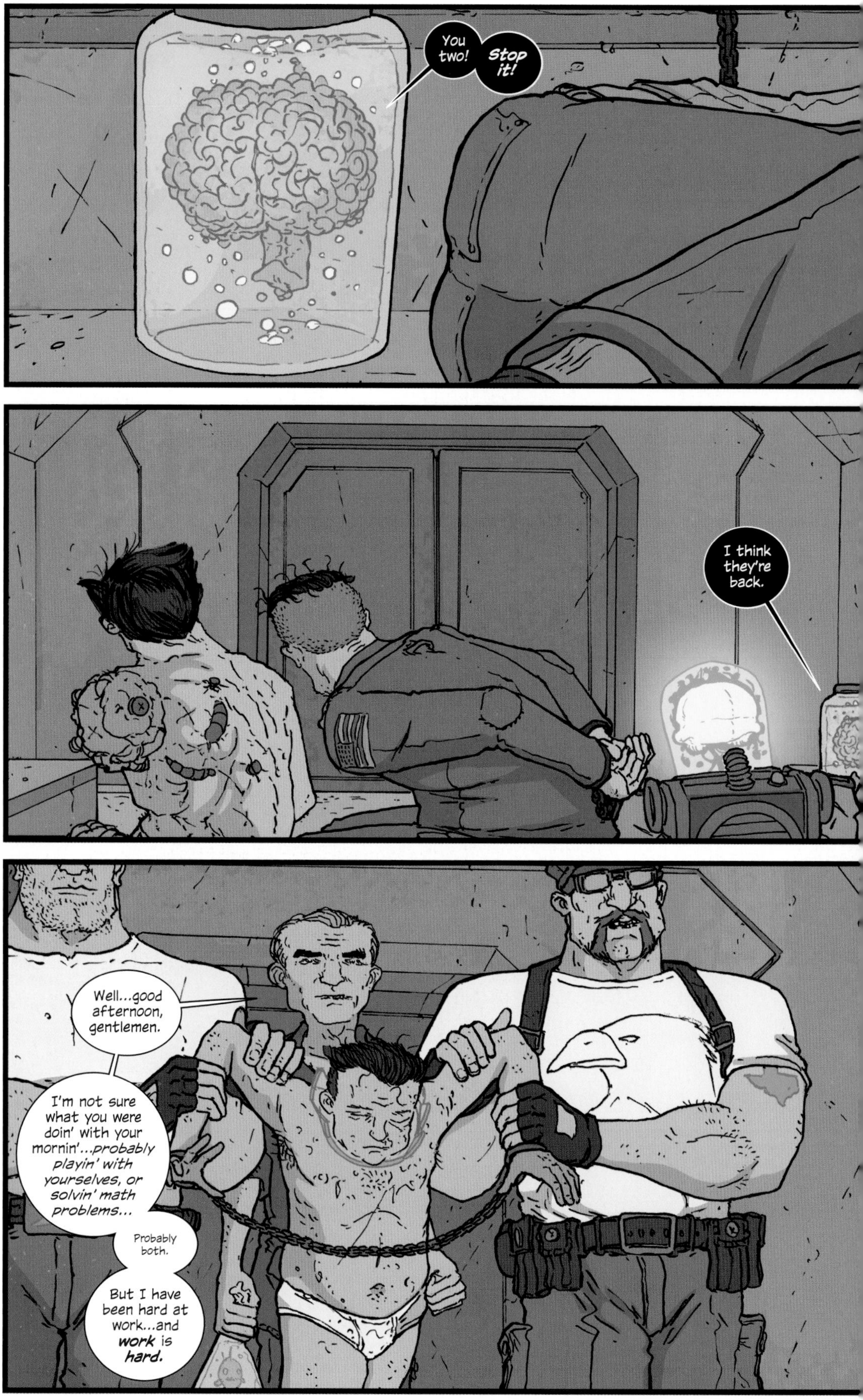
You two!
Stop it!
I think they're back.
Well...good afternoon, gentlemen.
I'm not sure what you were doin' with your mornin'...probably playin' with yourselves, or solvin' math problems...
Probably both.
But I have been hard at work...and work is hard.

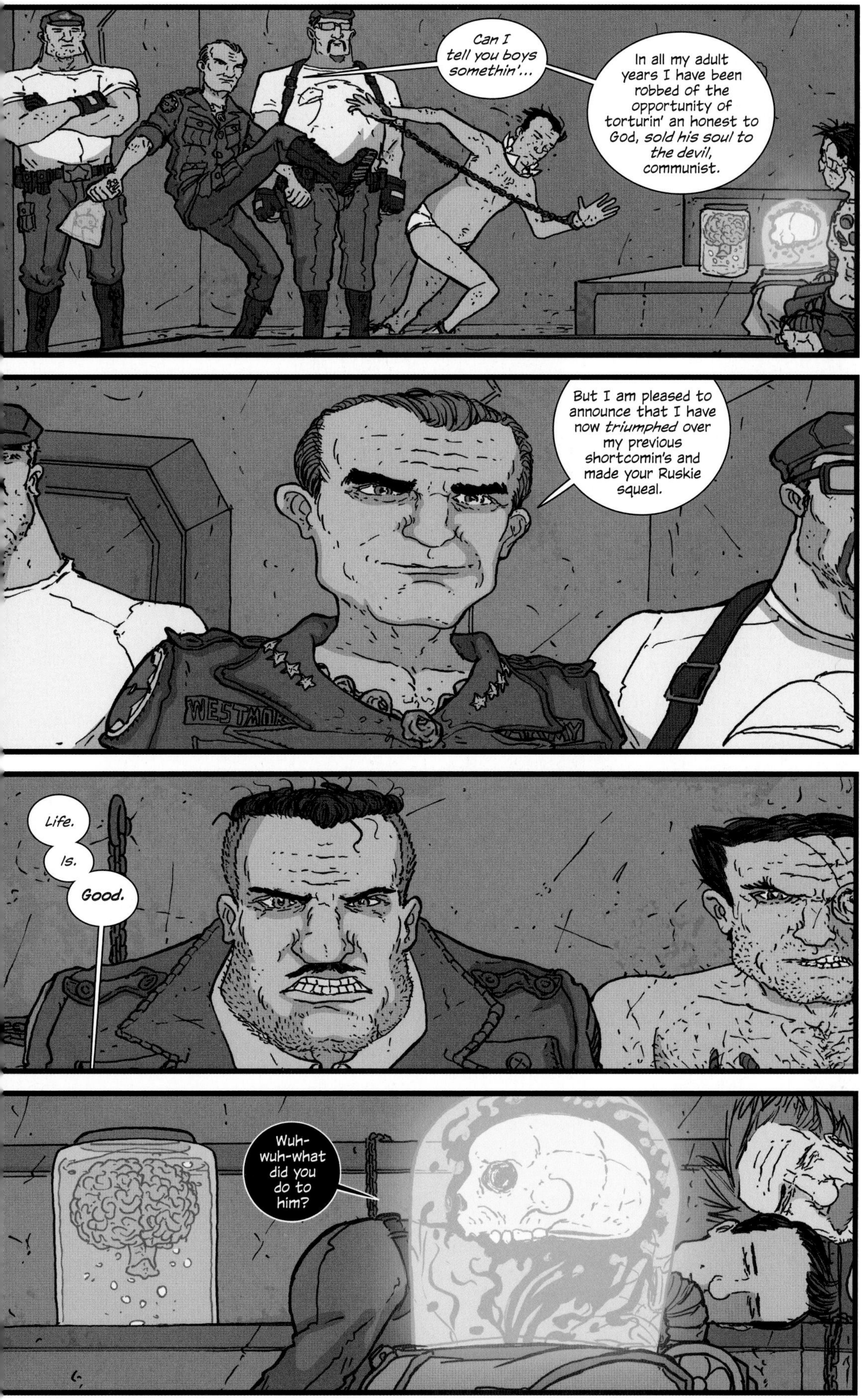
Can I tell you boys somethin'...
In all my adult years I have been robbed of the opportunity of torturin' an honest to God, *sold his soul to the devil,* communist.
But I am pleased to announce that I have now *triumphed* over my previous shortcomin's and made your Ruskie squeal.
WESTMO
Life.
Is.
Good.
Wuh-wuh-what did you do to him?

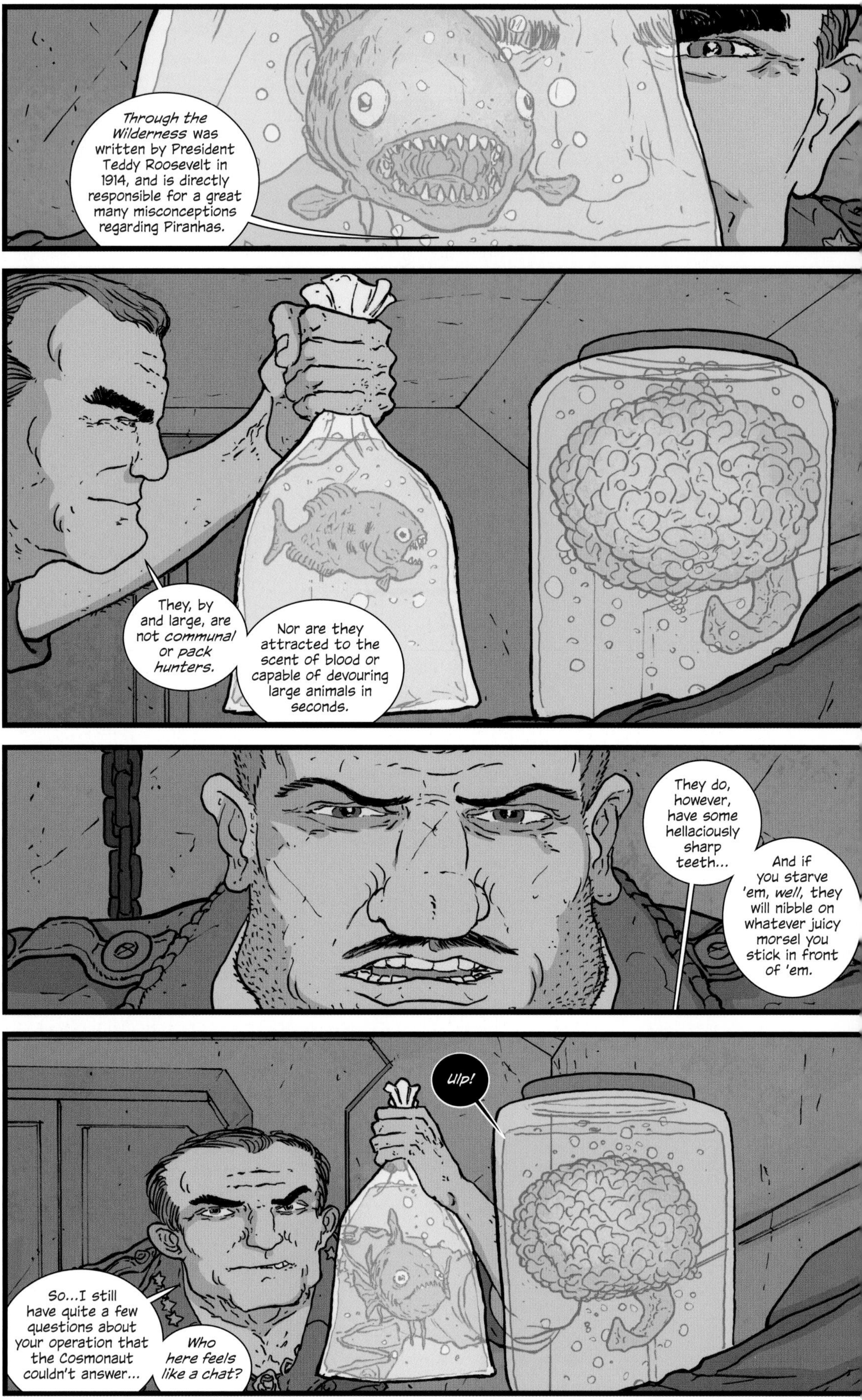
Through the Wilderness was written by President Teddy Roosevelt in 1914, and is directly responsible for a great many misconceptions regarding Piranhas.
They, by and large, are not *communal* or *pack hunters.*
Nor are they attracted to the scent of blood or capable of devouring large animals in seconds.
They do, however, have some hellaciously sharp teeth...
And if you starve 'em, *well,* they will nibble on whatever juicy morsel you stick in front of 'em.
Ulp!
So...I still have quite a few questions about your operation that the Cosmonaut couldn't answer...
Who here feels like a chat?

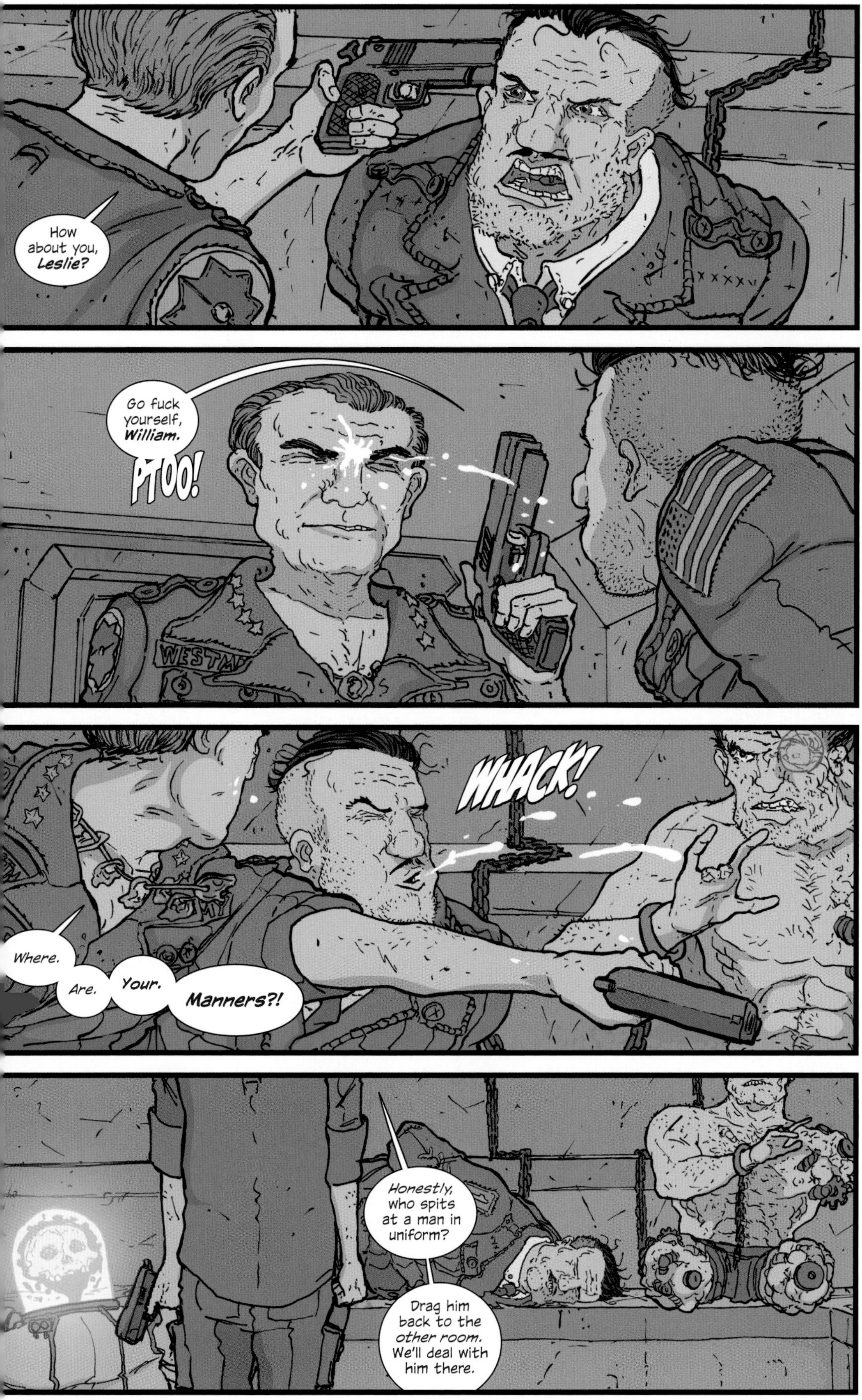

How about you, Leslie?
Go fuck yourself, William.
PTOO!
WHACK!
Where.
Are.
Your.
Manners?!
Honestly, who spits at a man in uniform?
Drag him back to the other room. We'll deal with him there.

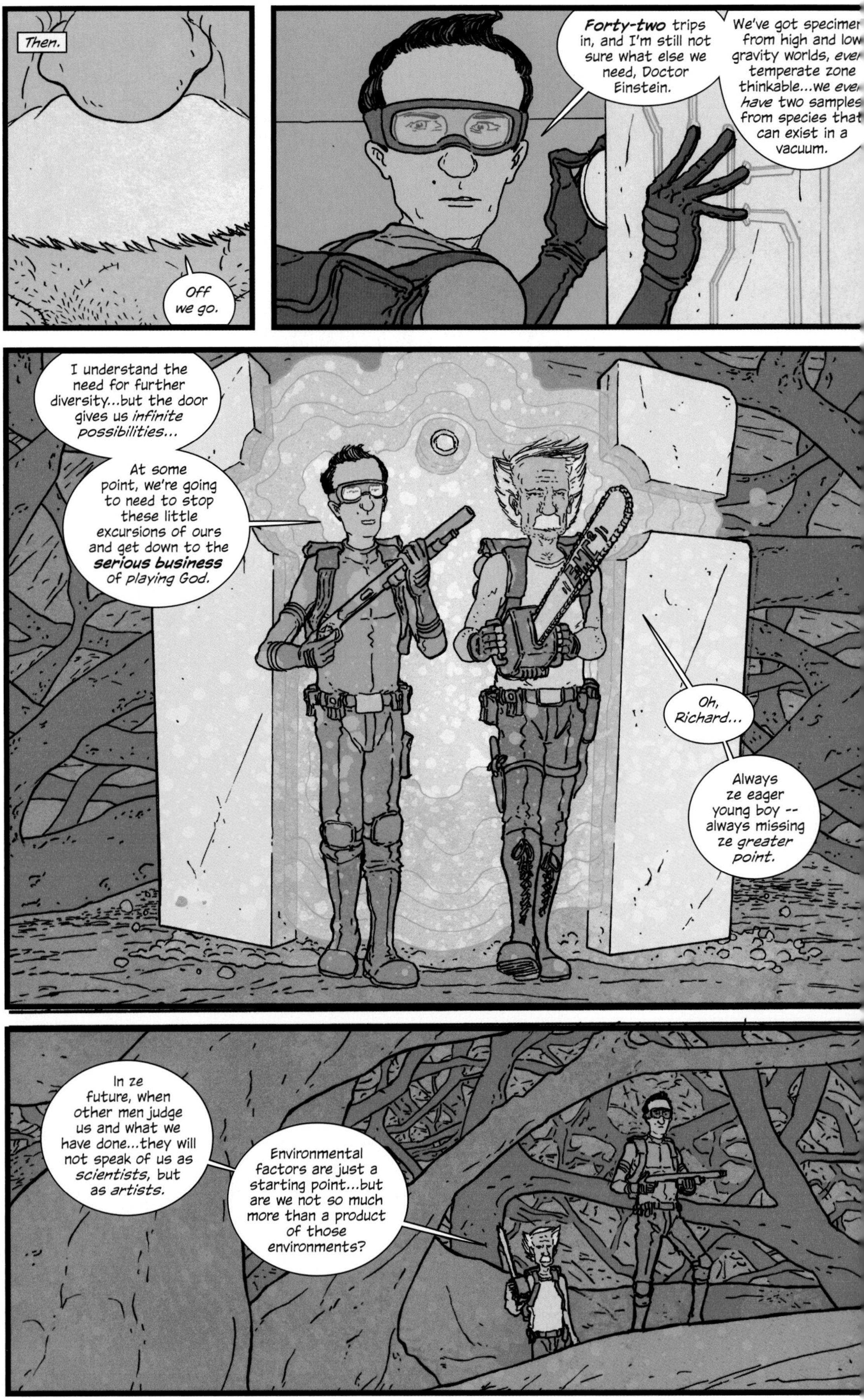

Then.
Off we go.
Forty-two trips in, and I'm still not sure what else we need, Doctor Einstein.
We've got specimen from high and low gravity worlds, ever temperate zone thinkable...we even have two samples from species that can exist in a vacuum.
I understand the need for further diversity...but the door gives us infinite possibilities...
At some point, we're going to need to stop these little excursions of ours and get down to the serious business of playing God.
Oh, Richard...
Always ze eager young boy -- always missing ze greater point.
In ze future, when other men judge us and what we have done...they will not speak of us as scientists, but as artists.
Environmental factors are just a starting point...but are we not so much more than a product of those environments?

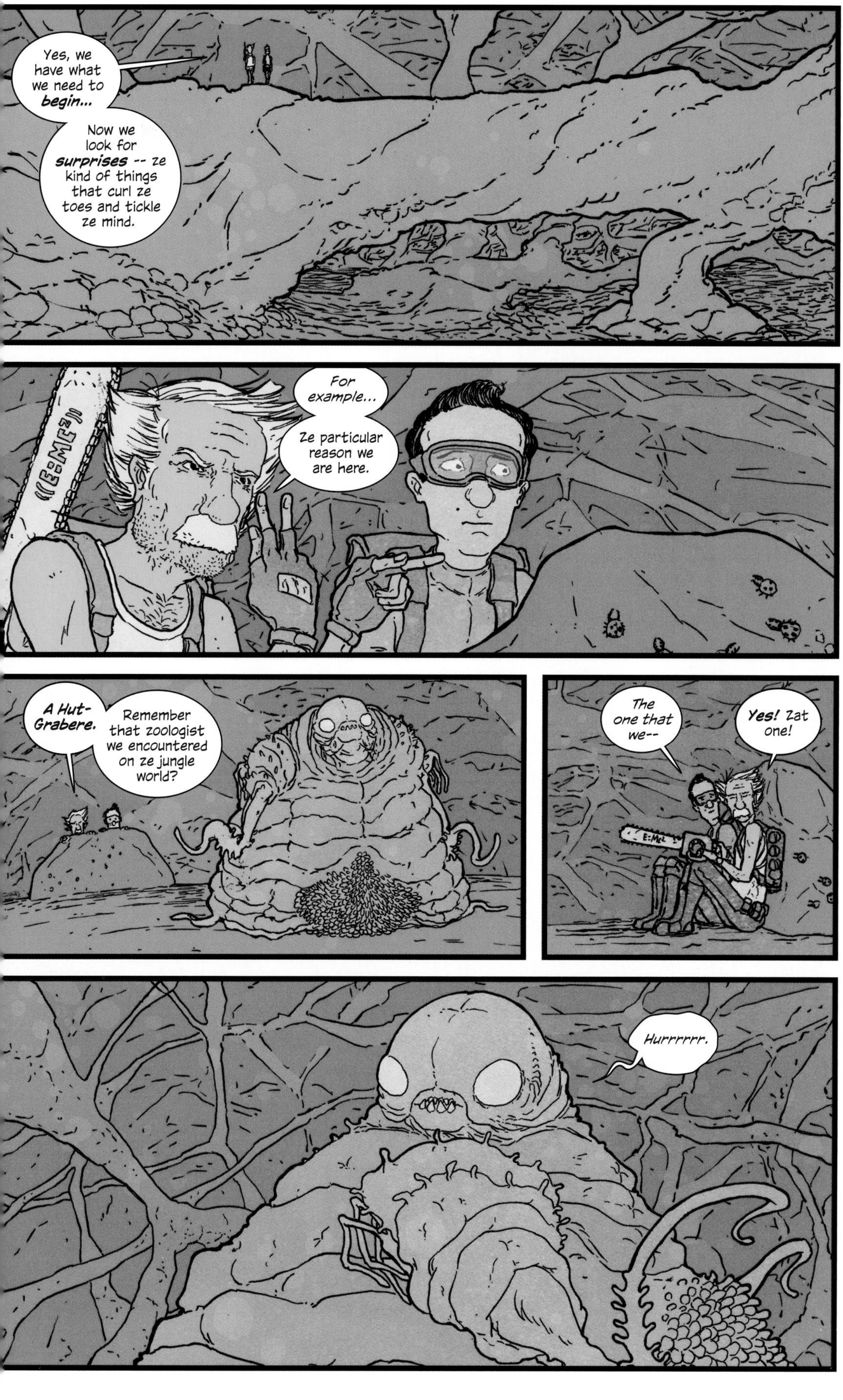
Yes, we have what we need to *begin...*
Now we look for *surprises* -- ze kind of things that curl ze toes and tickle ze mind.
For example...
Ze particular reason we are here.
E=MC²
A Hut-Grabere.
Remember that zoologist we encountered on ze jungle world?
The one that we--
Yes! Zat one!
E=MC²
Hurrrrrr.

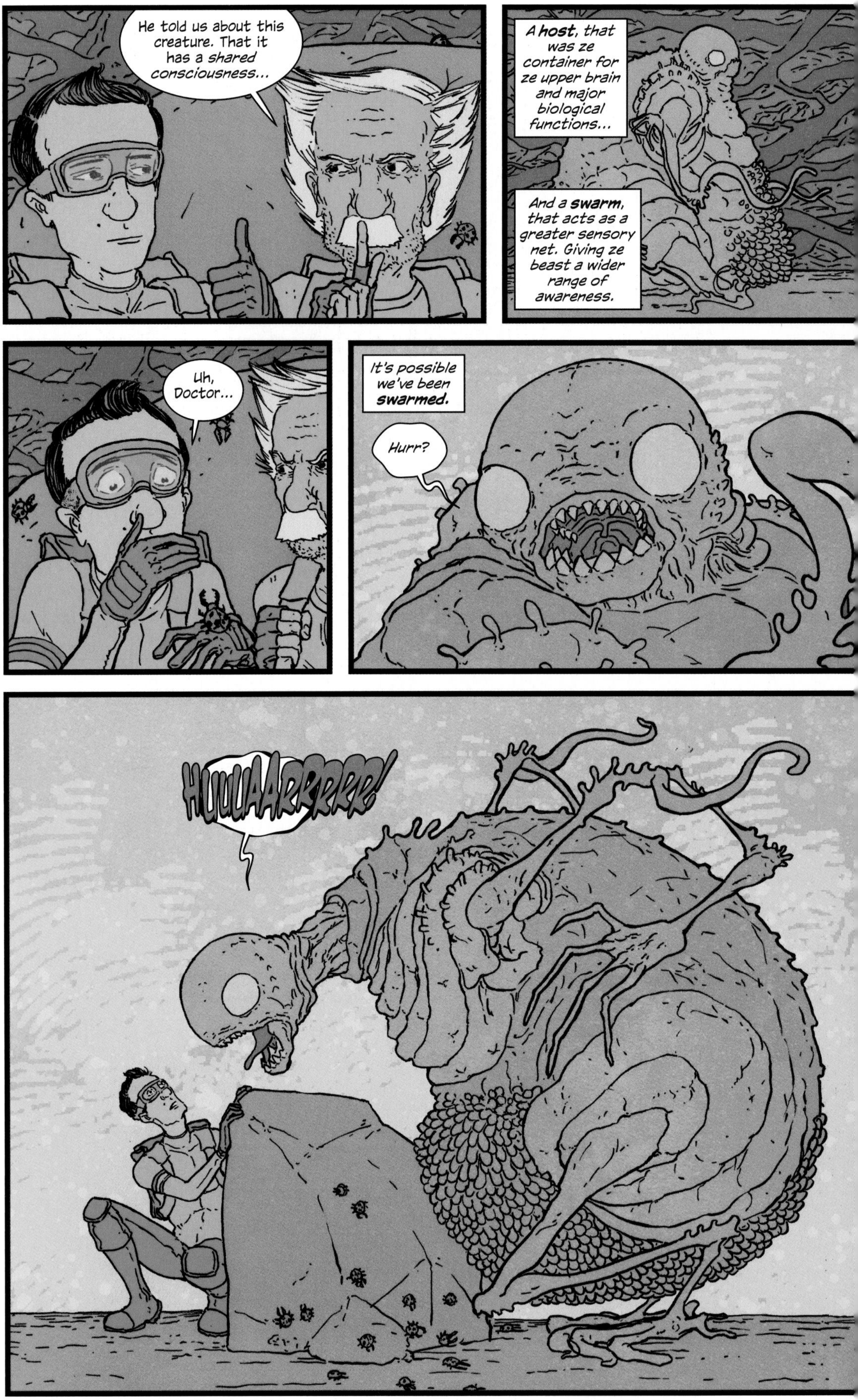
He told us about this creature. That it has a *shared* consciousness...
A **host**, that was ze container for ze upper brain and major biological functions...
And a **swarm**, that acts as a greater sensory net. Giving ze beast a wider range of awareness.
Uh, Doctor...
It's possible we've been **swarmed.**
Hurr?
HUUUAARRRRR!

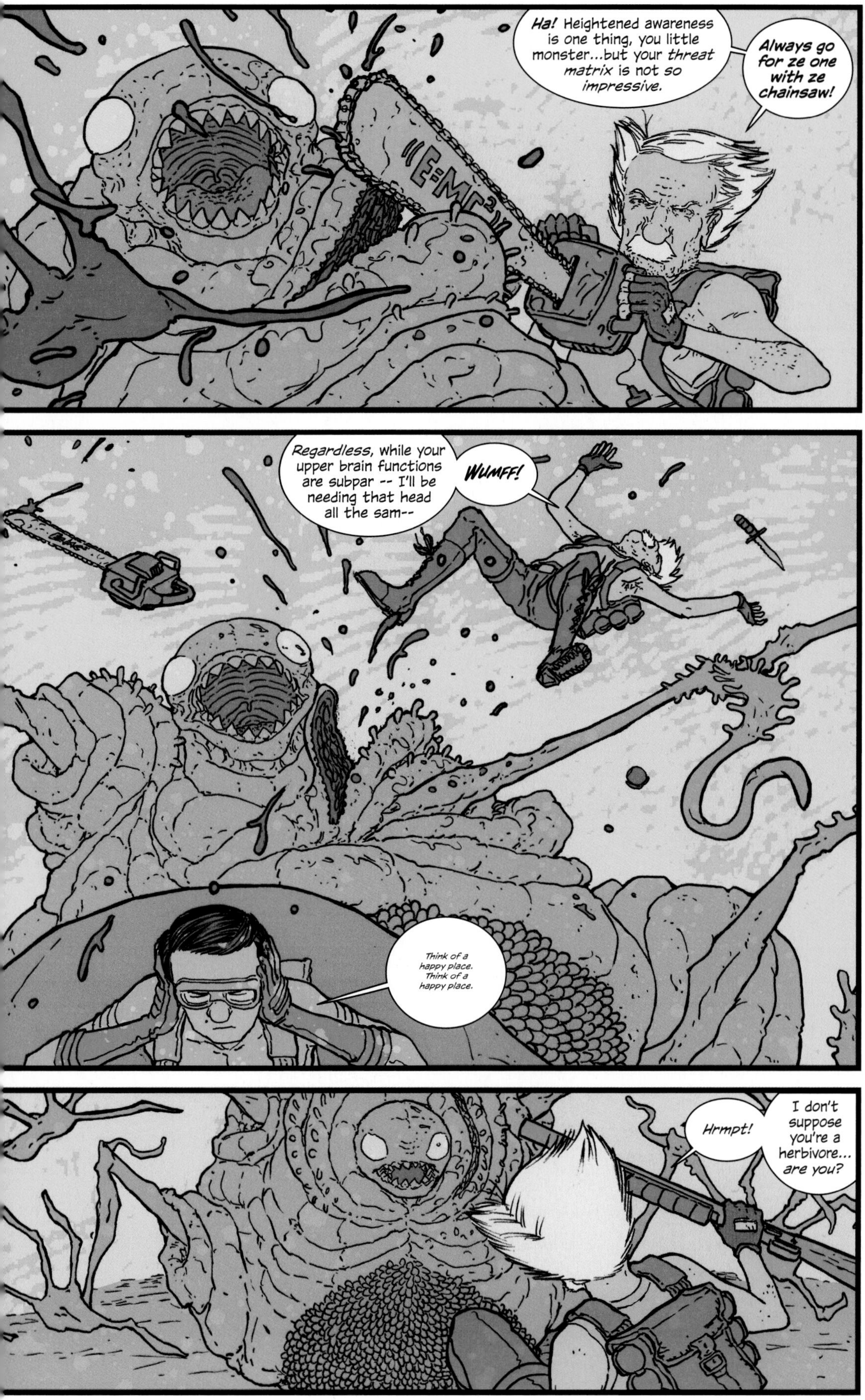

Ha! Heightened awareness is one thing, you little monster...but your *threat matrix* is not so *impressive.*
Always go for ze one with ze chainsaw!
"E=MC²"
Regardless, while your upper brain functions are subpar -- I'll be needing that head all the sam--
WUMFF!
Think of a happy place. Think of a happy place.
Hrmpt!
I don't suppose you're a herbivore... *are you?*

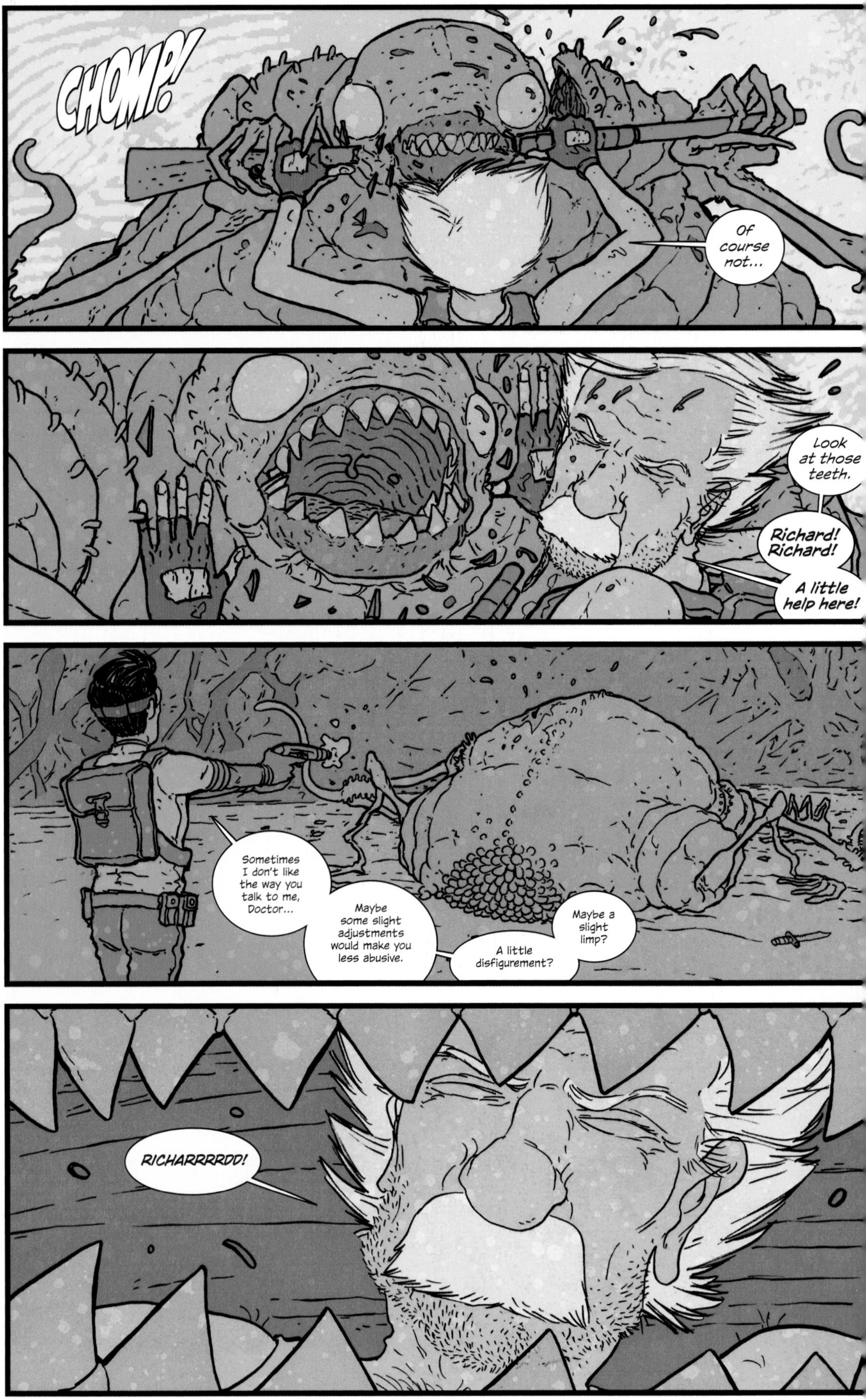
CHOMP!
Of course not...
Look at those teeth.
Richard! Richard!
A little help here!
Sometimes I don't like the way you talk to me, Doctor...
Maybe some slight adjustments would make you less abusive.
A little disfigurement?
Maybe a slight limp?
RICHARRRRDD!

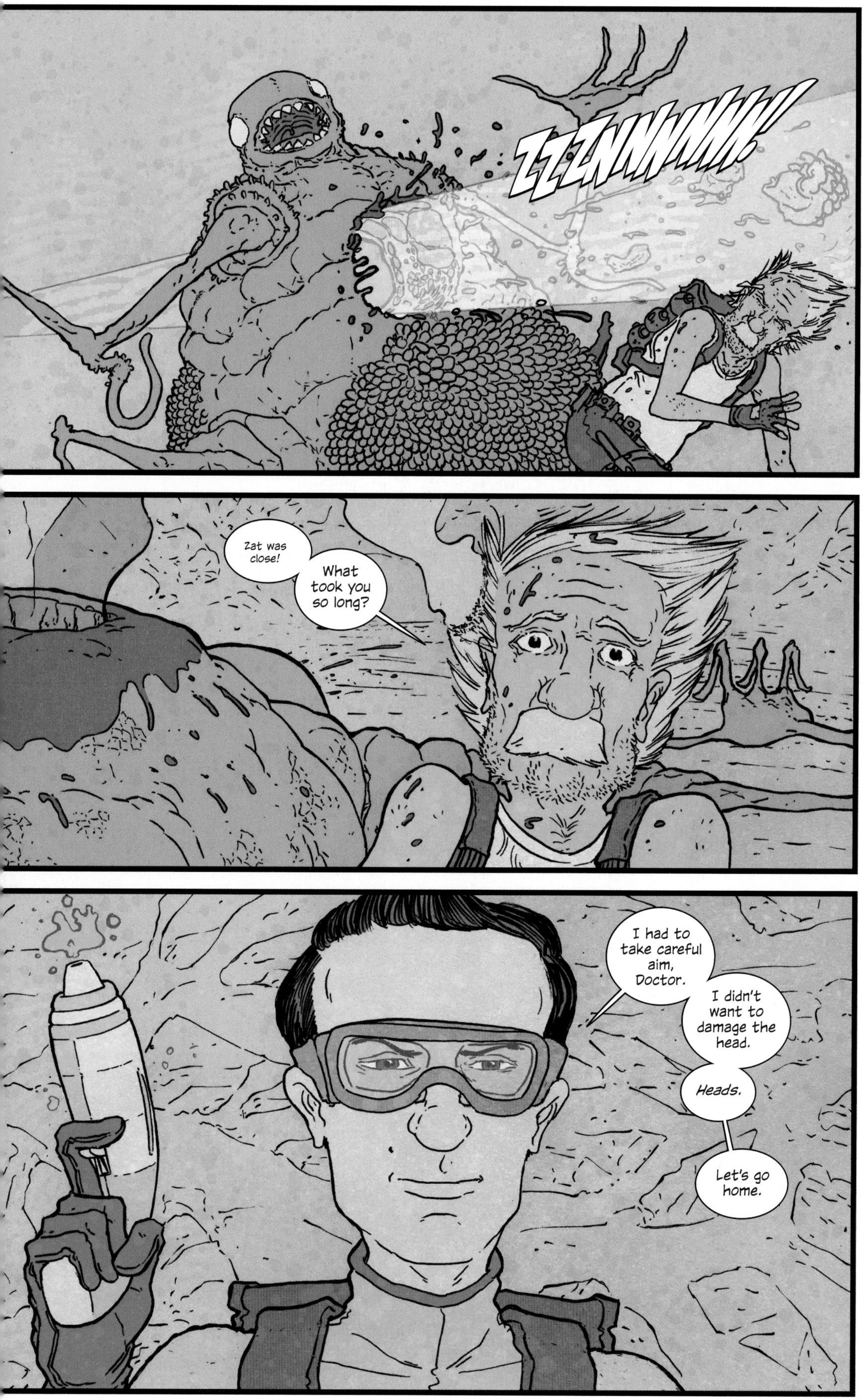
ZZZNNNNNNK!
Zat was close!
What took you so long?
I had to take careful aim, Doctor.
I didn't want to damage the head.
Heads.
Let's go home.

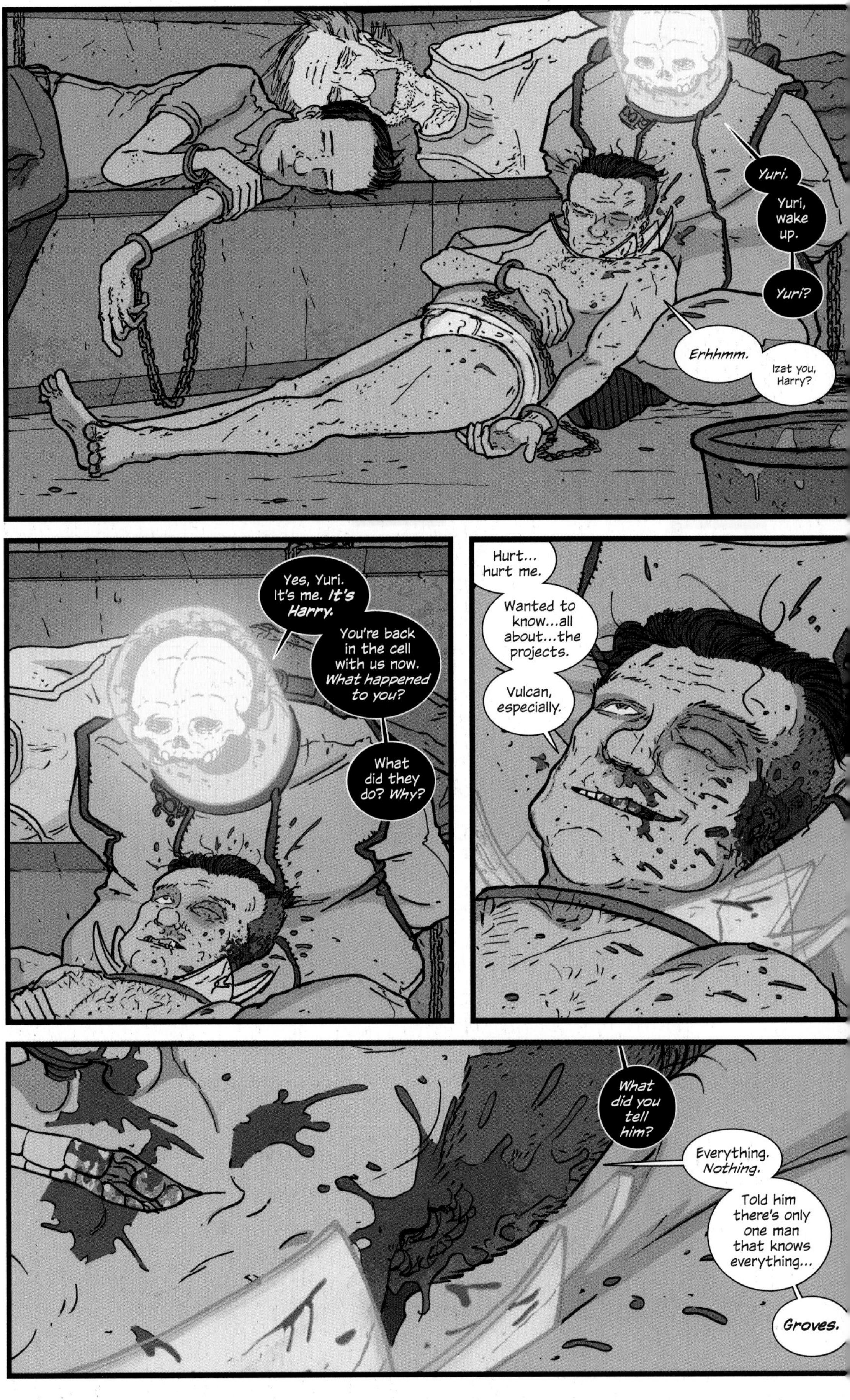

Yuri.
Yuri, wake up.
Yuri?
Erhhmm.
Izat you, Harry?
Yes, Yuri. It's me. It's Harry.
You're back in the cell with us now. What happened to you?
What did they do? Why?
Hurt... hurt me.
Wanted to know...all about...the projects.
Vulcan, especially.
What did you tell him?
Everything. Nothing.
Told him there's only one man that knows everything...
Groves.

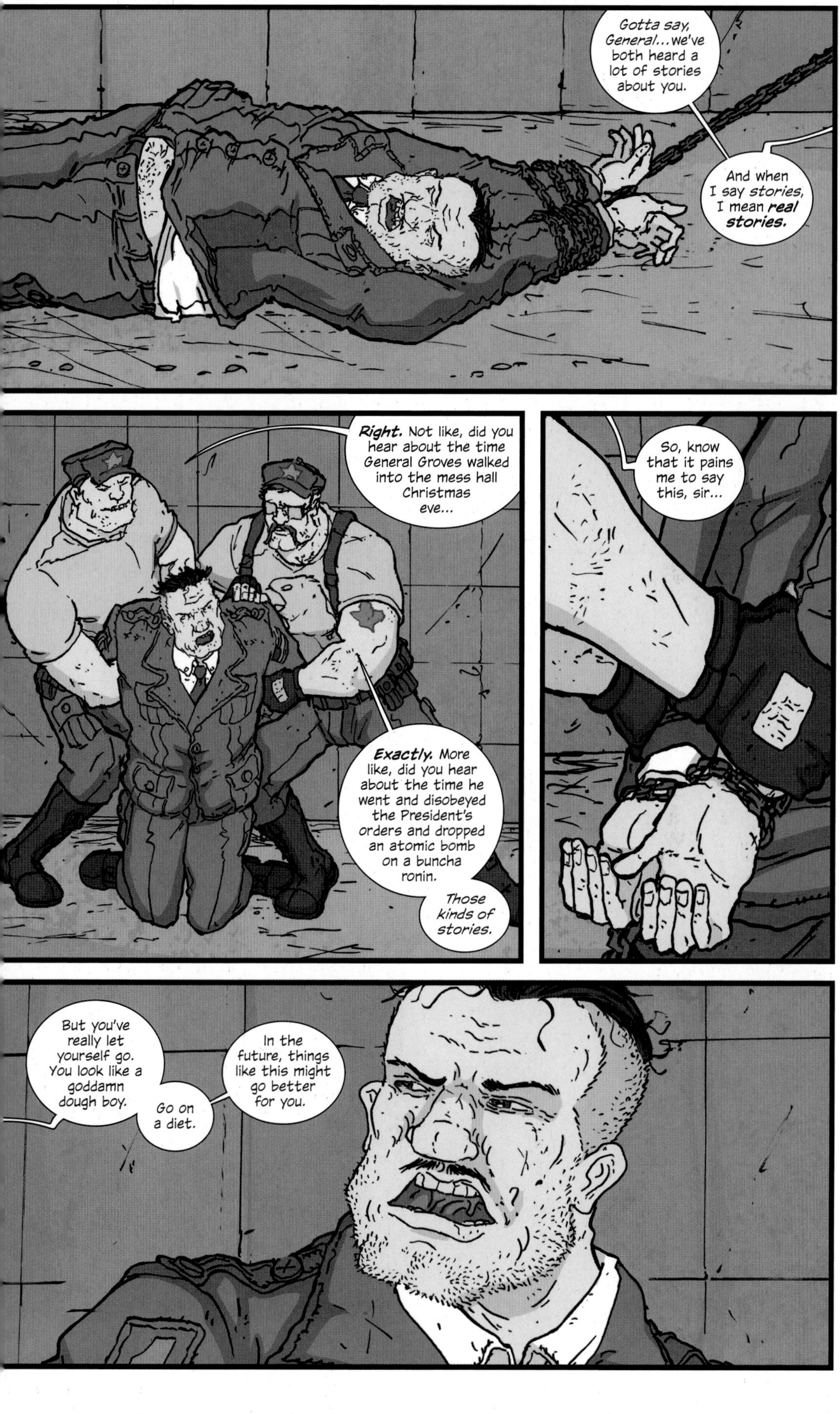
Gotta say, General...we've both heard a lot of stories about you.
And when I say *stories,* I mean ***real stories.***
Right. Not like, did you hear about the time General Groves walked into the mess hall Christmas eve...
Exactly. More like, did you hear about the time he went and disobeyed the President's orders and dropped an atomic bomb on a buncha ronin.
Those kinds of stories.
So, know that it pains me to say this, sir...
But you've really let yourself go. You look like a goddamn dough boy.
Go on a diet.
In the future, things like this might go better for you.

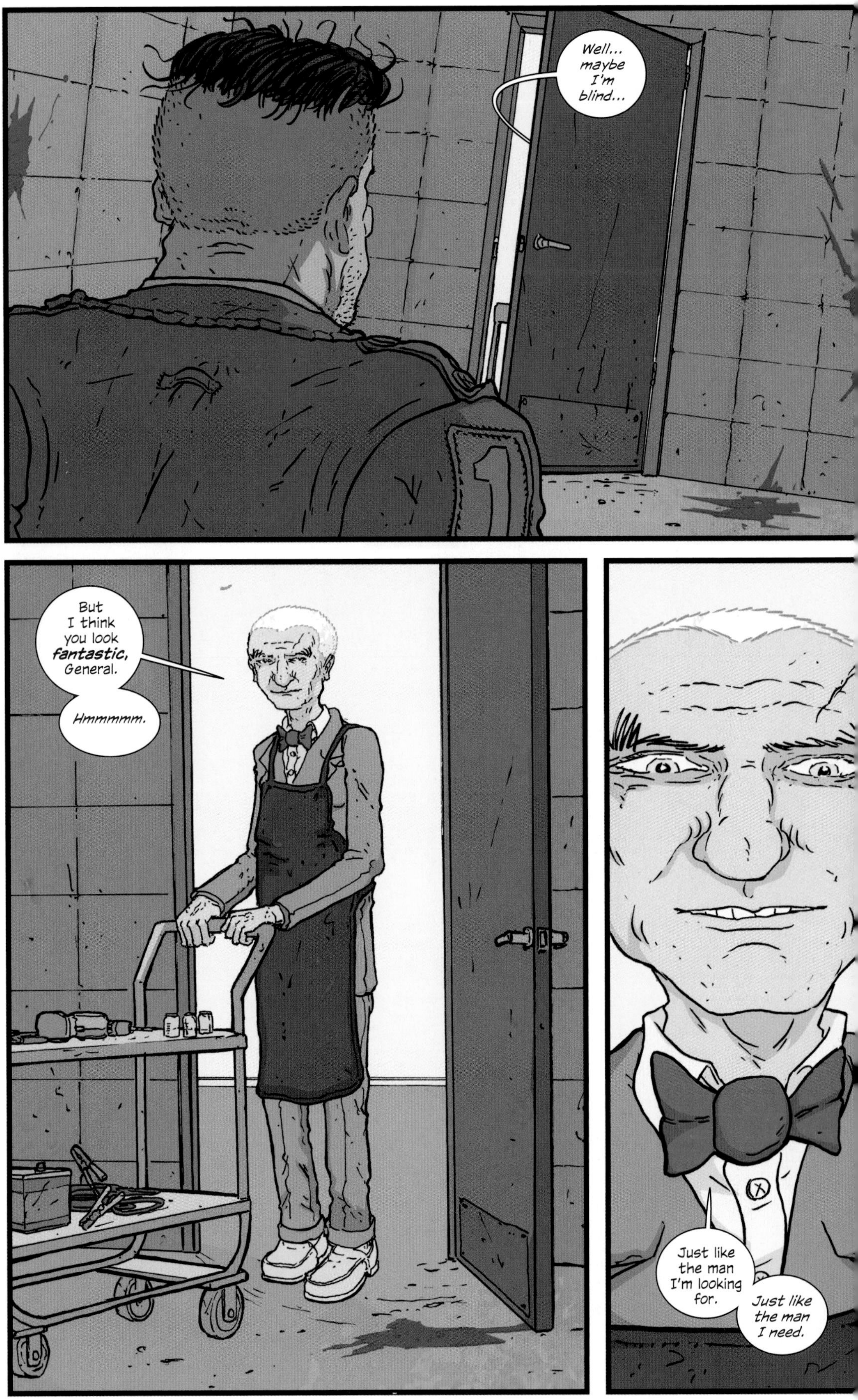
Well... maybe I'm blind...
But I think you look **fantastic,** General.
Hmmmmm.
Just like the man I'm looking for.
Just like the man I need.

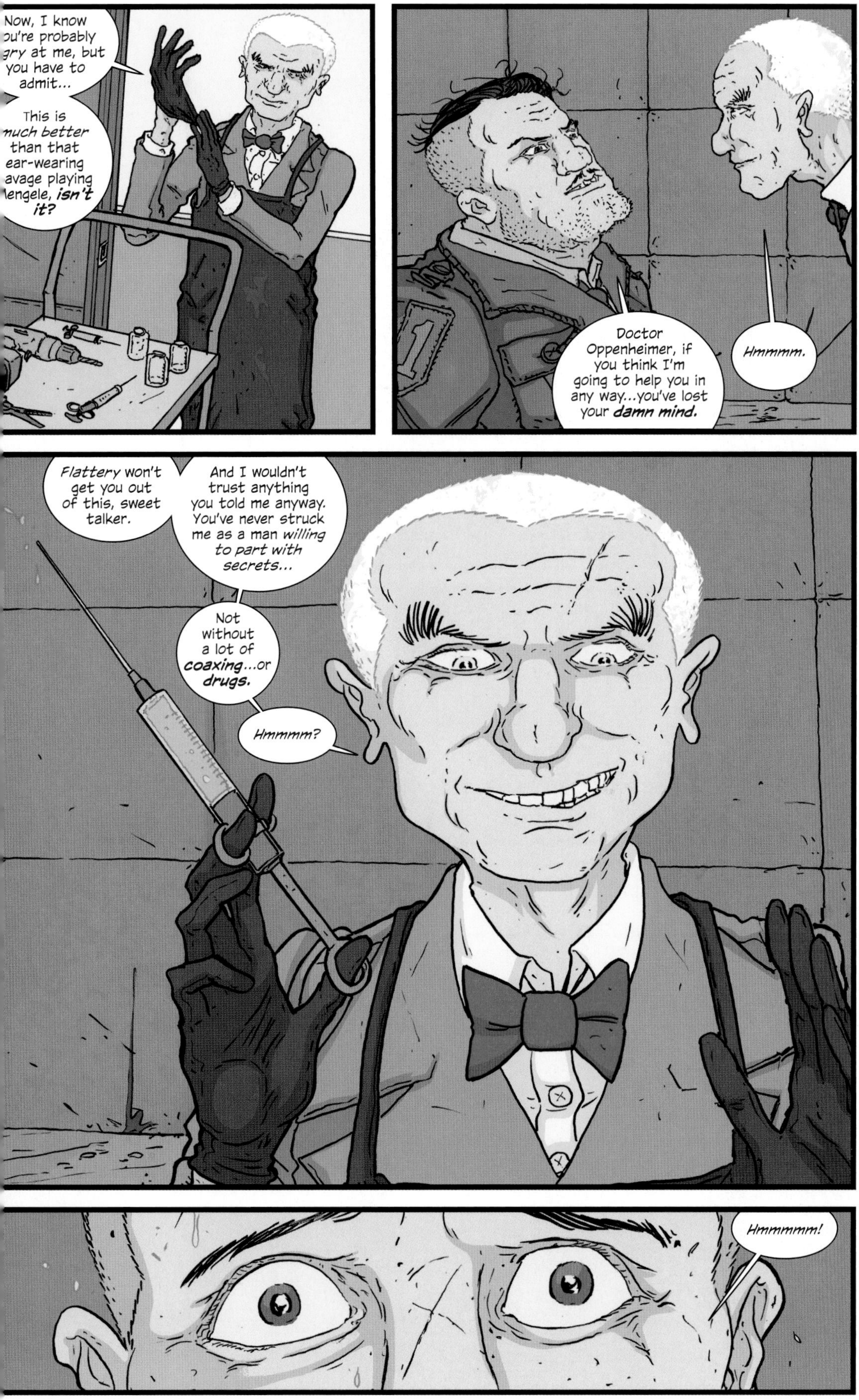
Now, I know ou're probably gry at me, but you have to admit...
This is much better than that ear-wearing avage playing lengele, isn't it?
Doctor Oppenheimer, if you think I'm going to help you in any way...you've lost your damn mind.
Hmmmm.
Flattery won't get you out of this, sweet talker.
And I wouldn't trust anything you told me anyway. You've never struck me as a man willing to part with secrets...
Not without a lot of coaxing...or drugs.
Hmmmm?
Hmmmmm!

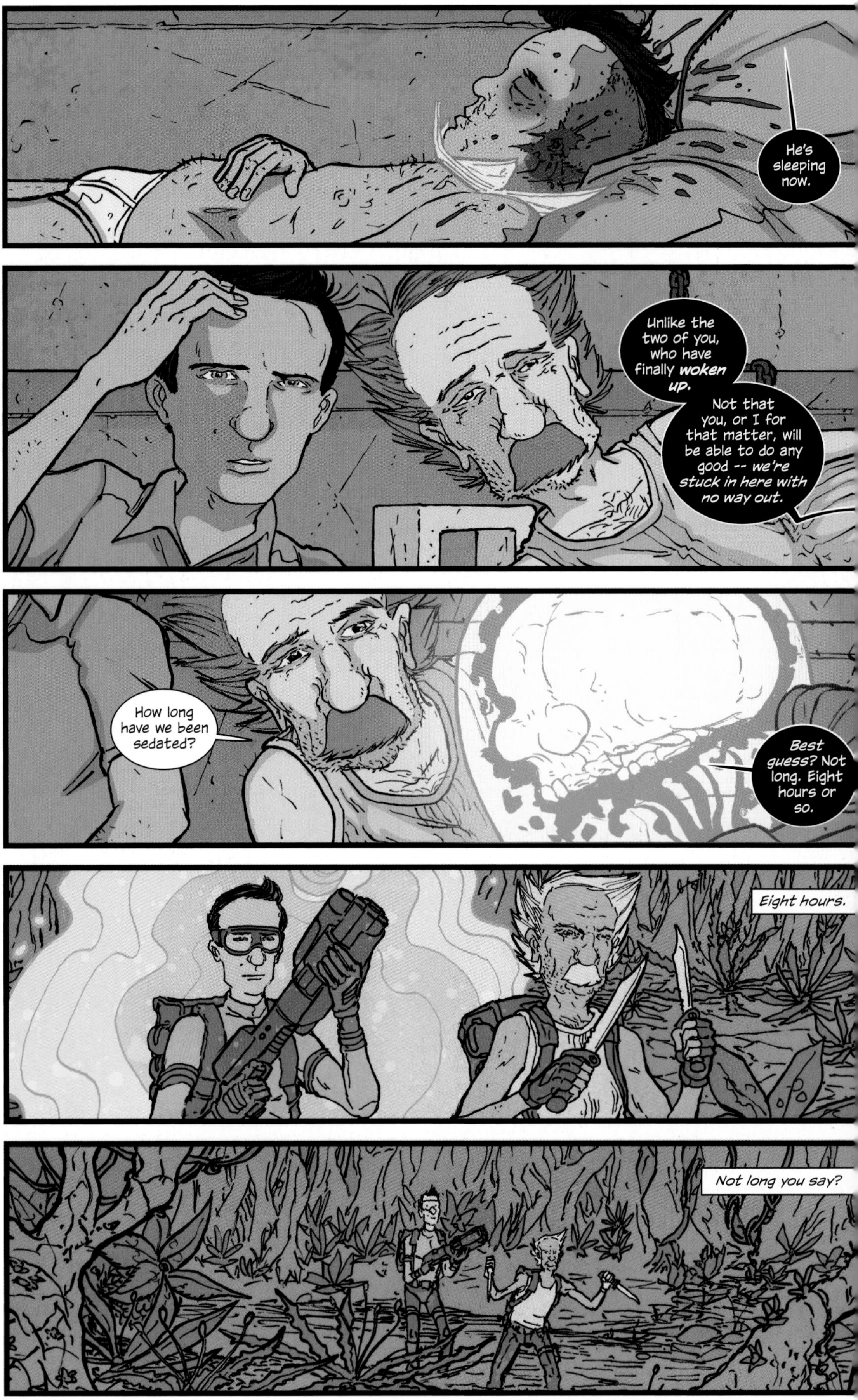
He's sleeping now.
Unlike the two of you, who have finally **woken up.**
Not that you, or I for that matter, will be able to do any good -- *we're stuck in here with no way out.*
How long have we been sedated?
Best guess? Not long. Eight hours or so.
Eight hours.
Not long you say?

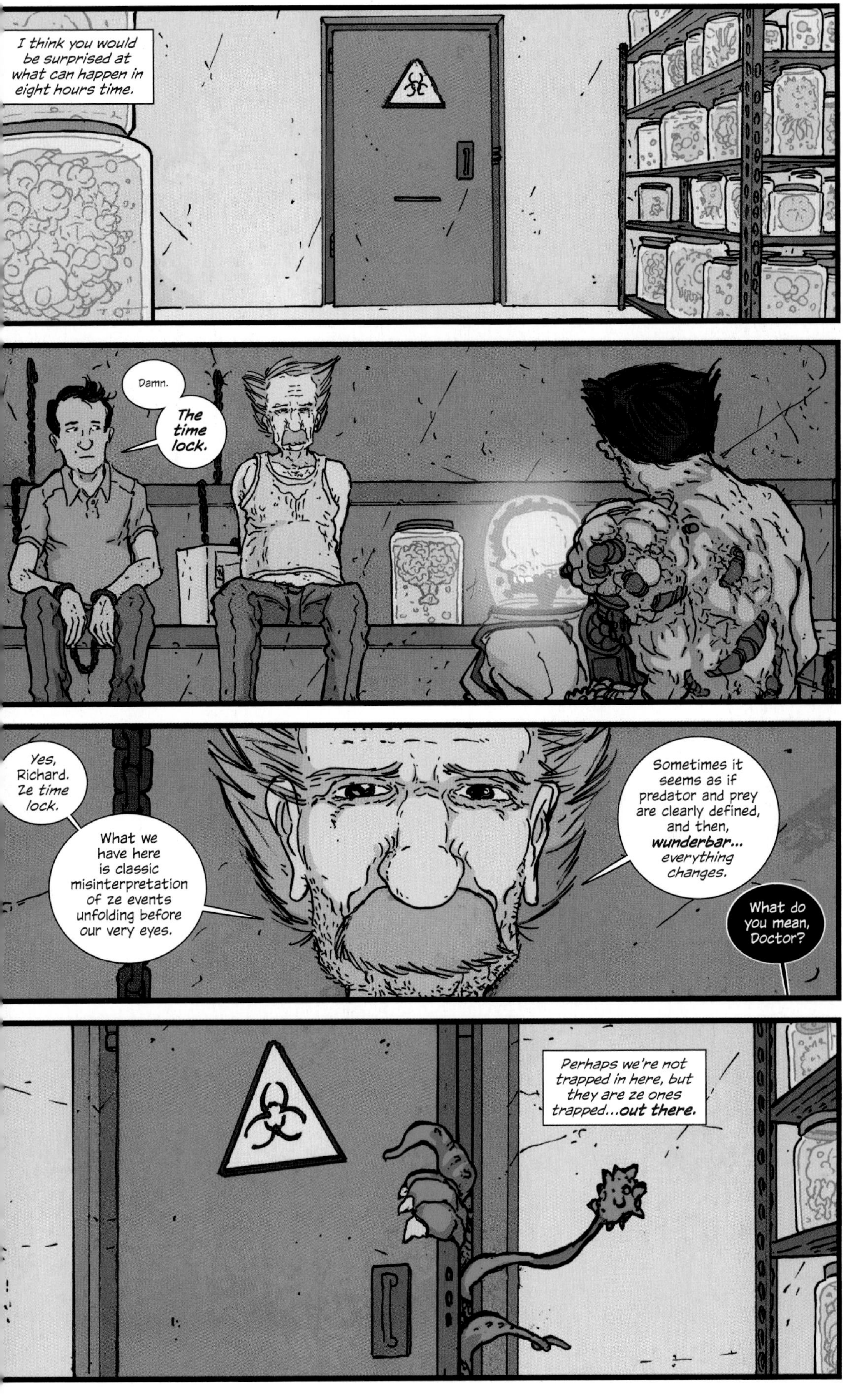

I think you would be surprised at what can happen in eight hours time.
Damn.
The time lock.
Yes, Richard. Ze time lock.
What we have here is classic misinterpretation of ze events unfolding before our very eyes.
Sometimes it seems as if predator and prey are clearly defined, and then, wunderbar... everything changes.
What do you mean, Doctor?
Perhaps we're not trapped in here, but they are ze ones trapped...out there.

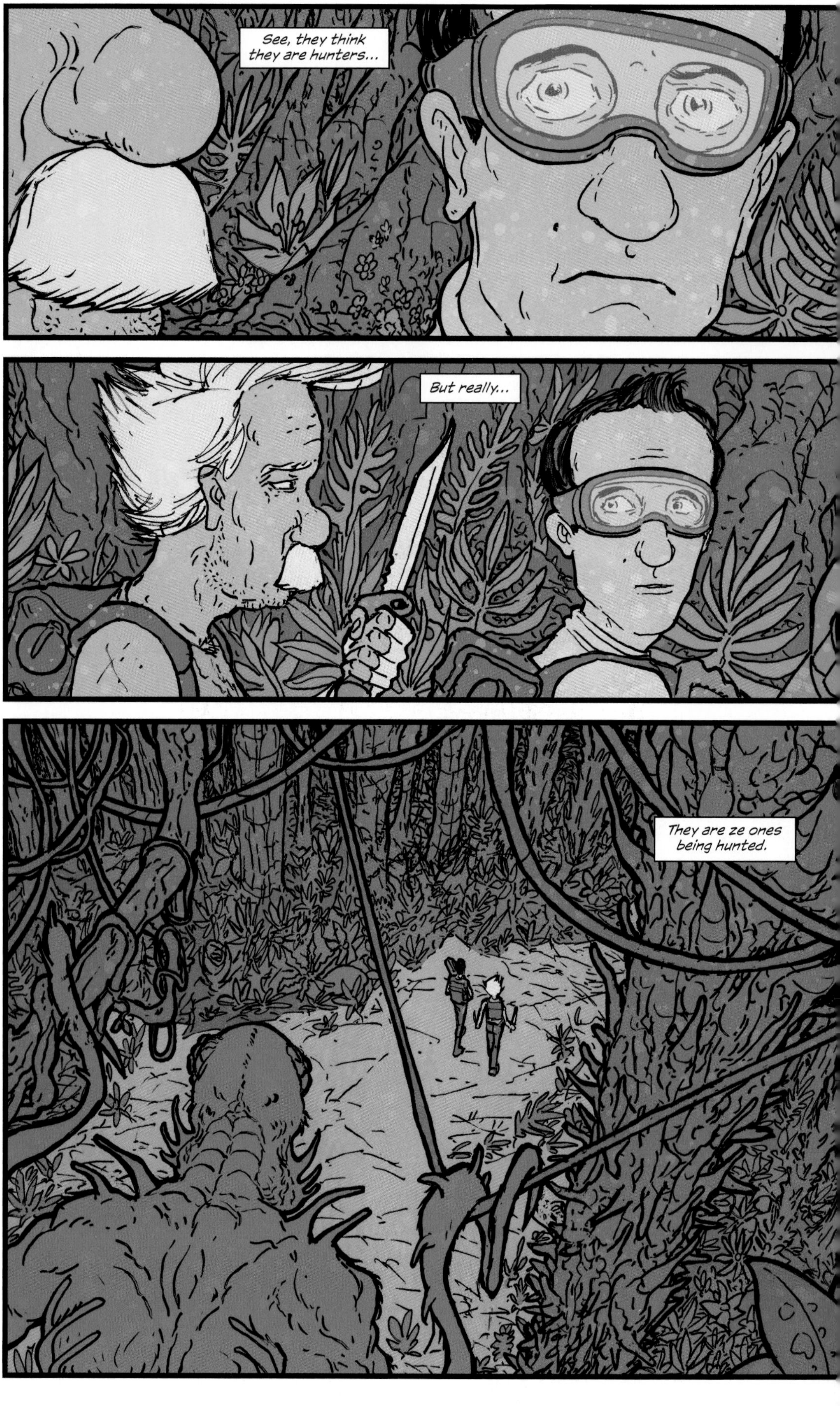
See, they think they are hunters...
But really...
They are ze ones being hunted.

"PROJECT ARES EXISTED OUTSIDE PROJECT CHARON. IN RETROSPECT, IT SAVED US ALL."

CLAVIS AUREA
THE RECORDED FEYNMAN

VOL. 4

SHALL WE GET
STARTED?

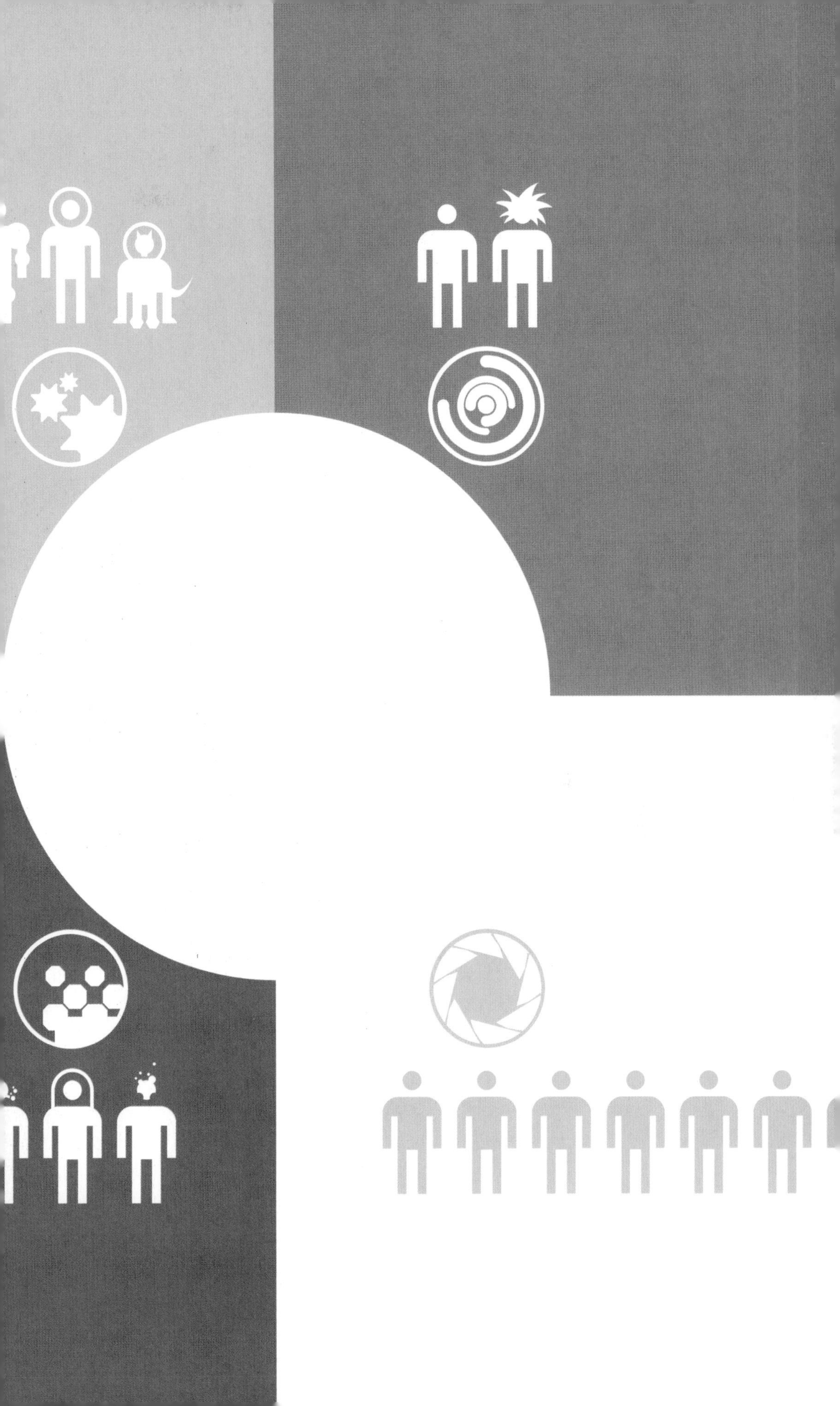

"THE WORKING THEORY WAS A FINISHED PRODUCT FROM WHICH WE COULD EXTRACT THE NECESSARY COMPONENTS FOR RAPID EVOLUTIONARY PROGRESS..."

CLAVIS AUREA
THE RECORDED FEYNMAN

VOL. 2

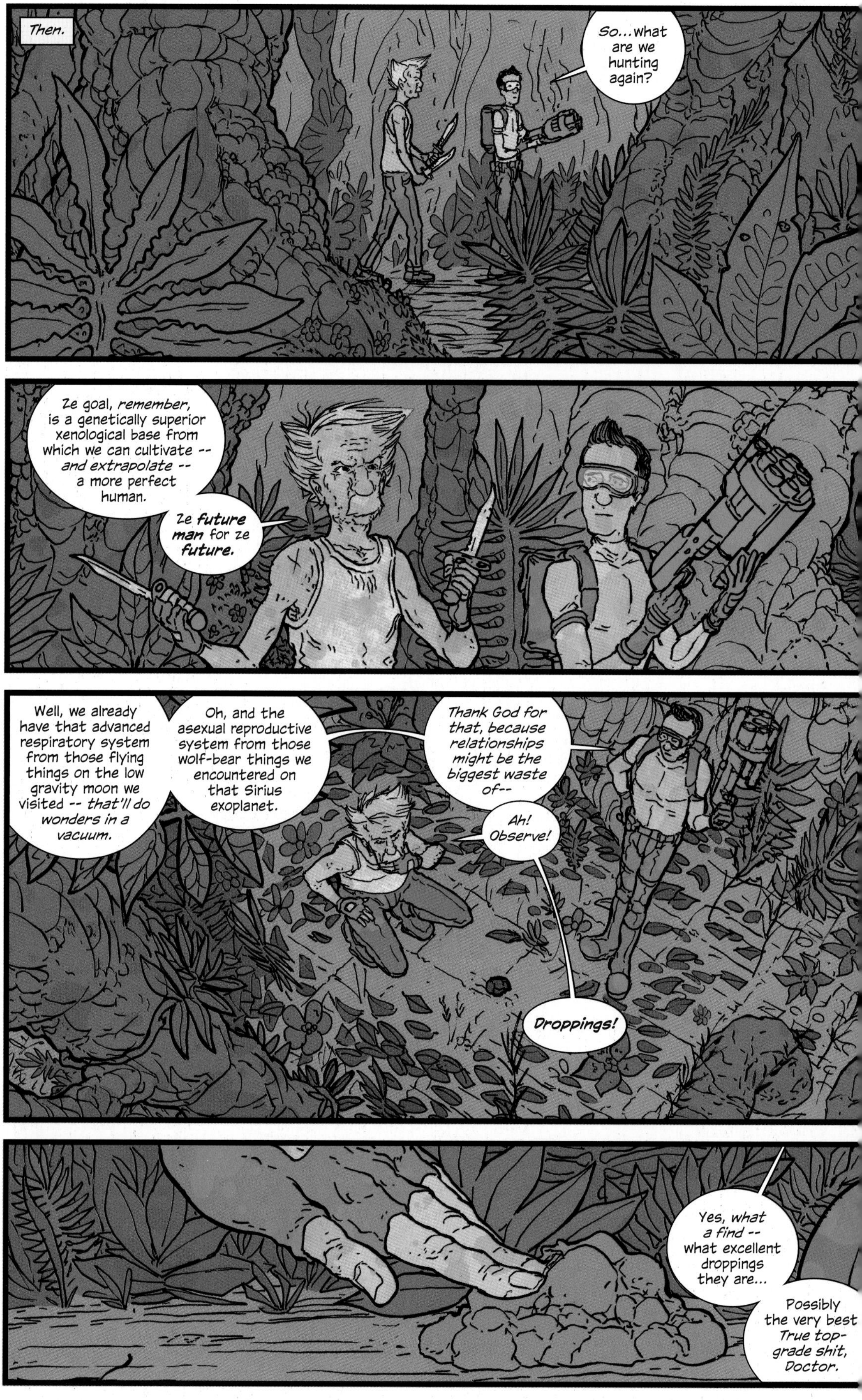
Then.
So...what are we hunting again?
Ze goal, *remember,* is a genetically superior xenological base from which we can cultivate -- *and extrapolate* -- a more perfect human.
Ze ***future man*** for ze ***future.***
Well, we already have that advanced respiratory system from those flying things on the low gravity moon we visited -- *that'll do wonders in a vacuum.*
Oh, and the asexual reproductive system from those wolf-bear things we encountered on that Sirius exoplanet.
Thank God for that, because relationships might be the biggest waste of--
Ah! Observe!
Droppings!
Yes, *what a find* -- what excellent droppings they are...
Possibly the very best
True top-grade shit, Doctor.

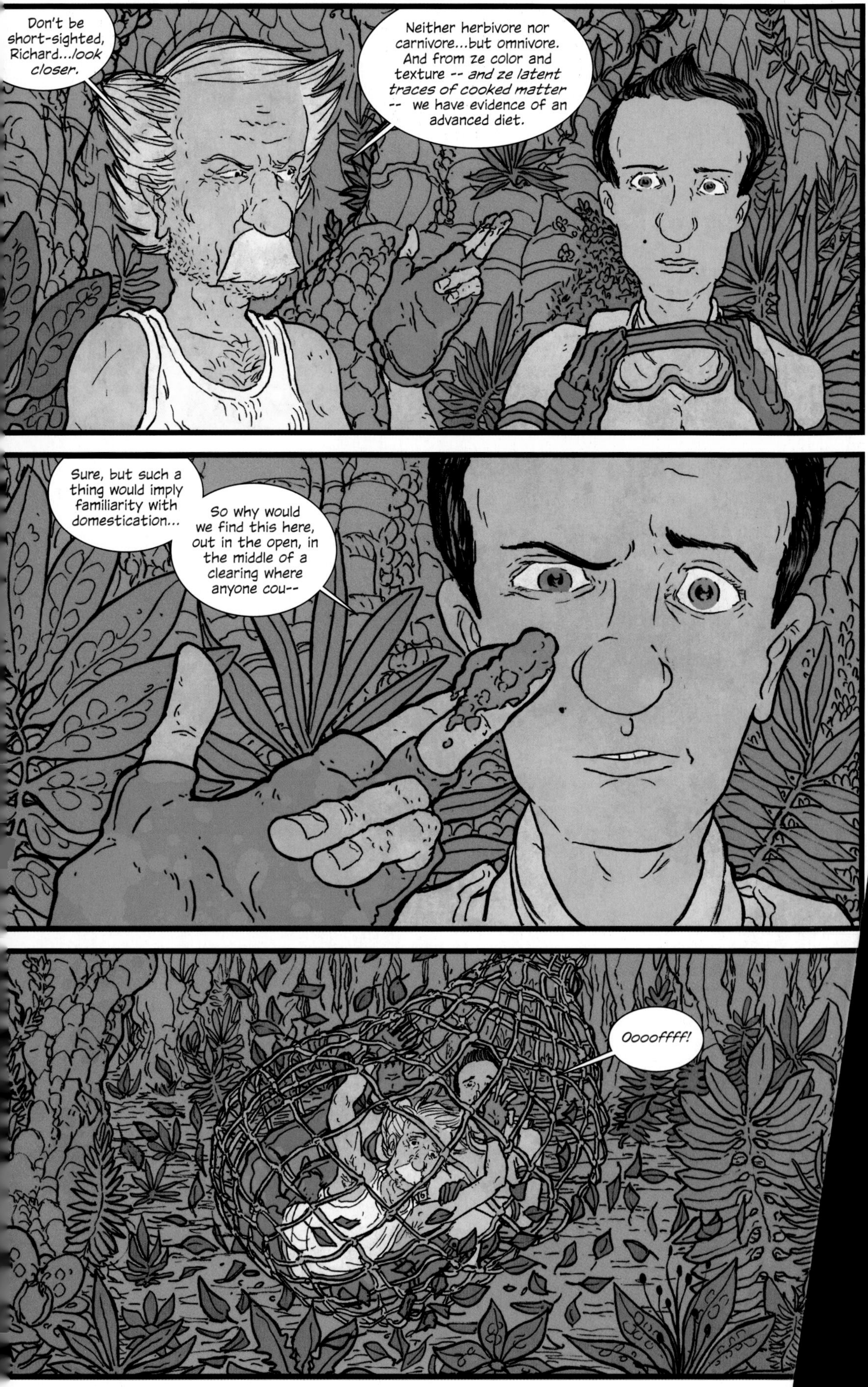
Don't be short-sighted, Richard...*look closer.*
Neither herbivore nor carnivore...but omnivore. And from ze color and texture -- *and ze latent traces of cooked matter* -- we have evidence of an advanced diet.
Sure, but such a thing would imply familiarity with domestication...
So why would we find this here, out in the open, in the middle of a clearing where anyone cou--
Ooooffff!

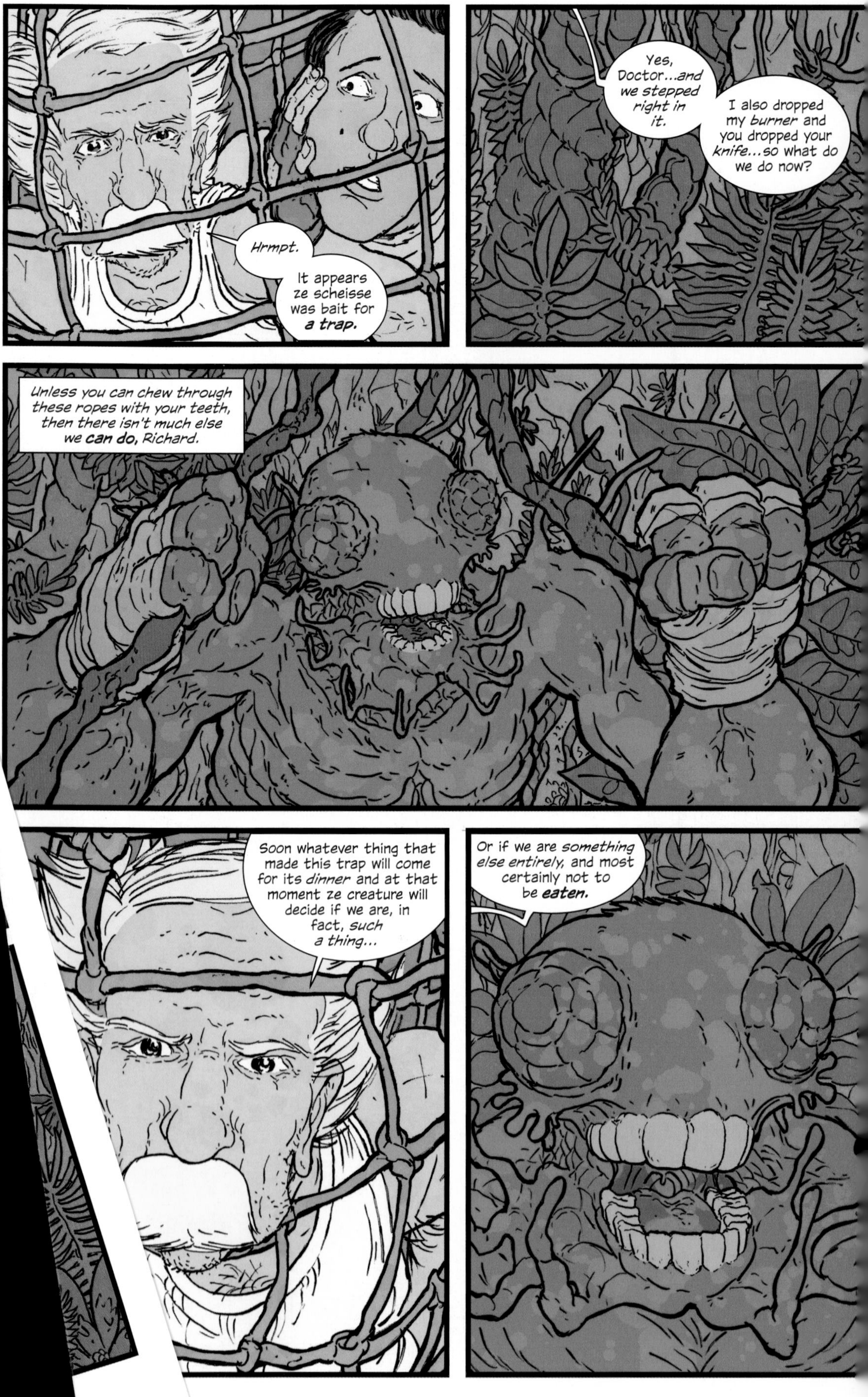
Hrmpt.
It appears ze scheisse was bait for a trap.
Yes, Doctor...and we stepped right in it.
I also dropped my burner and you dropped your knife...so what do we do now?
Unless you can chew through these ropes with your teeth, then there isn't much else we can do, Richard.
Soon whatever thing that made this trap will come for its dinner and at that moment ze creature will decide if we are, in fact, such a thing...
Or if we are something else entirely, and most certainly not to be eaten.

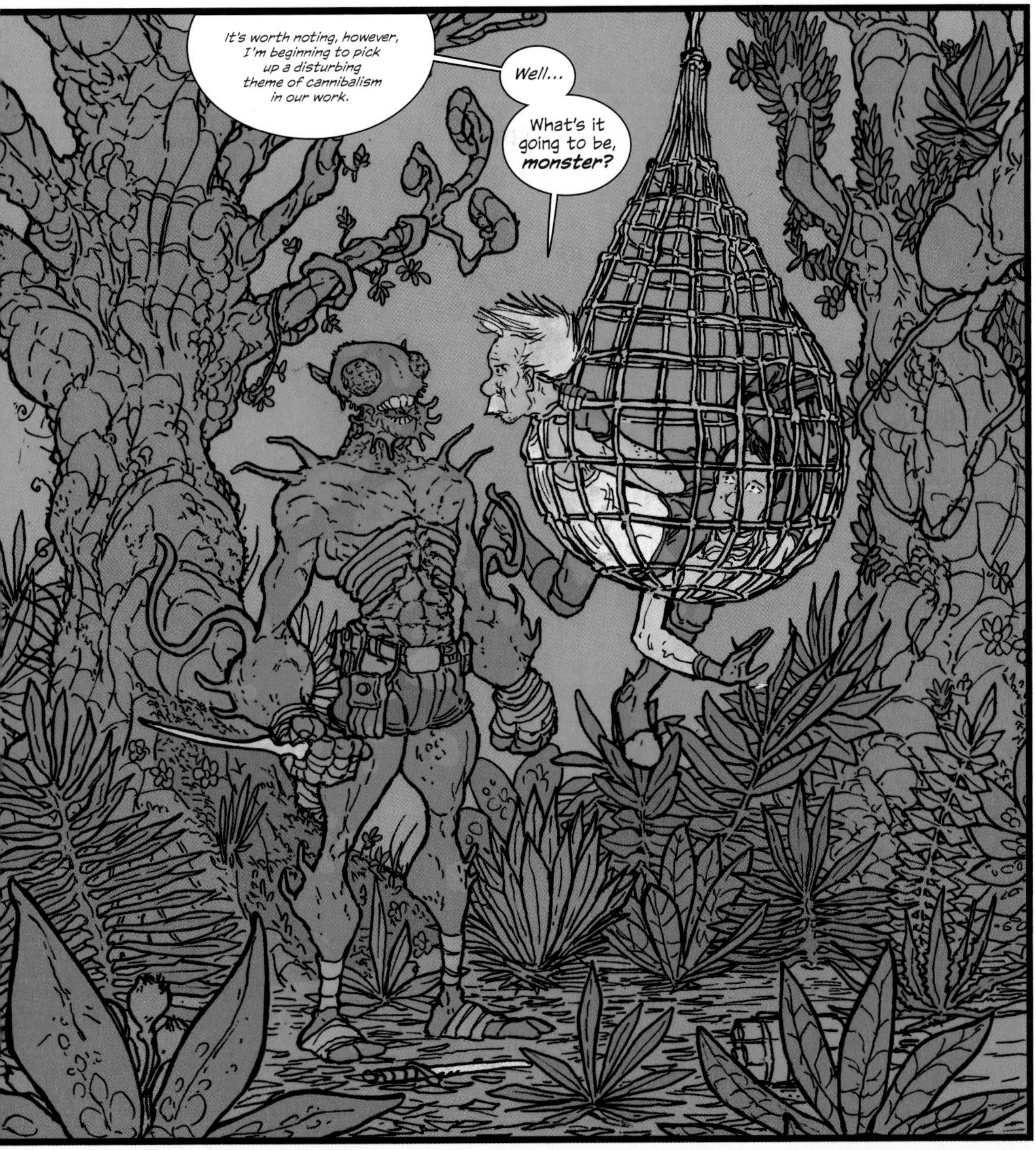
It's worth noting, however, I'm beginning to pick up a disturbing theme of cannibalism in our work.
Well...
What's it going to be, **monster?**

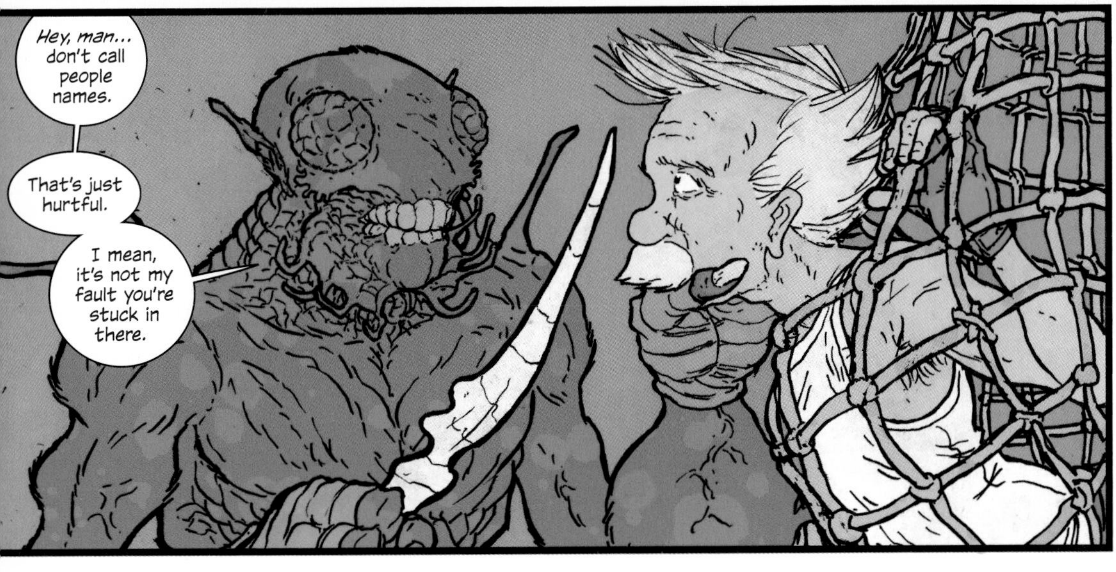
Hey, man... don't call people names.
That's just hurtful.
I mean, it's not my fault you're stuck in there.

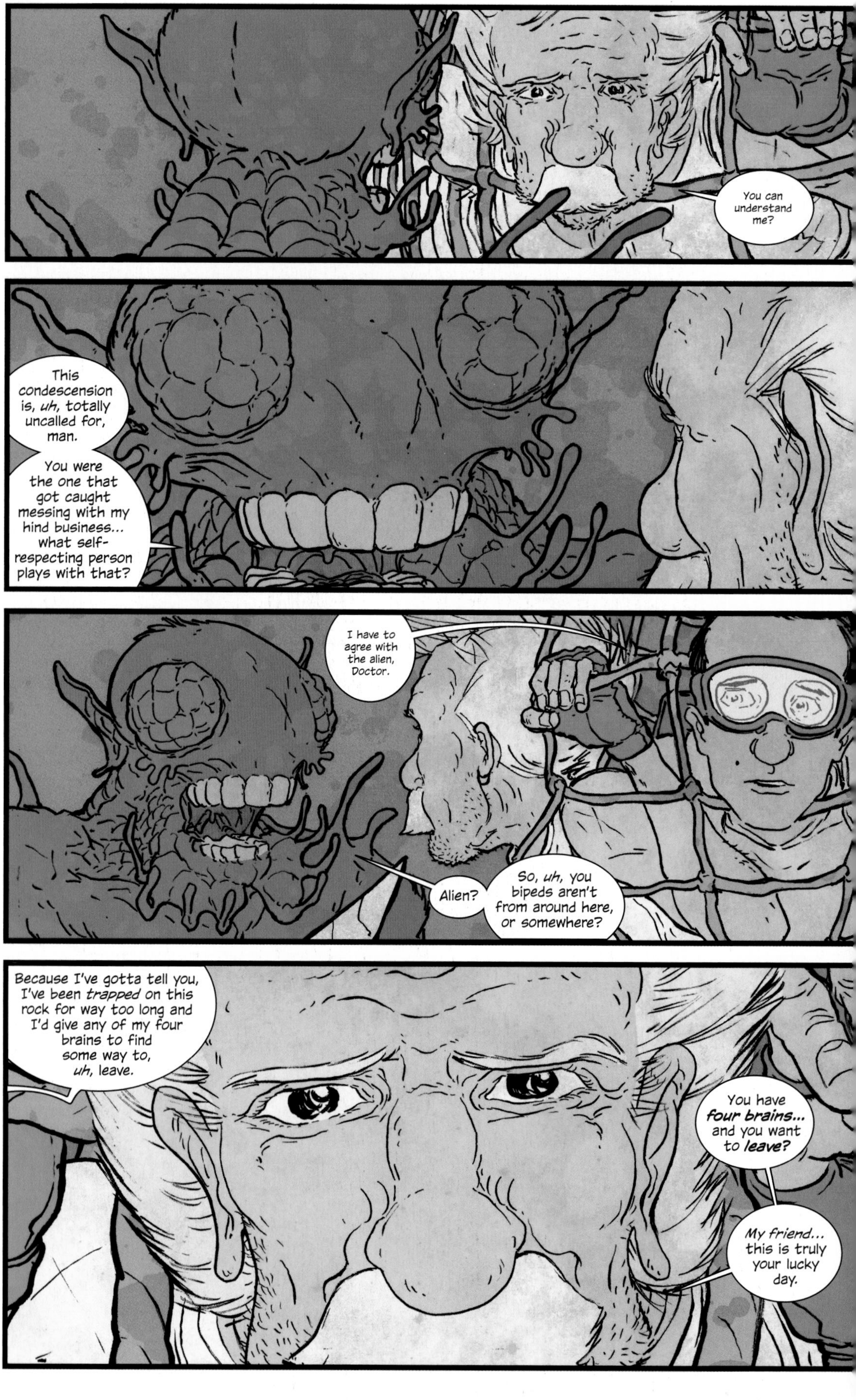
You can understand me?
This condescension is, *uh*, totally uncalled for, man.
You were the one that got caught messing with my hind business... what self-respecting person plays with that?
I have to agree with the alien, Doctor.
Alien?
So, *uh*, you bipeds aren't from around here, or somewhere?
Because I've gotta tell you, I've been *trapped* on this rock for way too long and I'd give any of my four brains to find some way to, *uh*, leave.
You have ***four brains...*** and you want to ***leave?***
My friend... this is truly your lucky day.

"...WE WERE SO VERY WRONG."

CLAVIS AUREA
THE RECORDED FEYNMAN | **VOL. 2**

17

WHAT WE MADE

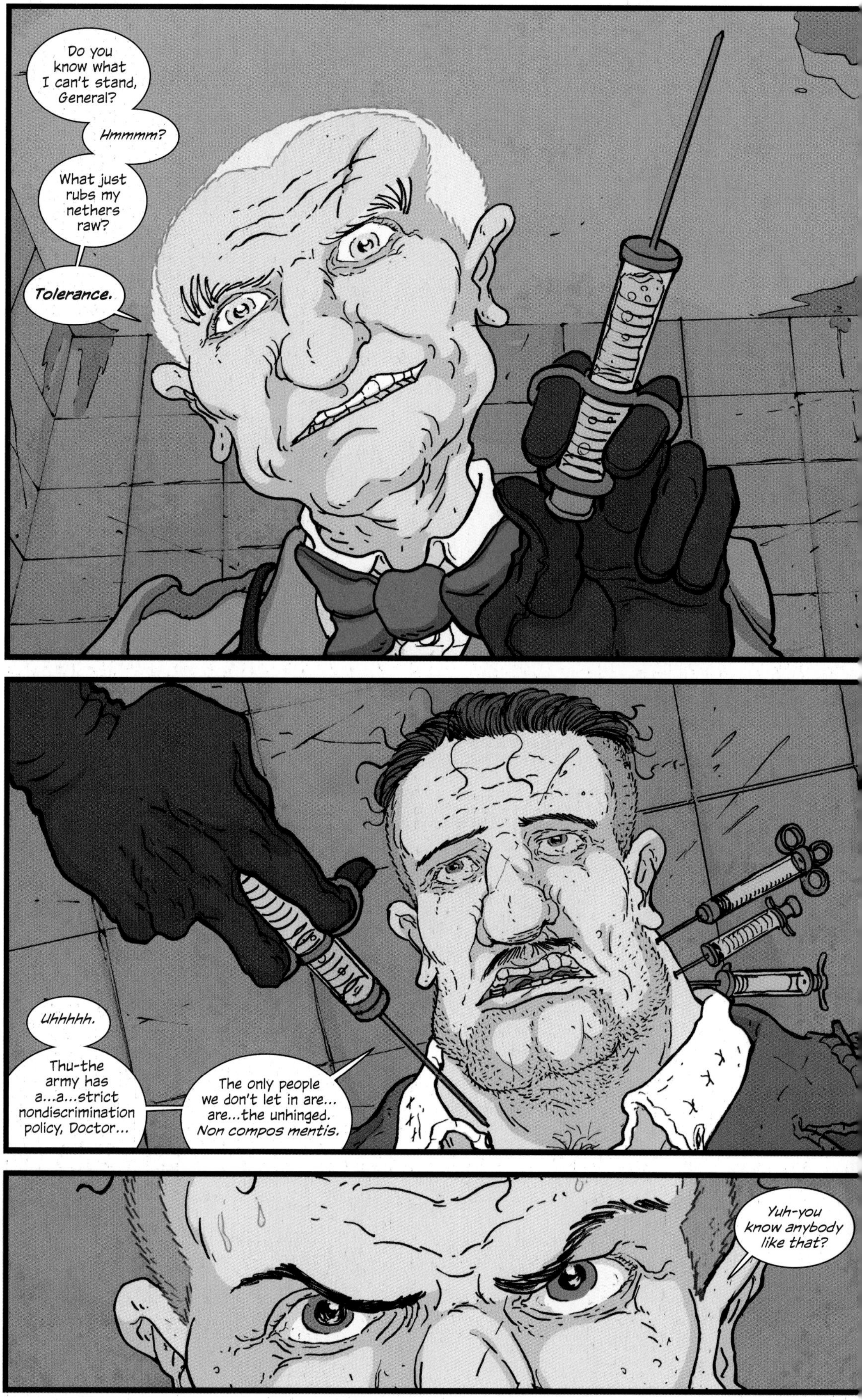
Do you know what I can't stand, General?
Hmmmm?
What just rubs my nethers raw?
Tolerance.
Uhhhhh.
Thu-the army has a...a...strict nondiscrimination policy, Doctor...
The only people we don't let in are... are...the unhinged. *Non compos mentis.*
Yuh-you know anybody like that?

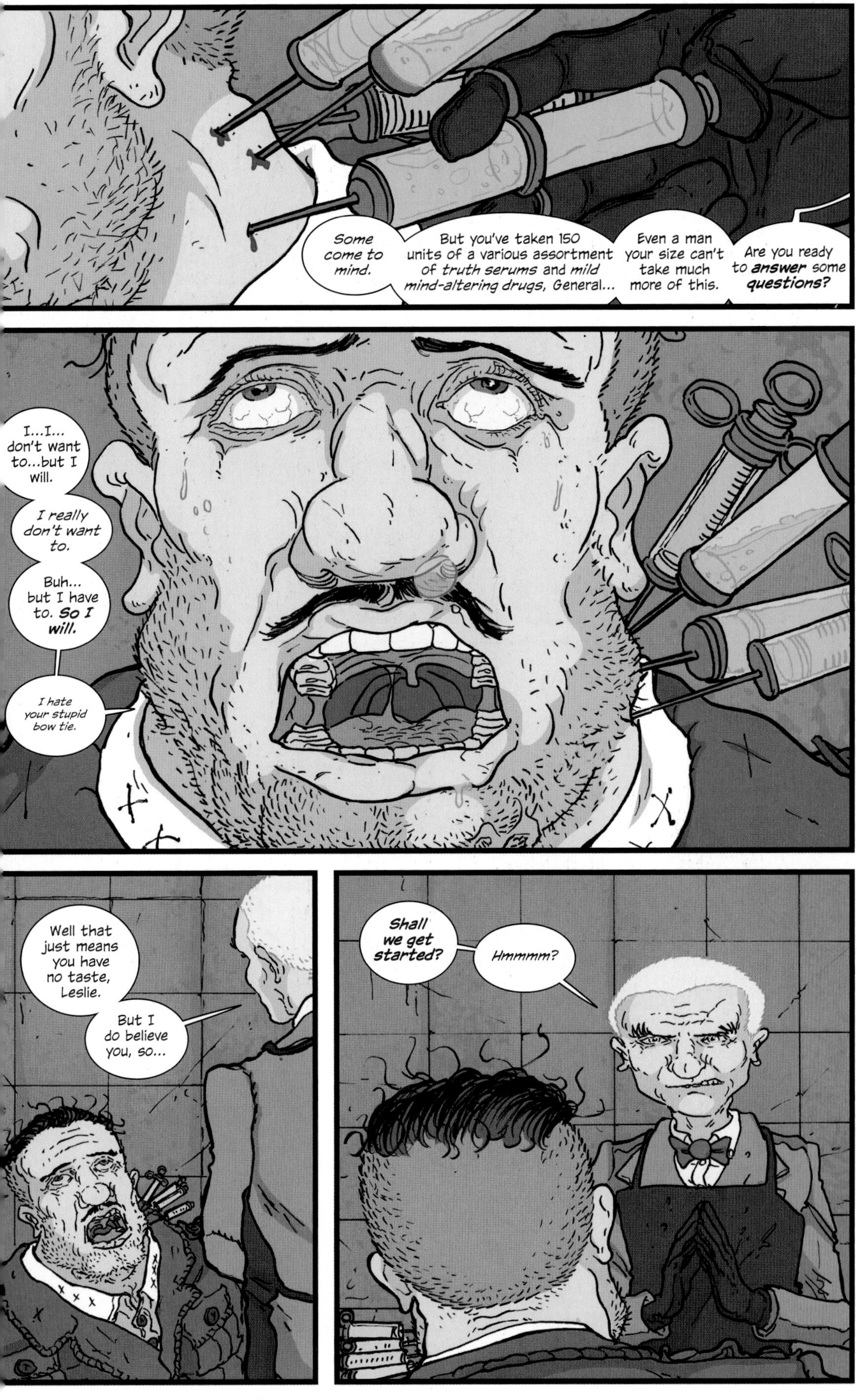
Some come to mind.
But you've taken 150 units of a various assortment of *truth serums* and *mild mind-altering drugs*, General...
Even a man your size can't take much more of this.
Are you ready to ***answer*** some ***questions?***
I...I... don't want to...but I will.
I really don't want to.
Buh... but I have to. ***So I will.***
I hate your stupid bow tie.
Well that just means you have no taste, Leslie.
But I do believe you, so...
Shall we get started?
Hmmmm?

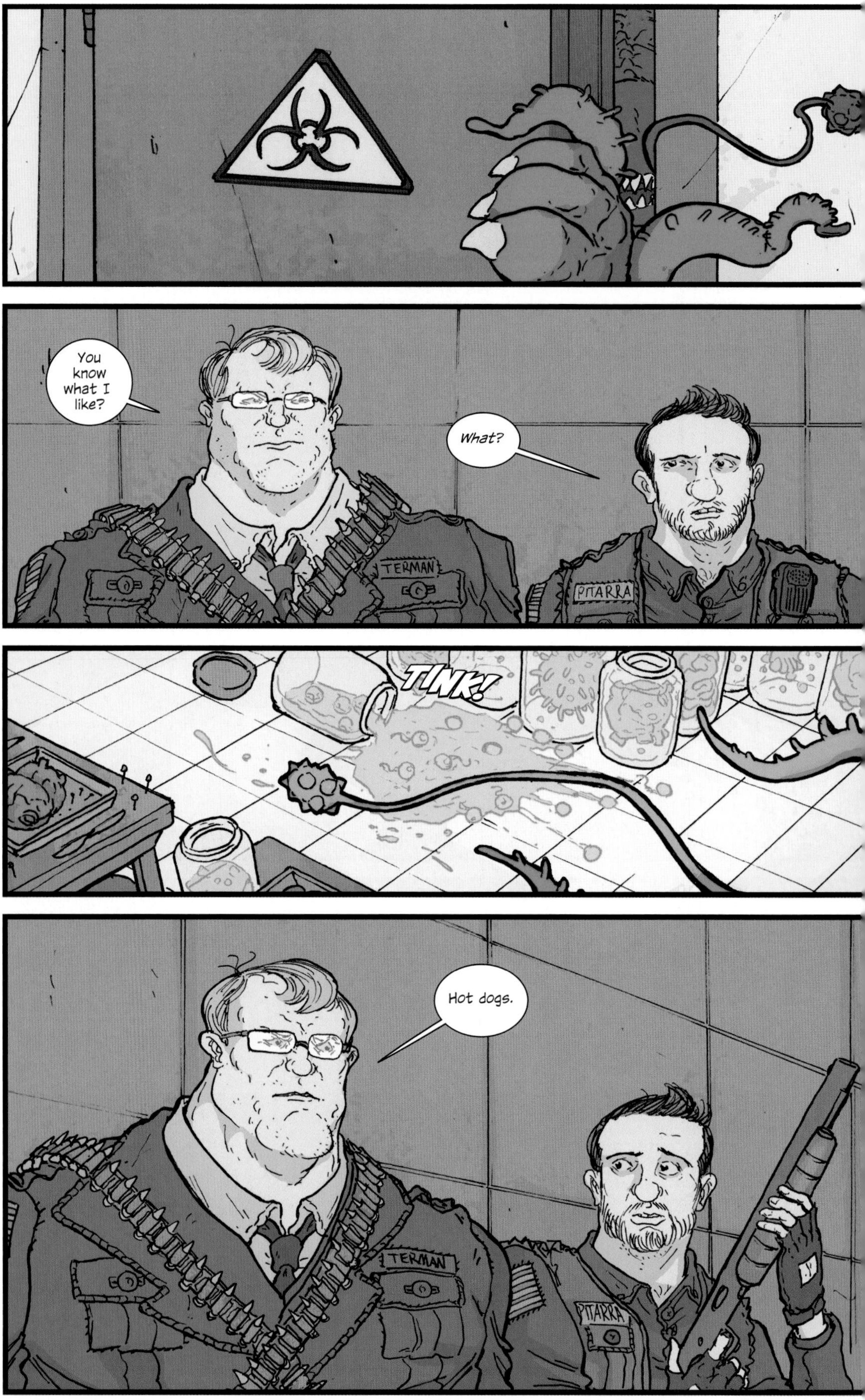
You know what I like?
What?
TERMAN
PITARRA
TINK!
Hot dogs.
TERMAN
PITARRA

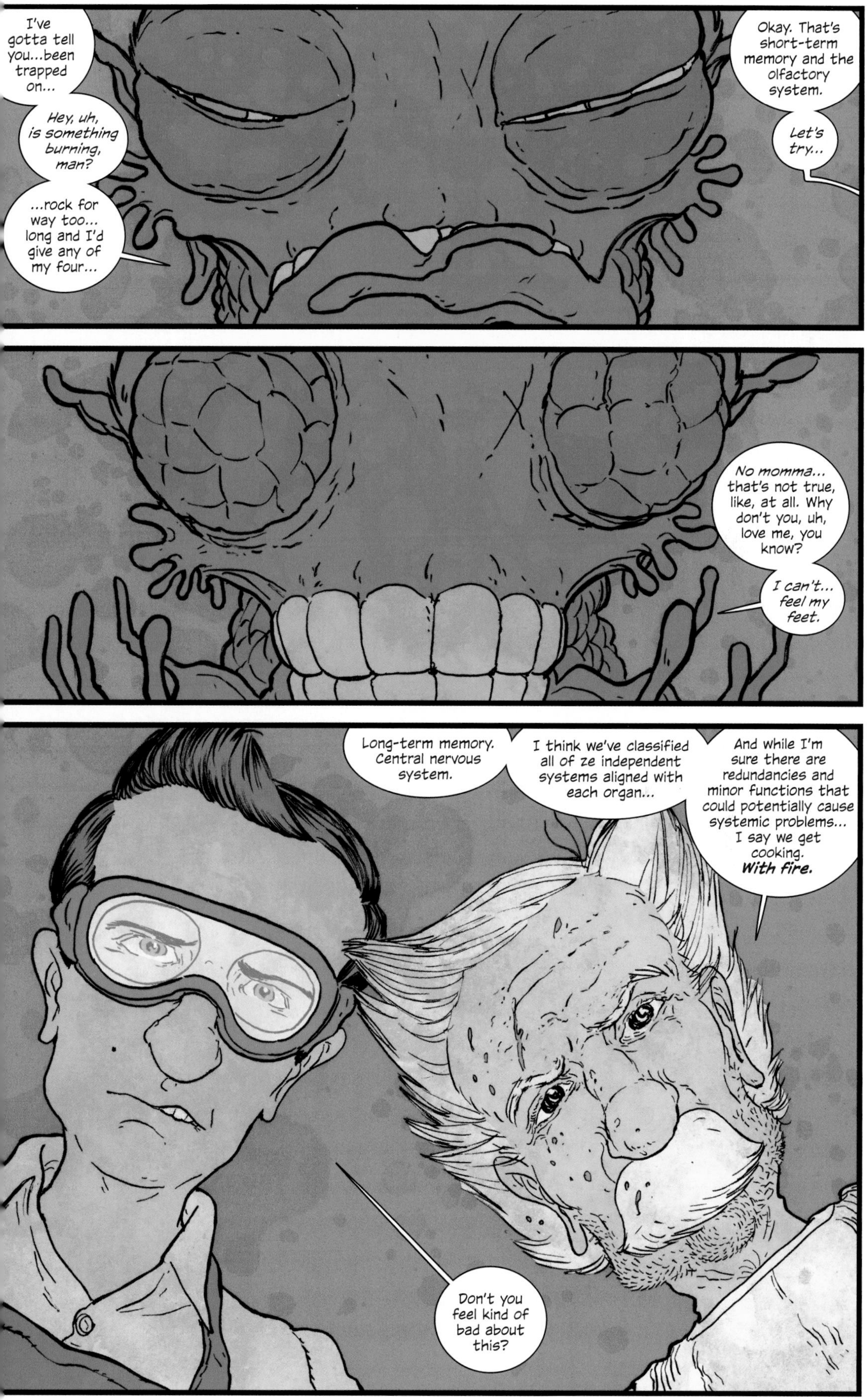

I've gotta tell you...been trapped on...
Hey, uh, is something burning, man?
...rock for way too... long and I'd give any of my four...
Okay. That's short-term memory and the olfactory system.
Let's try...
No momma... that's not true, like, at all. Why don't you, uh, love me, you know?
I can't... feel my feet.
Long-term memory. Central nervous system.
I think we've classified all of ze independent systems aligned with each organ...
And while I'm sure there are redundancies and minor functions that could potentially cause systemic problems... I say we get cooking. ***With fire.***
Don't you feel kind of bad about this?

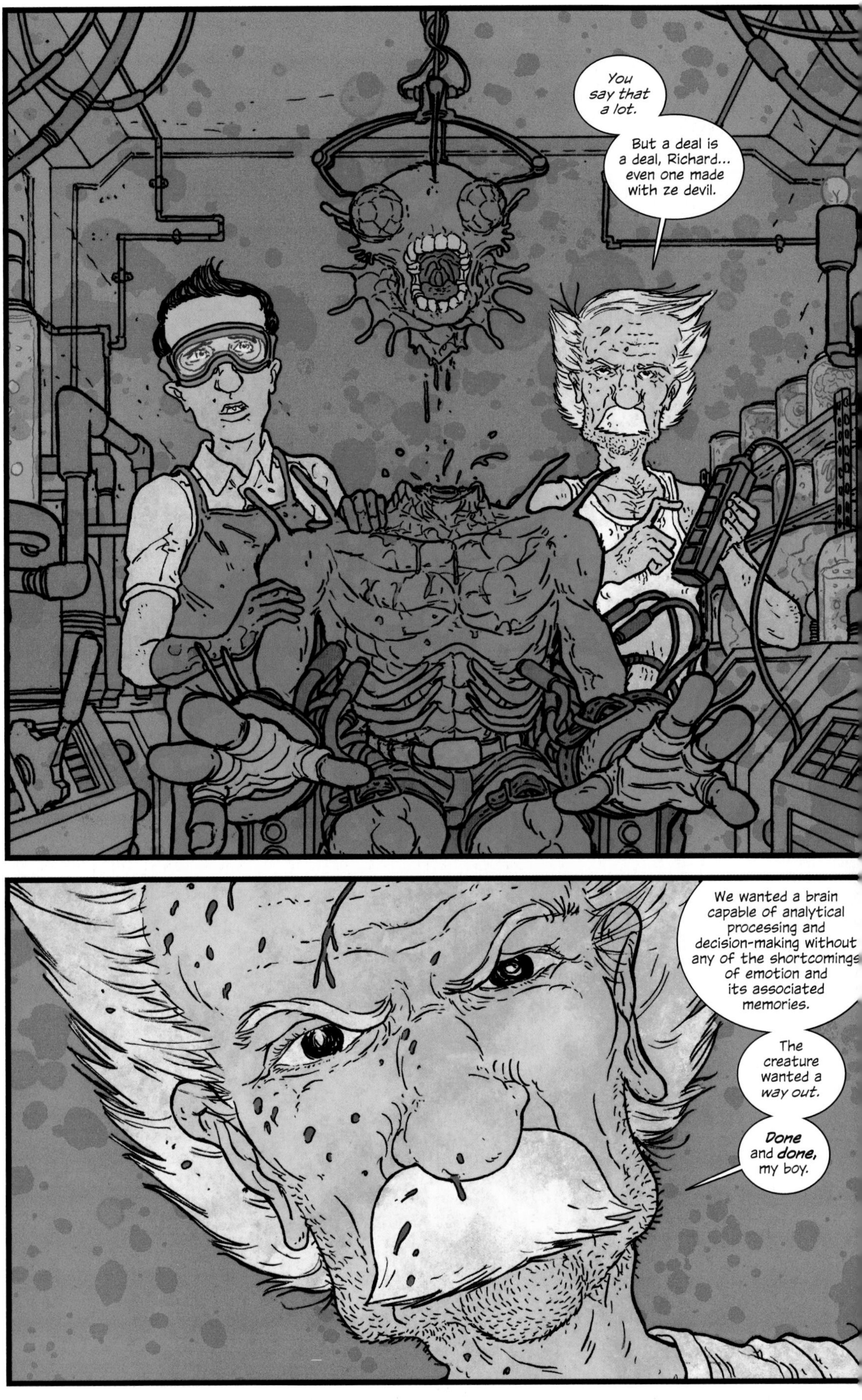
You say that a lot.
But a deal is a deal, Richard... even one made with ze devil.
We wanted a brain capable of analytical processing and decision-making without any of the shortcomings of emotion and its associated memories.
The creature wanted a way out.
Done and done, my boy.

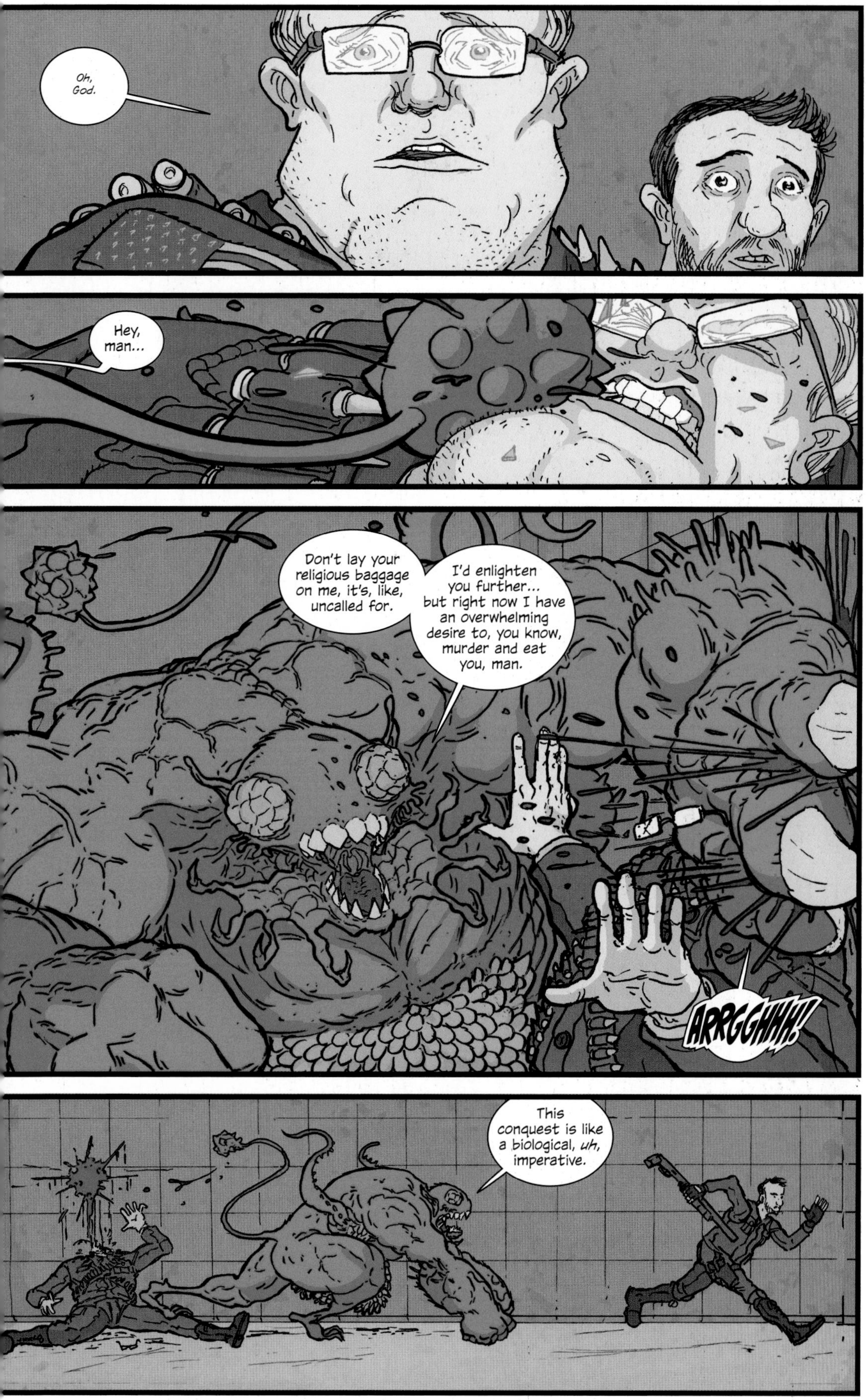

Oh, God.
Hey, man...
Don't lay your religious baggage on me, it's, like, uncalled for.
I'd enlighten you further... but right now I have an overwhelming desire to, you know, murder and eat you, man.
ARRGGHHH!
This conquest is like a biological, *uh*, imperative.

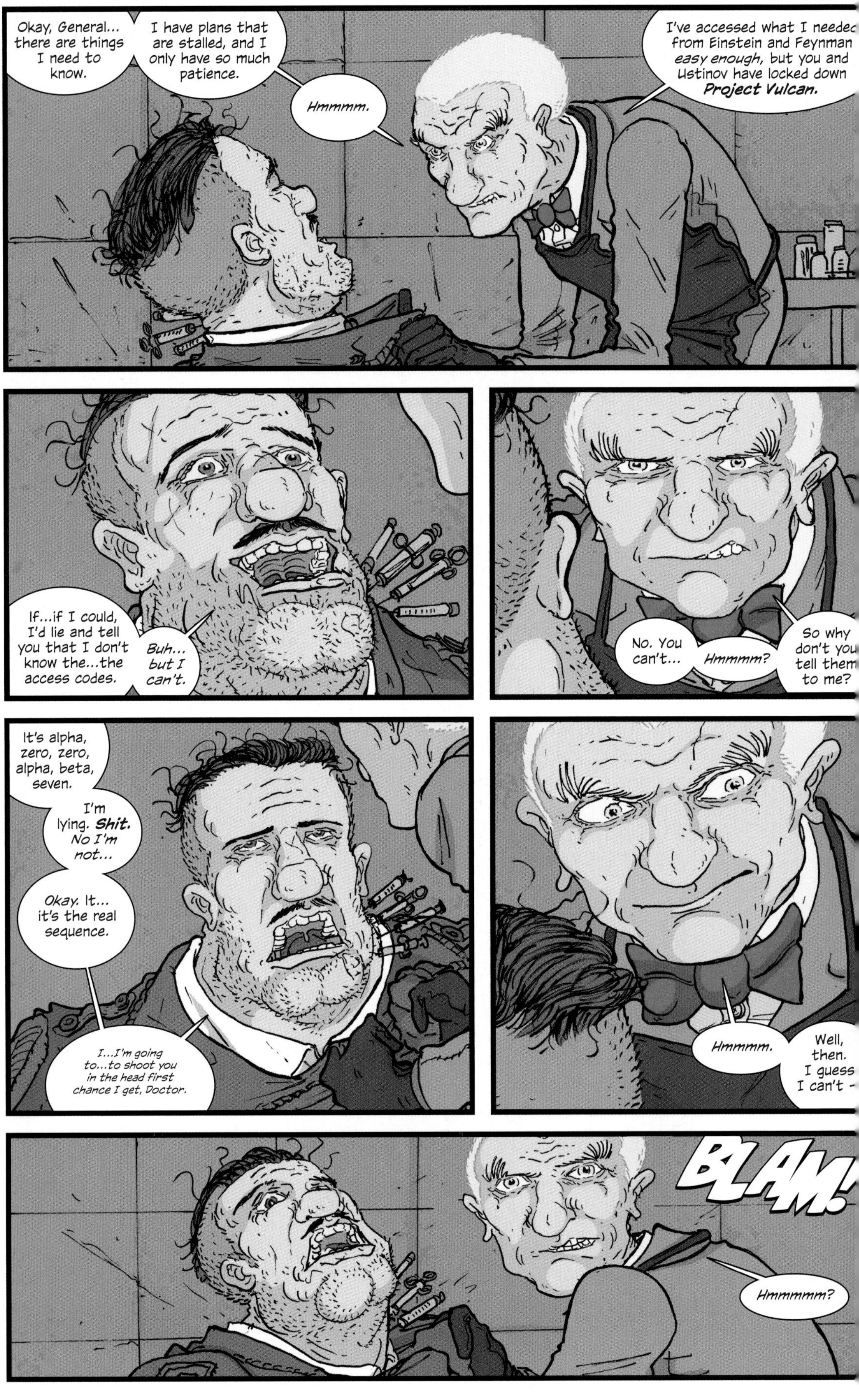

Okay, General... there are things I need to know.
I have plans that are stalled, and I only have so much patience.
Hmmmm.
I've accessed what I needed from Einstein and Feynman *easy enough*, but you and Ustinov have locked down ***Project Vulcan.***
If...if I could, I'd lie and tell you that I don't know the...the access codes.
Buh... but I can't.
No. You can't...
Hmmmm?
So why don't you tell them to me?
It's alpha, zero, zero, alpha, beta, seven.
I'm lying. ***Shit.*** *No I'm not...*
Okay. It... it's the real sequence.
I...I'm going to...to shoot you in the head first chance I get, Doctor.
Hmmmm.
Well, then. I guess I can't -
BLAM!
Hmmmmm?

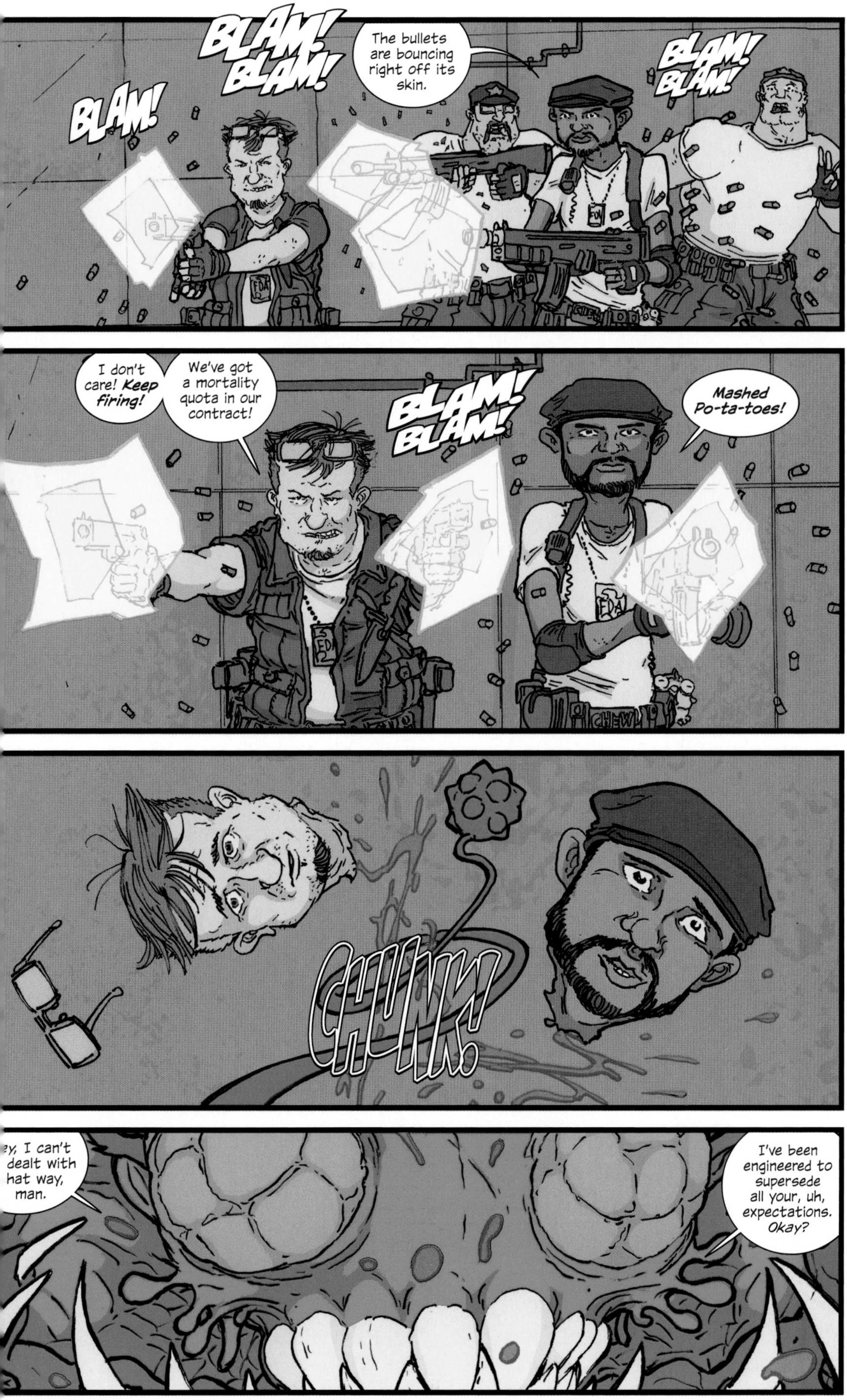

BLAM!
BLAM! BLAM!
The bullets are bouncing right off its skin.
BLAM! BLAM!
I don't care! Keep firing!
We've got a mortality quota in our contract!
BLAM! BLAM!
Mashed Po-ta-toes!
CHUNK!
ey, I can't dealt with hat way, man.
I've been engineered to supersede all your, uh, expectations. Okay?

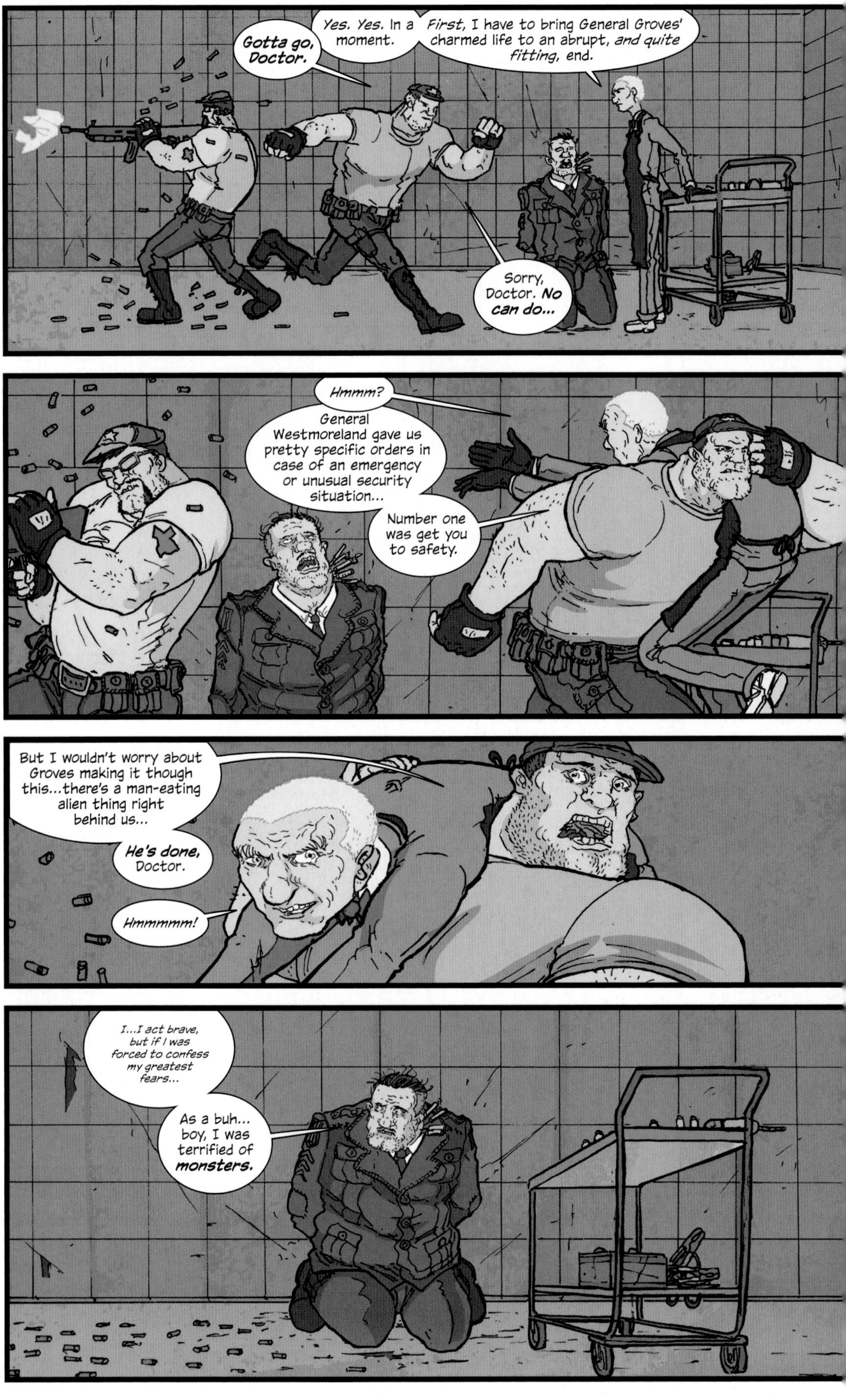
Gotta go, Doctor.
Yes. Yes. In a moment.
First, I have to bring General Groves' charmed life to an abrupt, and quite fitting, end.
Sorry, Doctor. No can do...
Hmmm?
General Westmoreland gave us pretty specific orders in case of an emergency or unusual security situation...
Number one was get you to safety.
But I wouldn't worry about Groves making it though this...there's a man-eating alien thing right behind us...
He's done, Doctor.
Hmmmmm!
I...I act brave, but if I was forced to confess my greatest fears...
As a buh... boy, I was terrified of monsters.

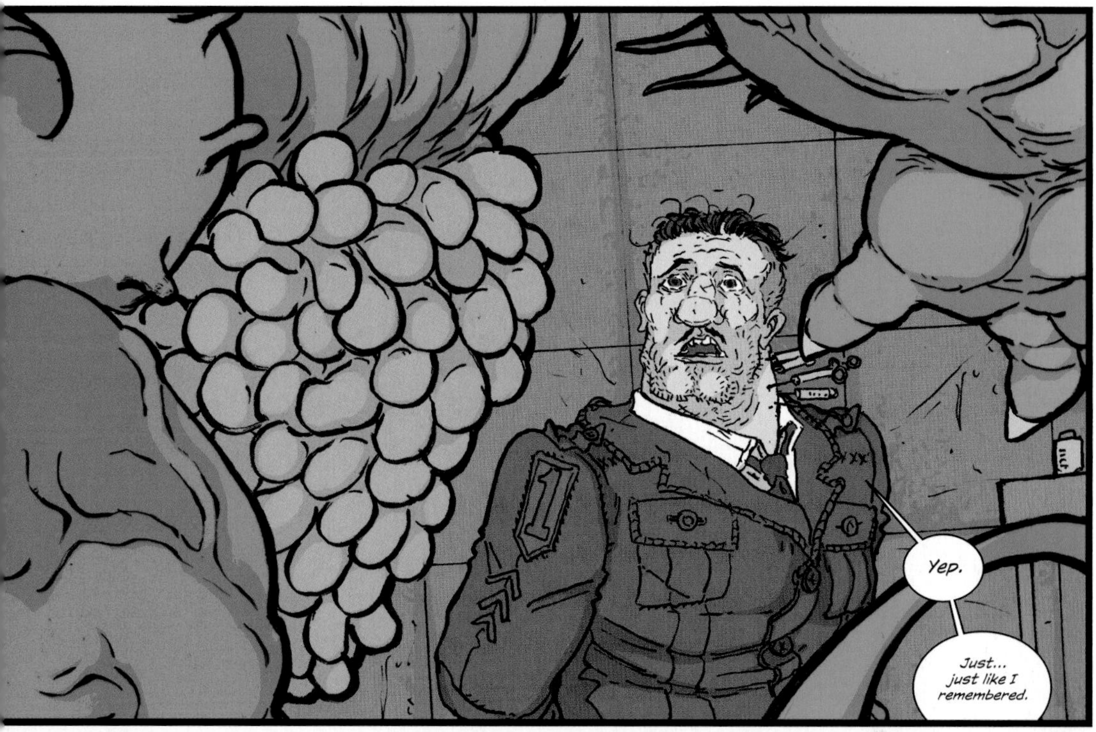
Yep.
Just... just like I remembered.

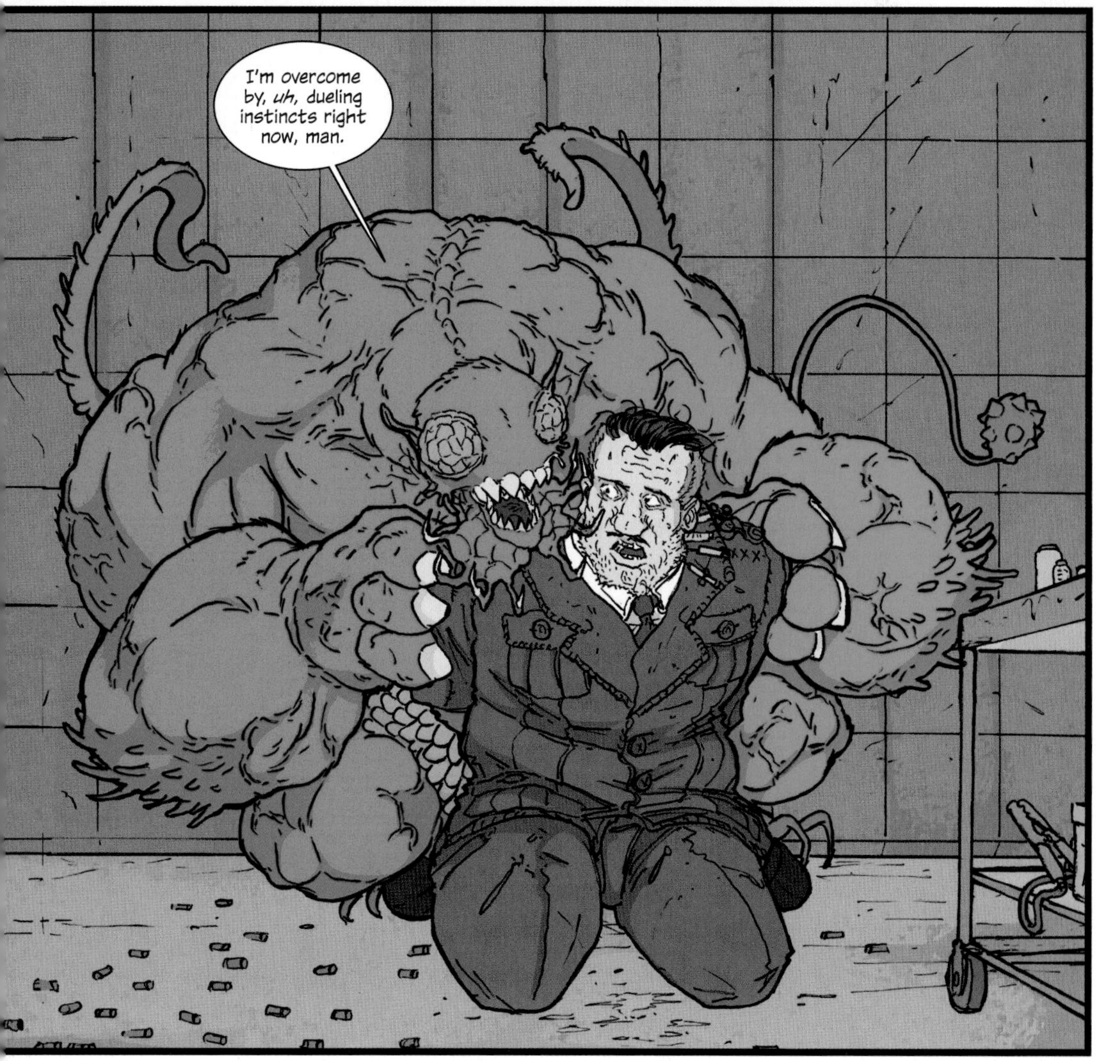
I'm overcome by, *uh*, dueling instincts right now, man.

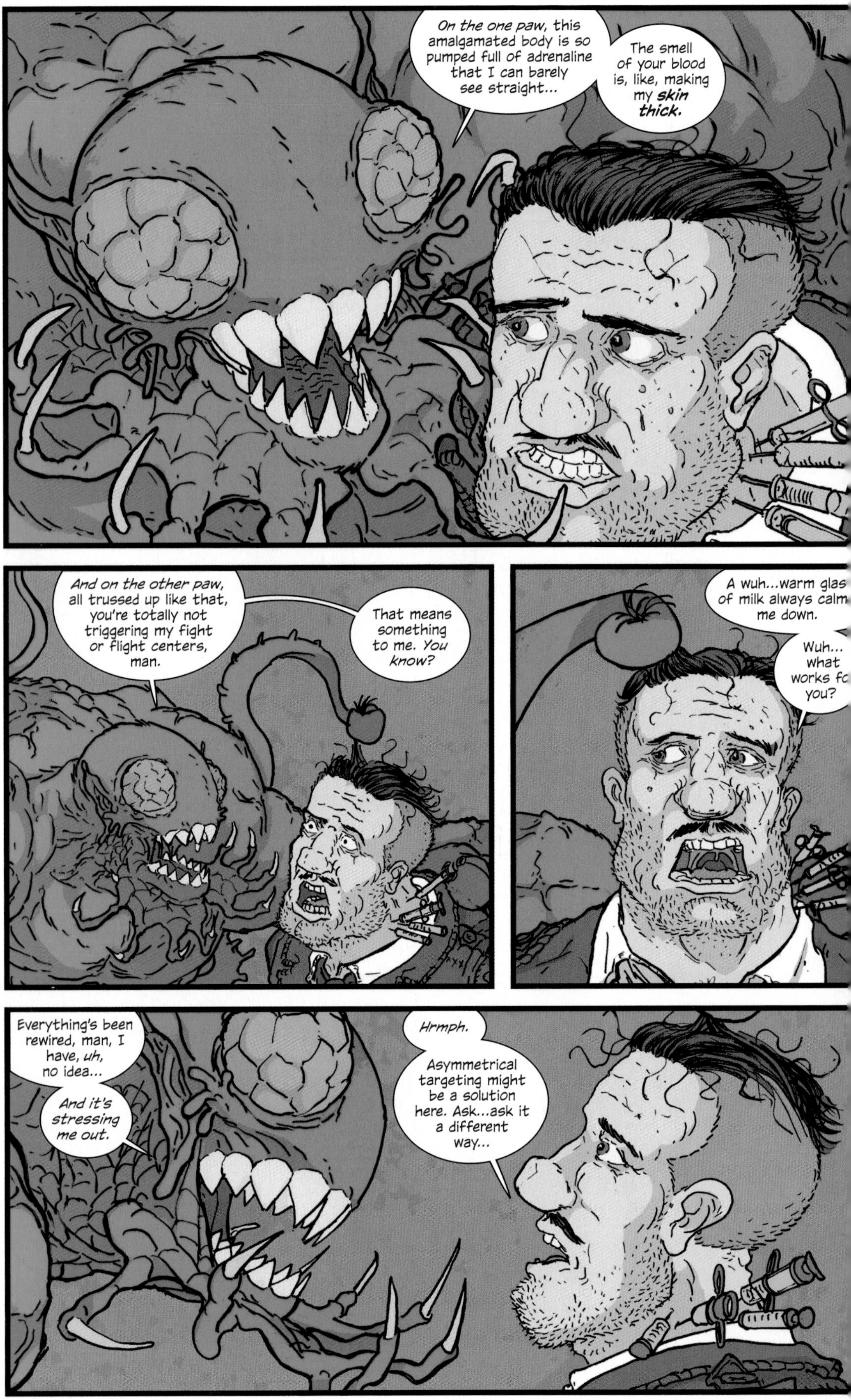
On the one paw, this amalgamated body is so pumped full of adrenaline that I can barely see straight...
The smell of your blood is, like, making my ***skin thick.***
And on the other paw, all trussed up like that, you're totally not triggering my fight or flight centers, man.
That means something to me. *You know?*
A wuh...warm glas of milk always calm me down.
Wuh... what works fc you?
Everything's been rewired, man, I have, *uh,* no idea...
And it's stressing me out.
Hrmph.
Asymmetrical targeting might be a solution here. Ask...ask it a different way...

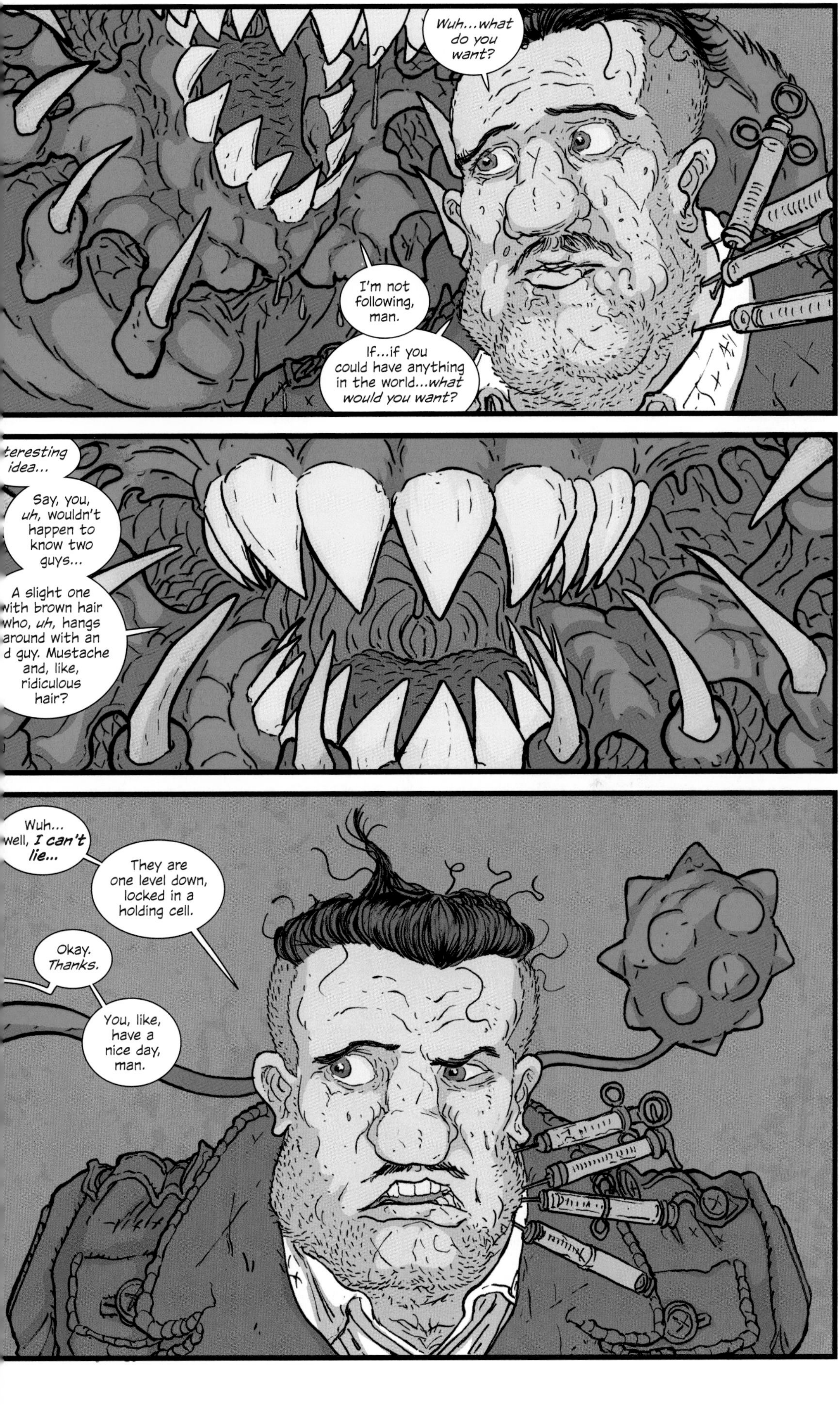
Wuh...what do you want?
I'm not following, man.
If...if you could have anything in the world...*what would you want?*
teresting idea...
Say, you, *uh*, wouldn't happen to know two guys...
A slight one with brown hair who, *uh*, hangs around with an d guy. Mustache and, like, ridiculous hair?
Wuh... well, ***I can't lie...***
They are one level down, locked in a holding cell.
Okay. *Thanks.*
You, like, have a nice day, man.

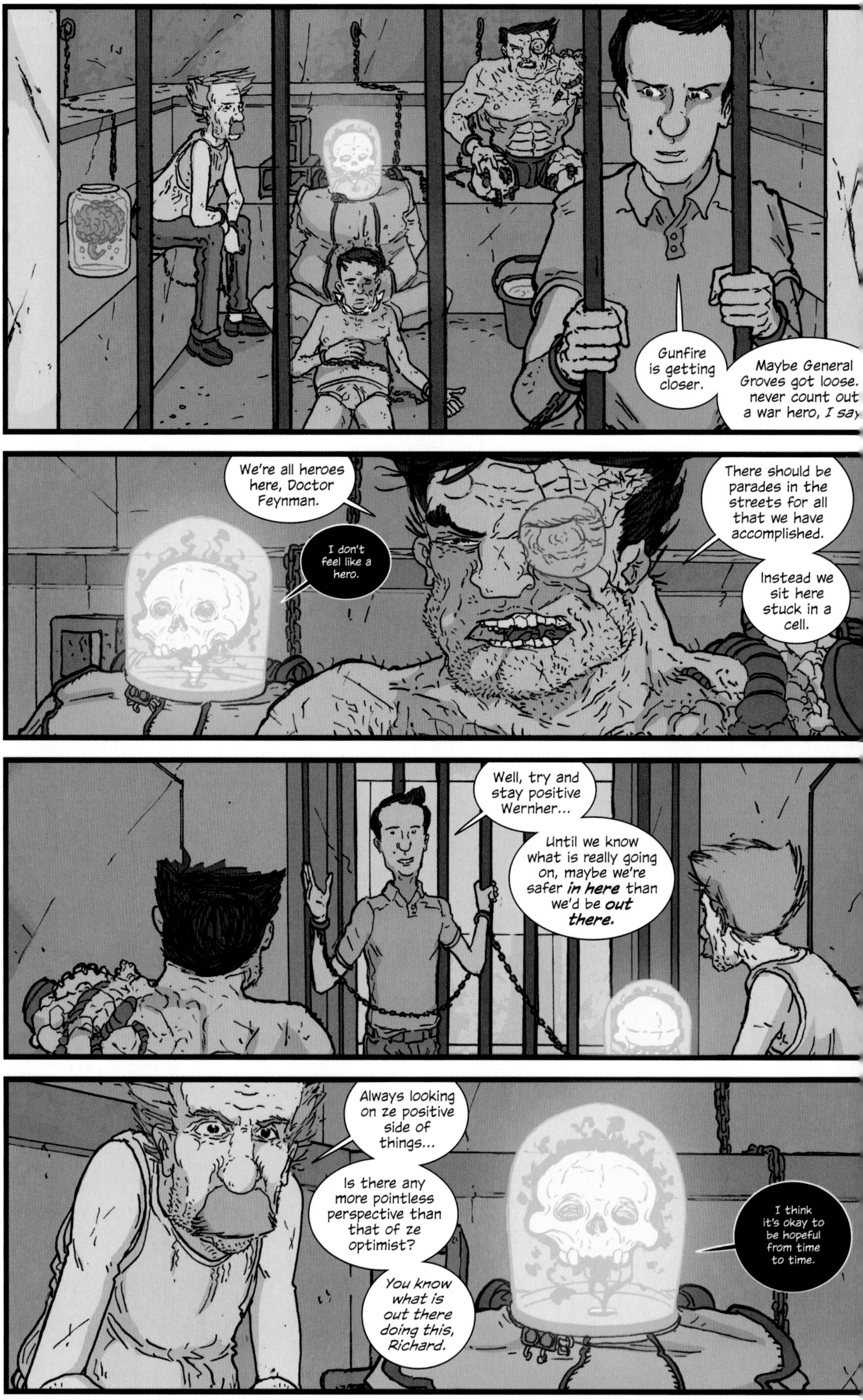

Gunfire is getting closer.
Maybe General Groves got loose. never count out a war hero, *I say*
We're all heroes here, Doctor Feynman.
I don't feel like a hero.
There should be parades in the streets for all that we have accomplished.
Instead we sit here stuck in a cell.
Well, try and stay positive Wernher...
Until we know what is really going on, maybe we're safer ***in here*** than we'd be ***out there.***
Always looking on ze positive side of things...
Is there any more pointless perspective than that of ze optimist?
You know what is out there doing this, Richard.
I think it's okay to be hopeful from time to time.

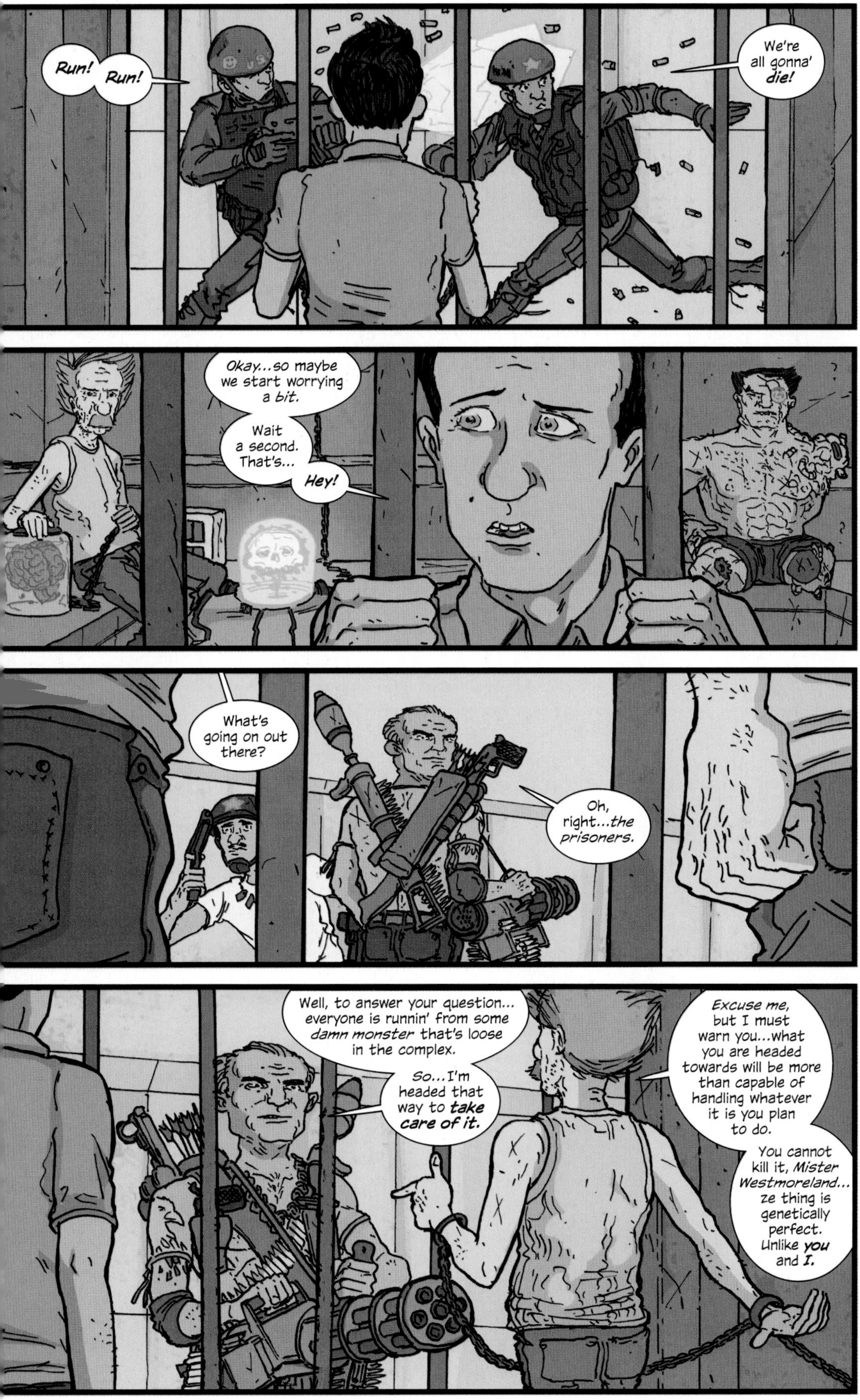
Run!
Run!
We're all gonna' die!
Okay...so maybe we start worrying a bit.
Wait a second. That's...
Hey!
What's going on out there?
Oh, right...the prisoners.
Well, to answer your question... everyone is runnin' from some damn monster that's loose in the complex.
So...I'm headed that way to take care of it.
Excuse me, but I must warn you...what you are headed towards will be more than capable of handling whatever it is you plan to do.
You cannot kill it, Mister Westmoreland... ze thing is genetically perfect. Unlike you and I.

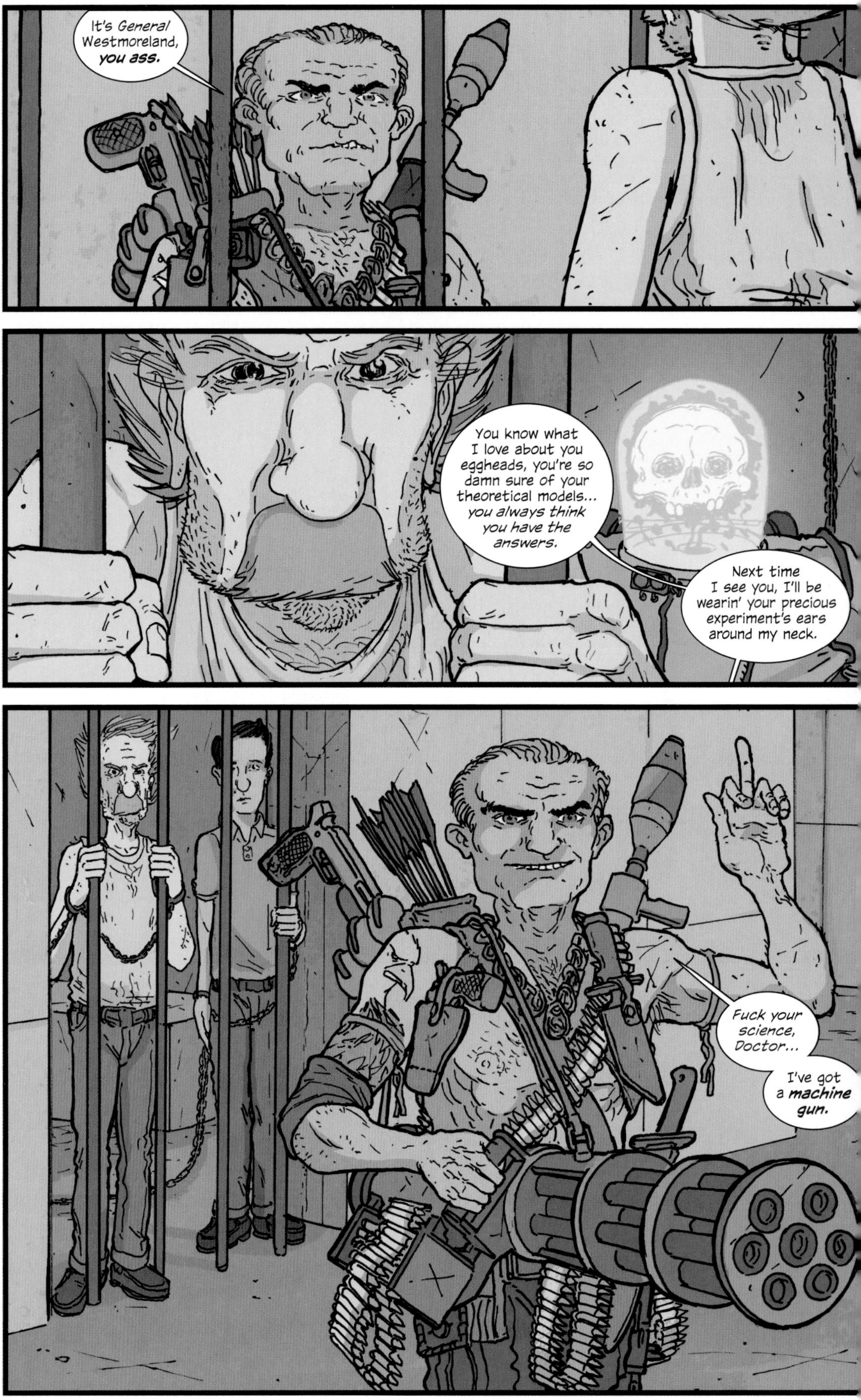
It's *General* Westmoreland, ***you ass.***
You know what I love about you eggheads, you're so damn sure of your theoretical models... *you always think you have the answers.*
Next time I see you, I'll be wearin' your precious experiment's ears around my neck.
Fuck your science, Doctor...
I've got a ***machine gun.***

"WE WERE TRAPPED, AND CAPTIVITY WOULD LEAD TO COMPROMISE. COMPROMISE WOULD LEAD TO BETRAYAL. BETRAYAL WOULD LEAD TO MURDER.

SUCH IS THE WORLD. "

CLAVIS AUREA
THE RECORDED FEYNMAN | **VOL. 4**

I AM NOT A GOOD MAN

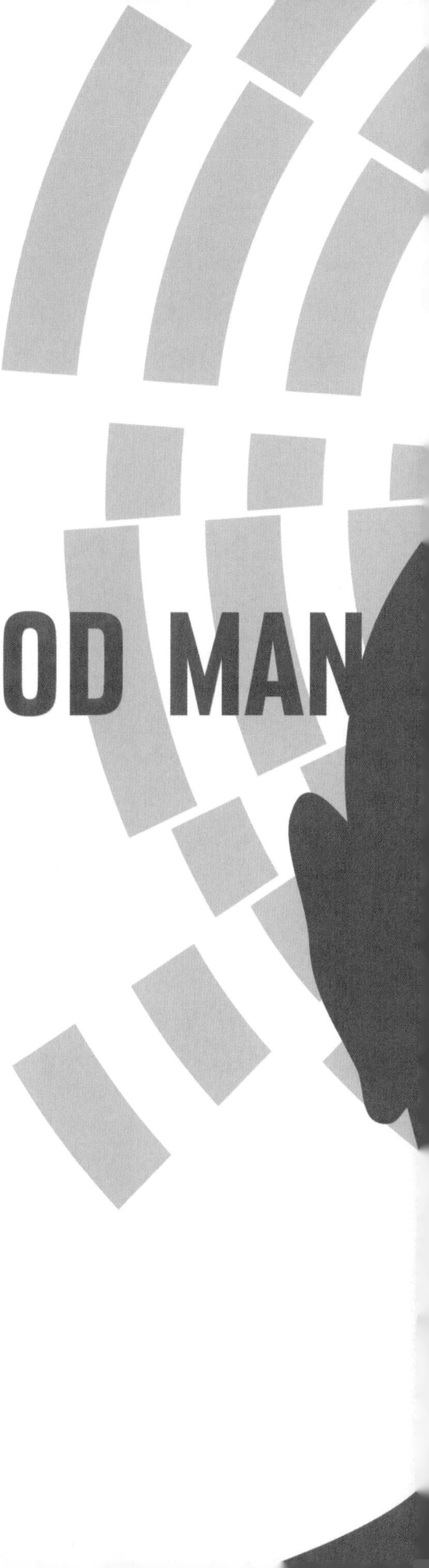

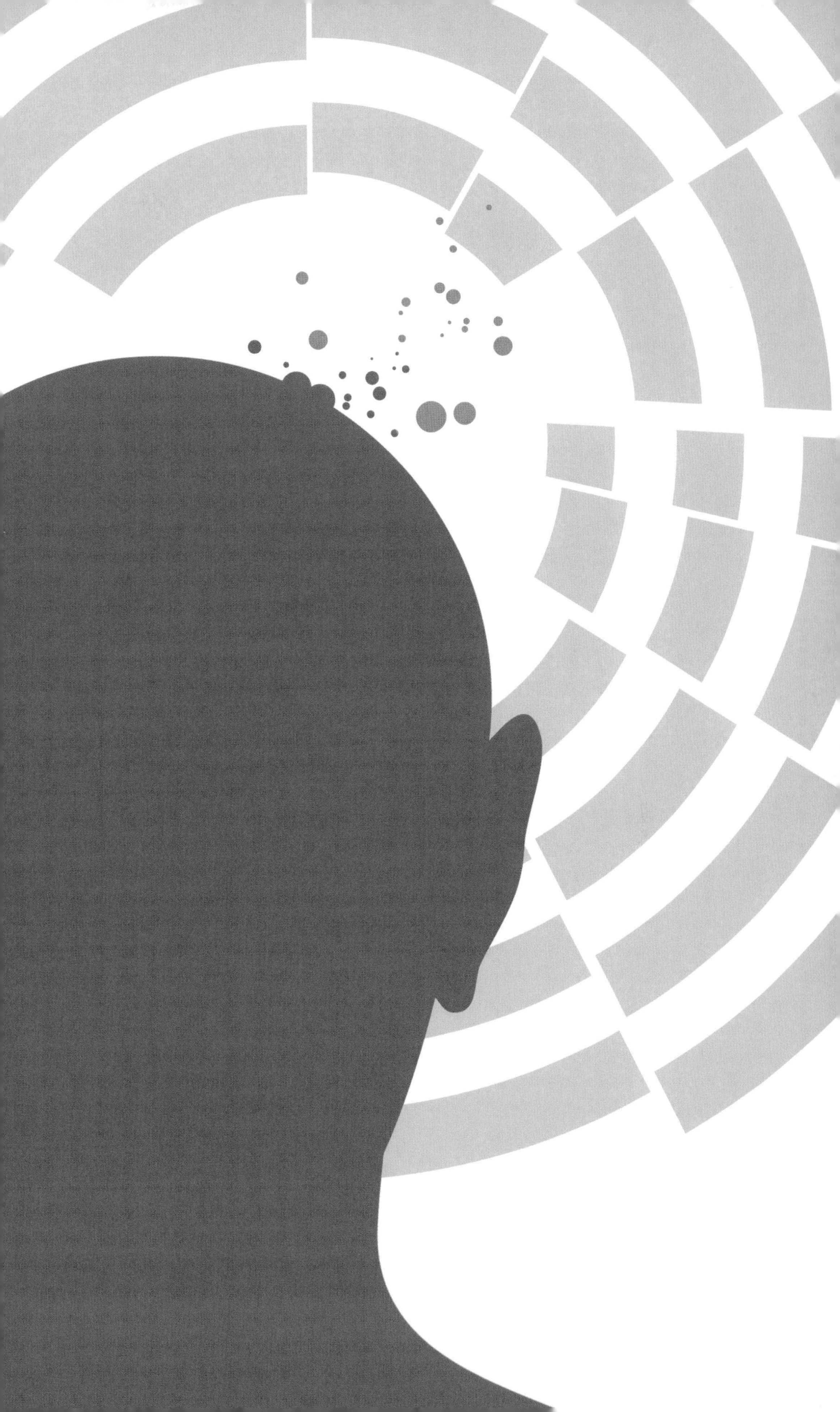

"HMMMMMM."

CLAVIS AUREA
THE RECORDED FEYNMAN | **VOL. 3**

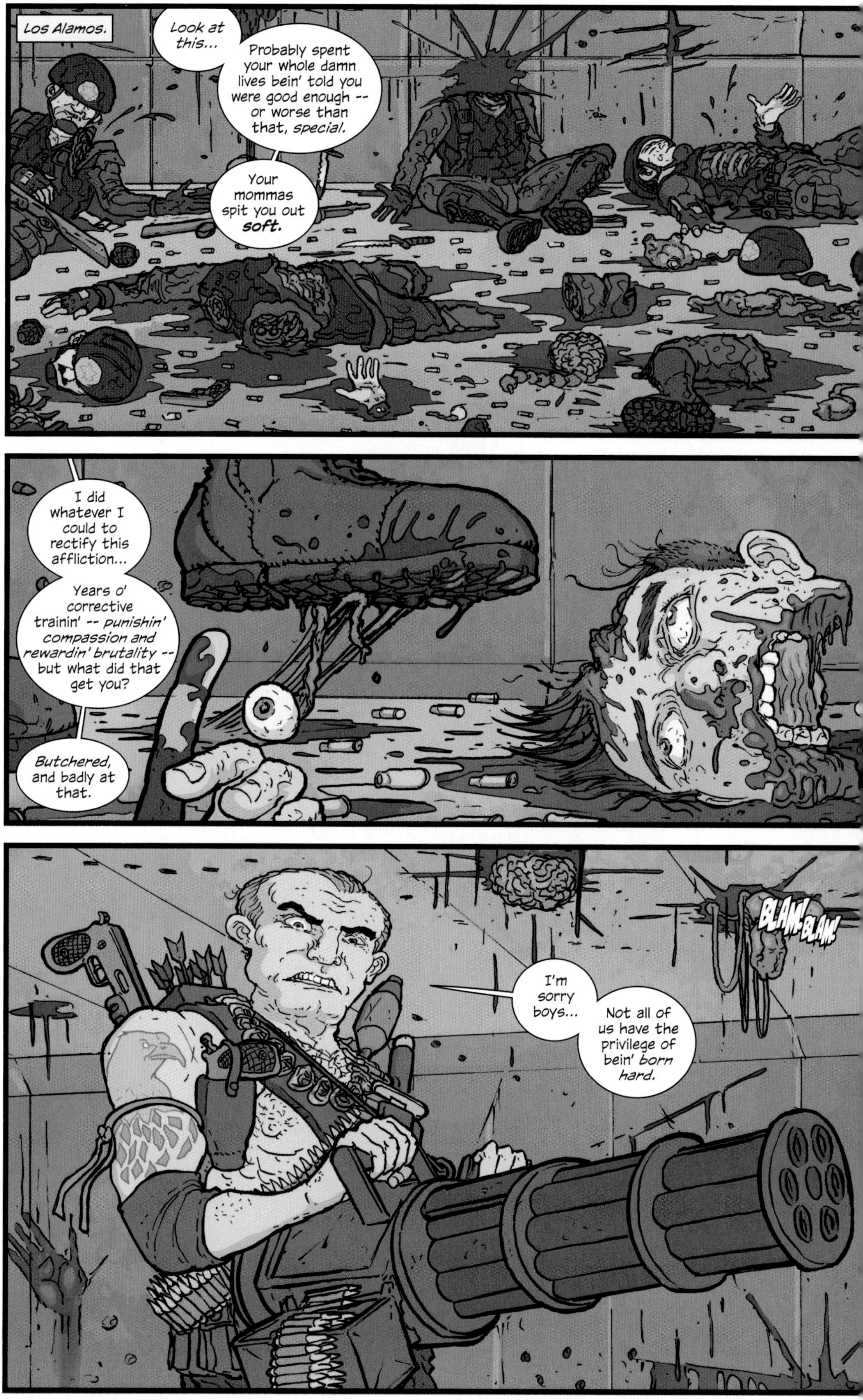
Los Alamos.
Look at this...
Probably spent your whole damn lives bein' told you were good enough -- or worse than that, *special.*
Your mommas spit you out **soft.**
I did whatever I could to rectify this affliction...
Years o' corrective trainin' -- *punishin' compassion and rewardin' brutality* -- but what did that get you?
Butchered, and badly at that.
BLAM! BLAM!
I'm sorry boys...
Not all of us have the privilege of bein' *born hard.*

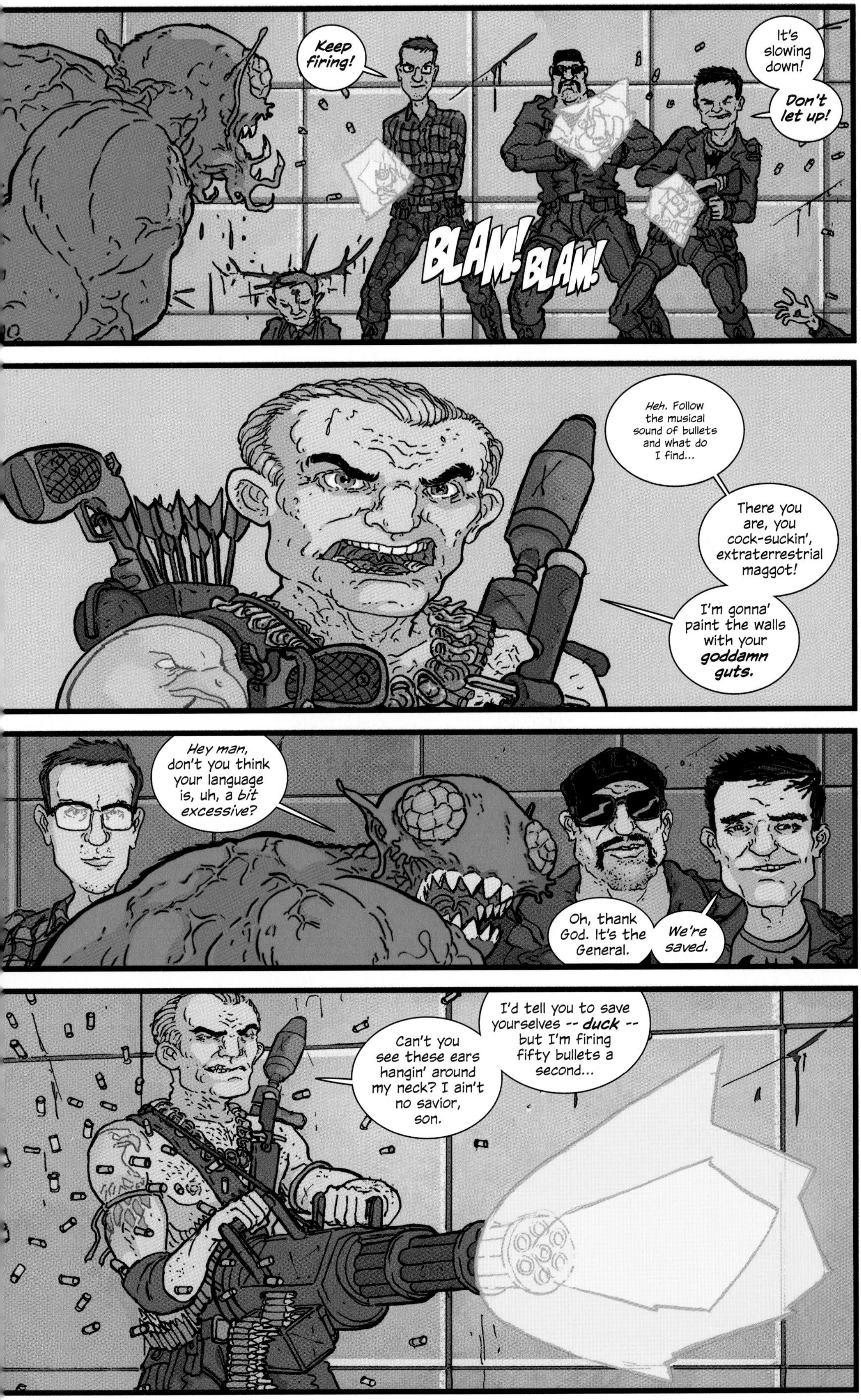
Keep firing!
It's slowing down!
Don't let up!
BLAM! BLAM!
Heh. Follow the musical sound of bullets and what do I find...
There you are, you cock-suckin', extraterrestrial maggot!
I'm gonna' paint the walls with your goddamn guts.
Hey man, don't you think your language is, uh, a bit excessive?
Oh, thank God. It's the General.
We're saved.
Can't you see these ears hangin' around my neck? I ain't no savior, son.
I'd tell you to save yourselves -- duck -- but I'm firing fifty bullets a second...

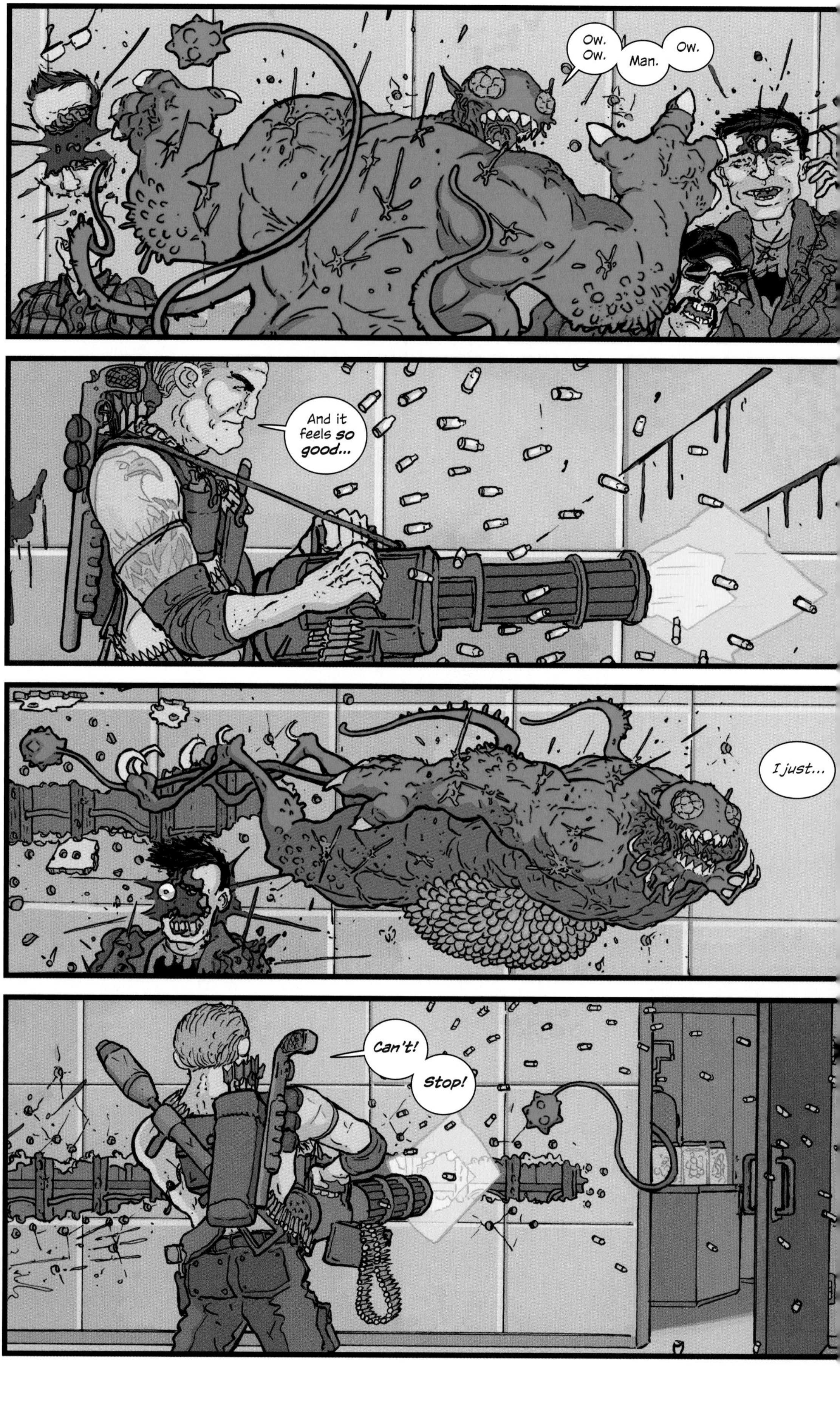
Ow.
Ow.
Man.
Ow.
And it feels so good...
I just...
Can't!
Stop!

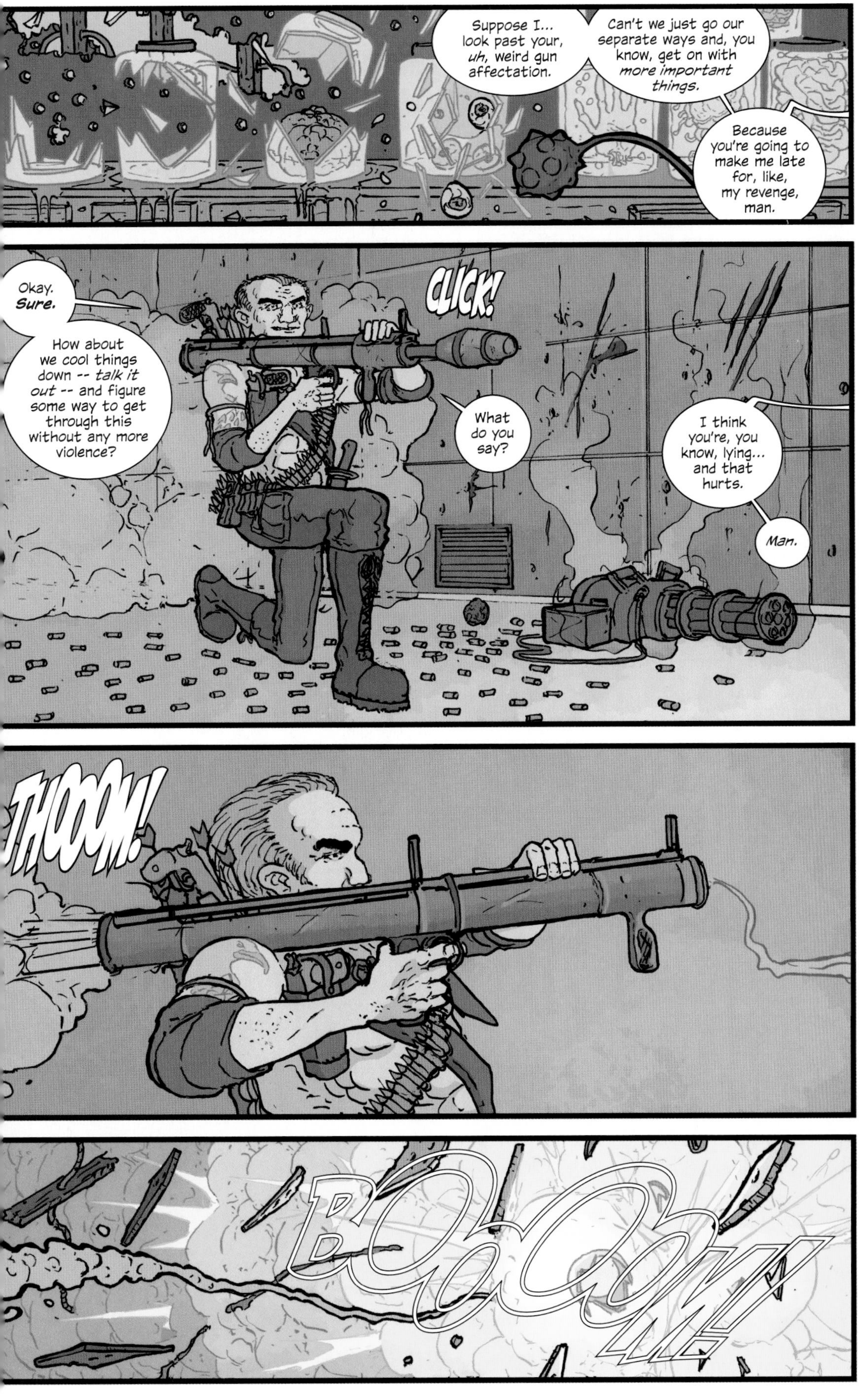

Suppose I... look past your, *uh,* weird gun affectation.
Can't we just go our separate ways and, you know, get on with *more important things.*
Because you're going to make me late for, like, my revenge, man.
Okay. **Sure.**
How about we cool things down -- *talk it out* -- and figure some way to get through this without any more violence?
CLICK!
What do you say?
I think you're, you know, lying... and that hurts.
Man.
THOOOM!
BOOOOM!

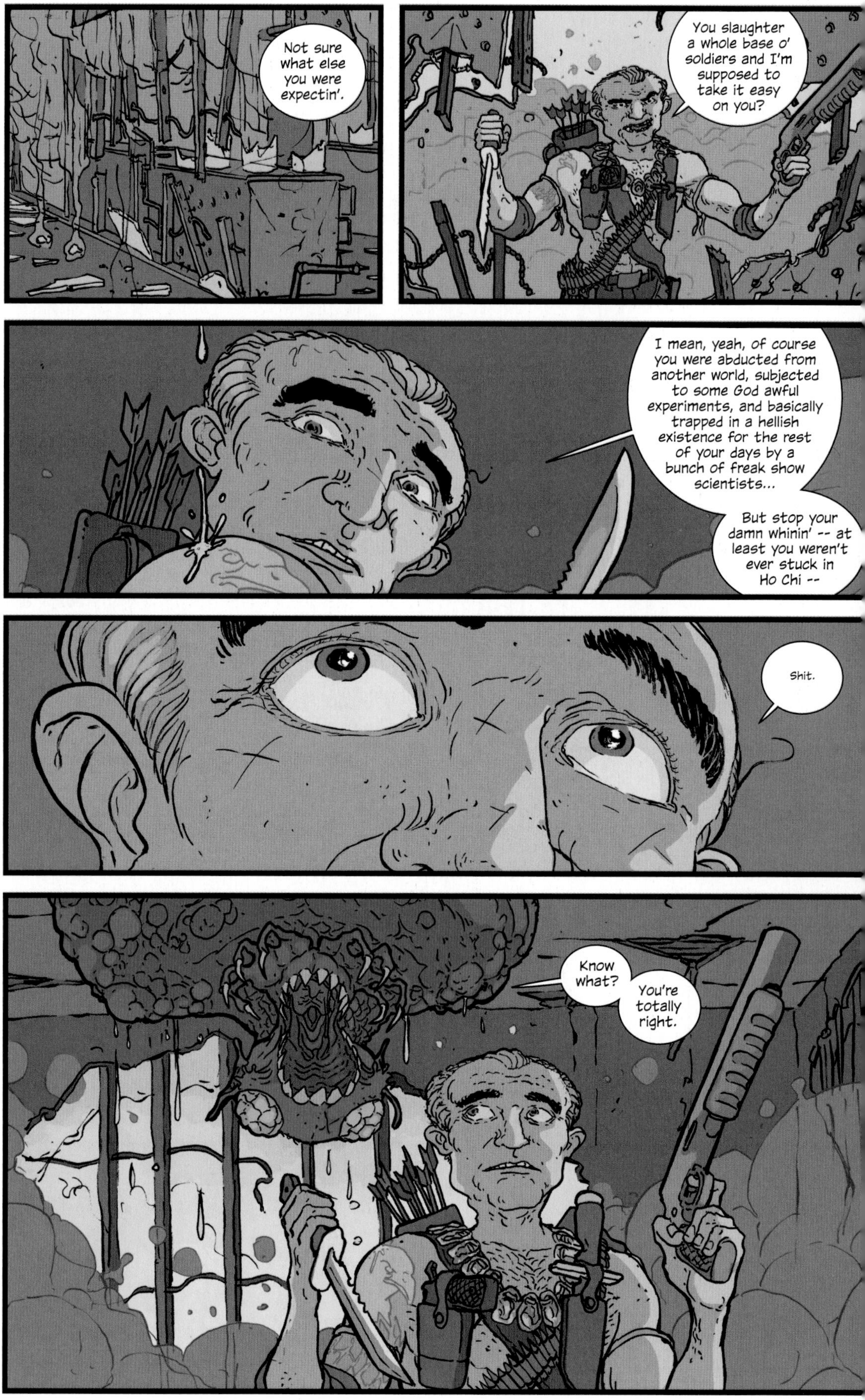
Not sure what else you were expectin'.
You slaughter a whole base o' soldiers and I'm supposed to take it easy on you?
I mean, yeah, of course you were abducted from another world, subjected to some God awful experiments, and basically trapped in a hellish existence for the rest of your days by a bunch of freak show scientists...
But stop your damn whinin' -- at least you weren't ever stuck in Ho Chi --
Shit.
Know what?
You're totally right.

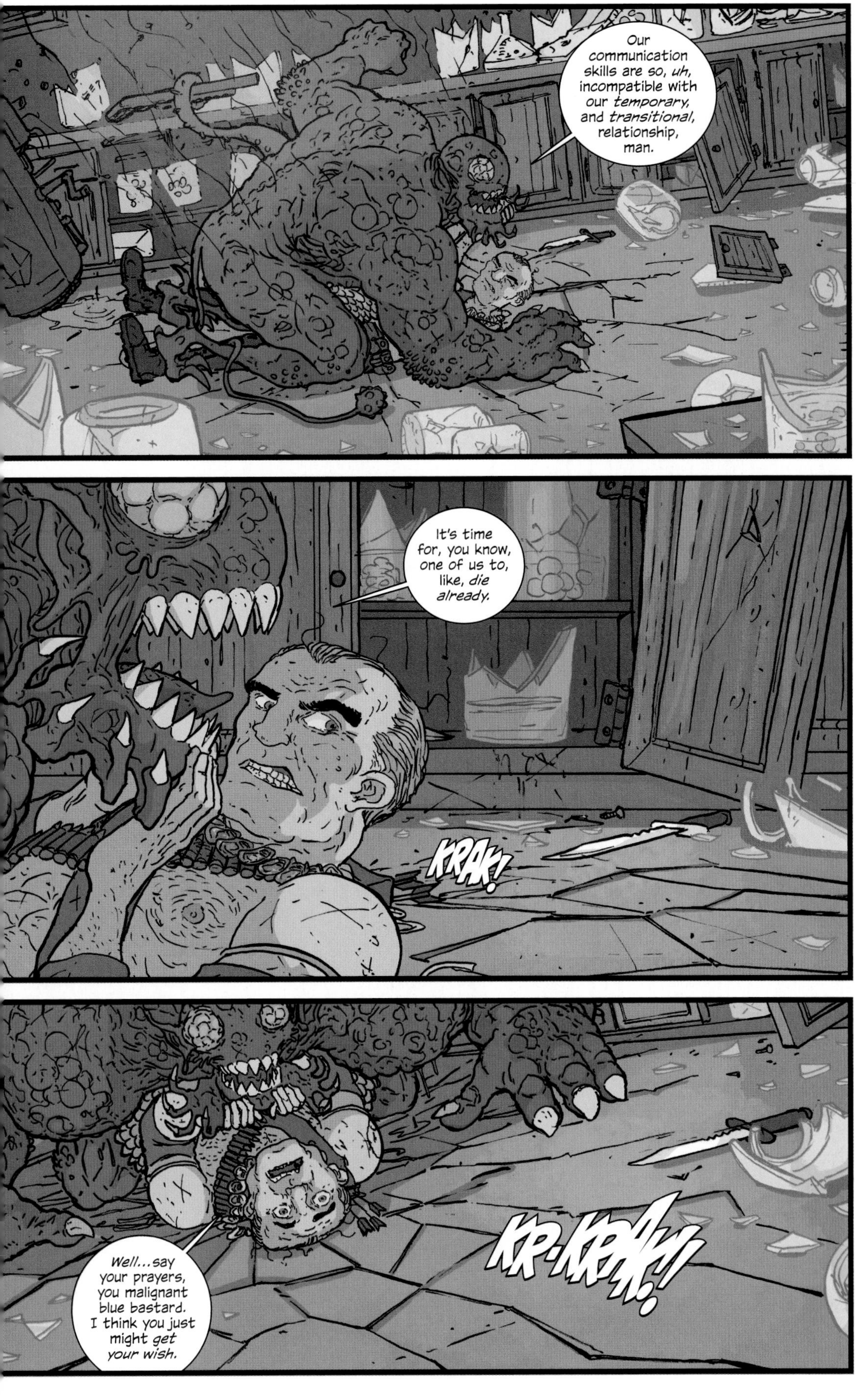
Our communication skills are so, *uh*, incompatible with our *temporary*, and *transitional*, relationship, man.
It's time for, you know, one of us to, like, *die already*.
KRAK!
Well...say your prayers, you malignant blue bastard. I think you just might *get your wish*.
KR-KRAK!

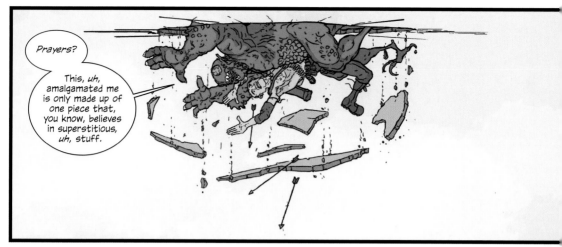

Prayers?

This, *uh*, amalgamated me is only made up of one piece that, you know, believes in superstitious, *uh*, stuff.

You might think that recent experiences would have, uh, soured us on science...

And until now you'd be wrong.

But I confess. This gravity is, like, depressing, man.

I guess we're, I dunno, done for.

Hrmpt!

So just like the Vietcong, you're a godless monster. **Shoulda guessed.** Do you wanna know how I got these lucky souvenirs I wear around my neck?

Preparation and answered prayers.

Enjoy the fall, you damn heathen.

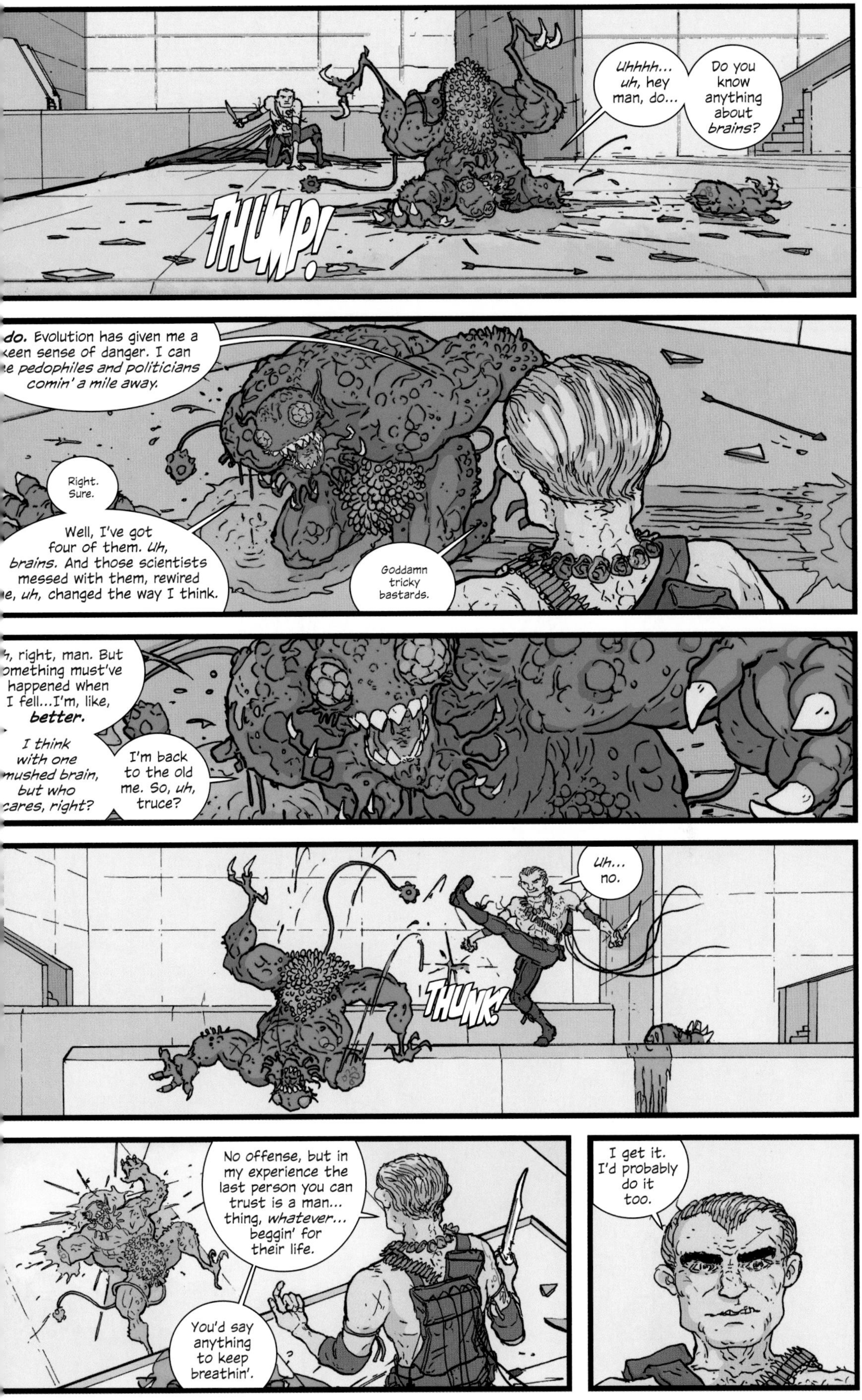
THUMP!
Uhhhh... uh, hey man, do...
Do you know anything about brains?
do. Evolution has given me a een sense of danger. I can e pedophiles and politicians comin' a mile away.
Right. Sure.
Well, I've got four of them. Uh, brains. And those scientists messed with them, rewired e, uh, changed the way I think.
Goddamn tricky bastards.
, right, man. But omething must've happened when I fell...I'm, like, better.
I think with one mushed brain, but who cares, right?
I'm back to the old me. So, uh, truce?
THUNK!
Uh... no.
No offense, but in my experience the last person you can trust is a man... thing, whatever... beggin' for their life.
You'd say anything to keep breathin'.
I get it. I'd probably do it too.

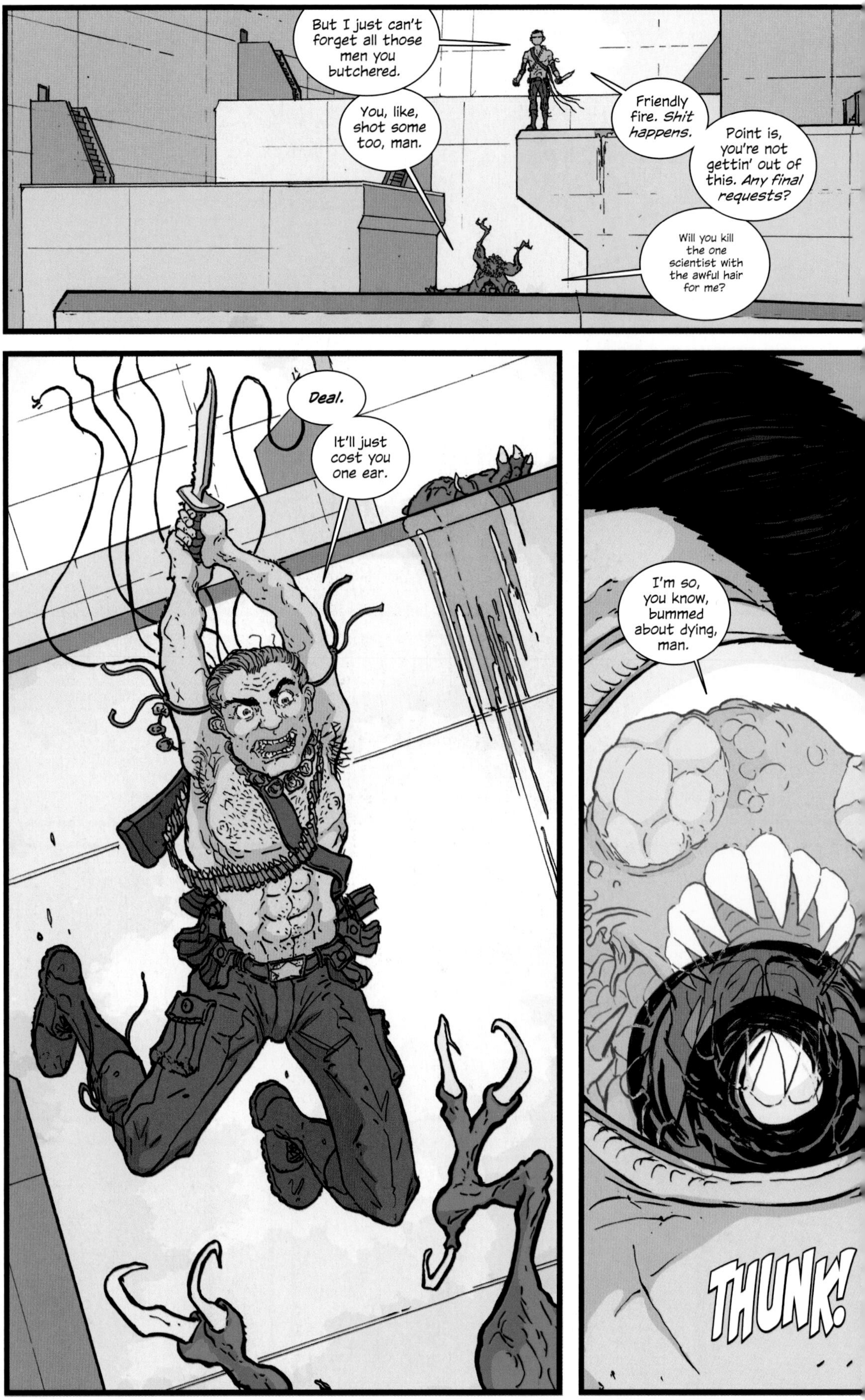
But I just can't forget all those men you butchered.
You, like, shot some too, man.
Friendly fire. *Shit happens.*
Point is, you're not gettin' out of this. *Any final requests?*
Will you kill the one scientist with the awful hair for me?
Deal.
It'll just cost you one ear.
I'm so, you know, bummed about dying, man.
THUNK!

"HMMMMMMMMMMMM!"

CLAVIS AUREA
THE RECORDED FEYNMAN | VOL. 3

18

ASSASSINATION

"HMMMMMMMMMMMM?"

CLAVIS AUREA
THE RECORDED FEYNMAN | VOL. 3

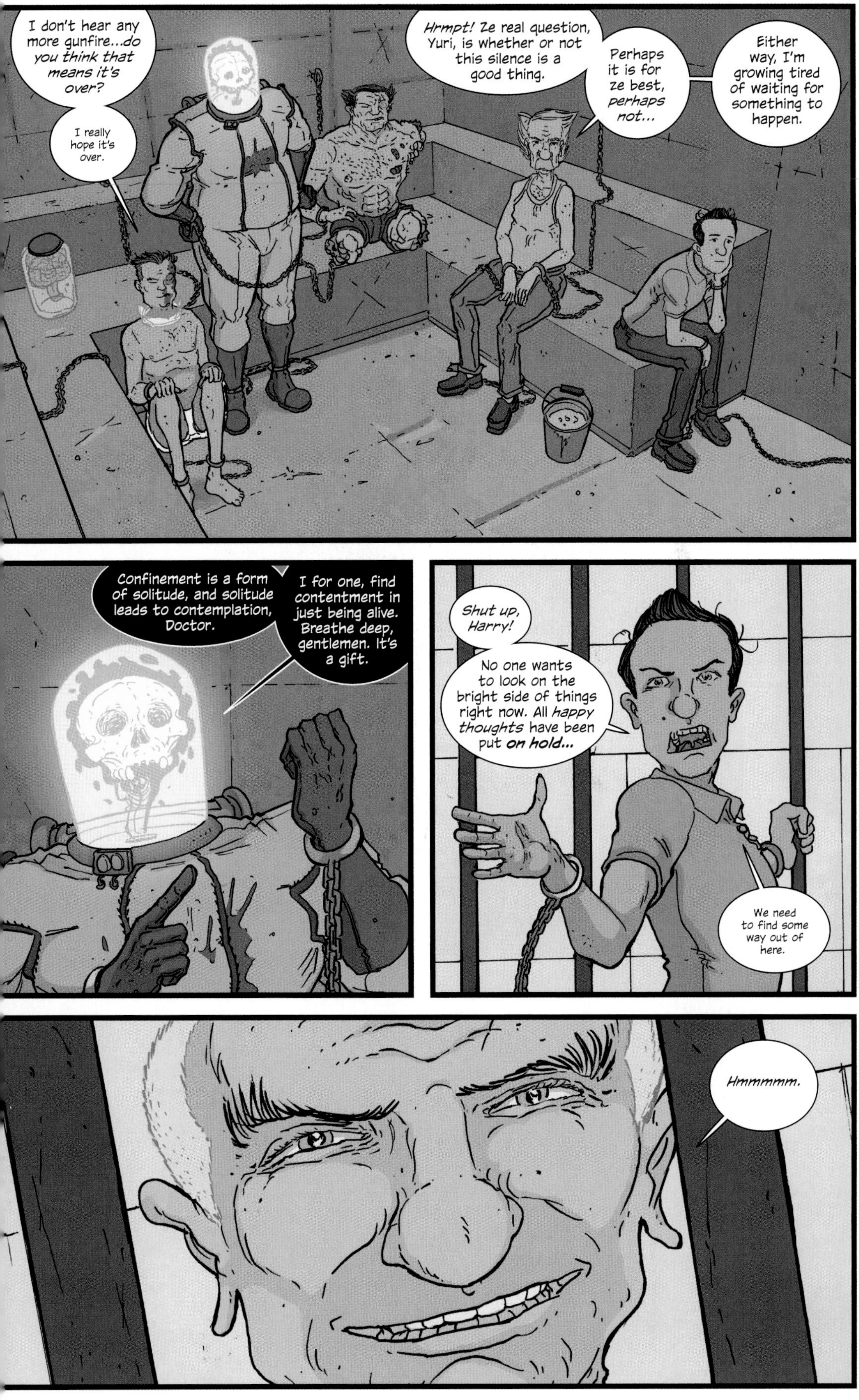
I don't hear any more gunfire...*do you think that means it's over?*
I really hope it's over.
Hrmpt! Ze real question, Yuri, is whether or not this silence is a good thing.
Perhaps it is for ze best, *perhaps not...*
Either way, I'm growing tired of waiting for something to happen.
Confinement is a form of solitude, and solitude leads to contemplation, Doctor.
I for one, find contentment in just being alive. Breathe deep, gentlemen. It's a gift.
Shut up, Harry!
No one wants to look on the bright side of things right now. All *happy thoughts* have been put ***on hold...***
We need to find some way out of here.
Hmmmmm.

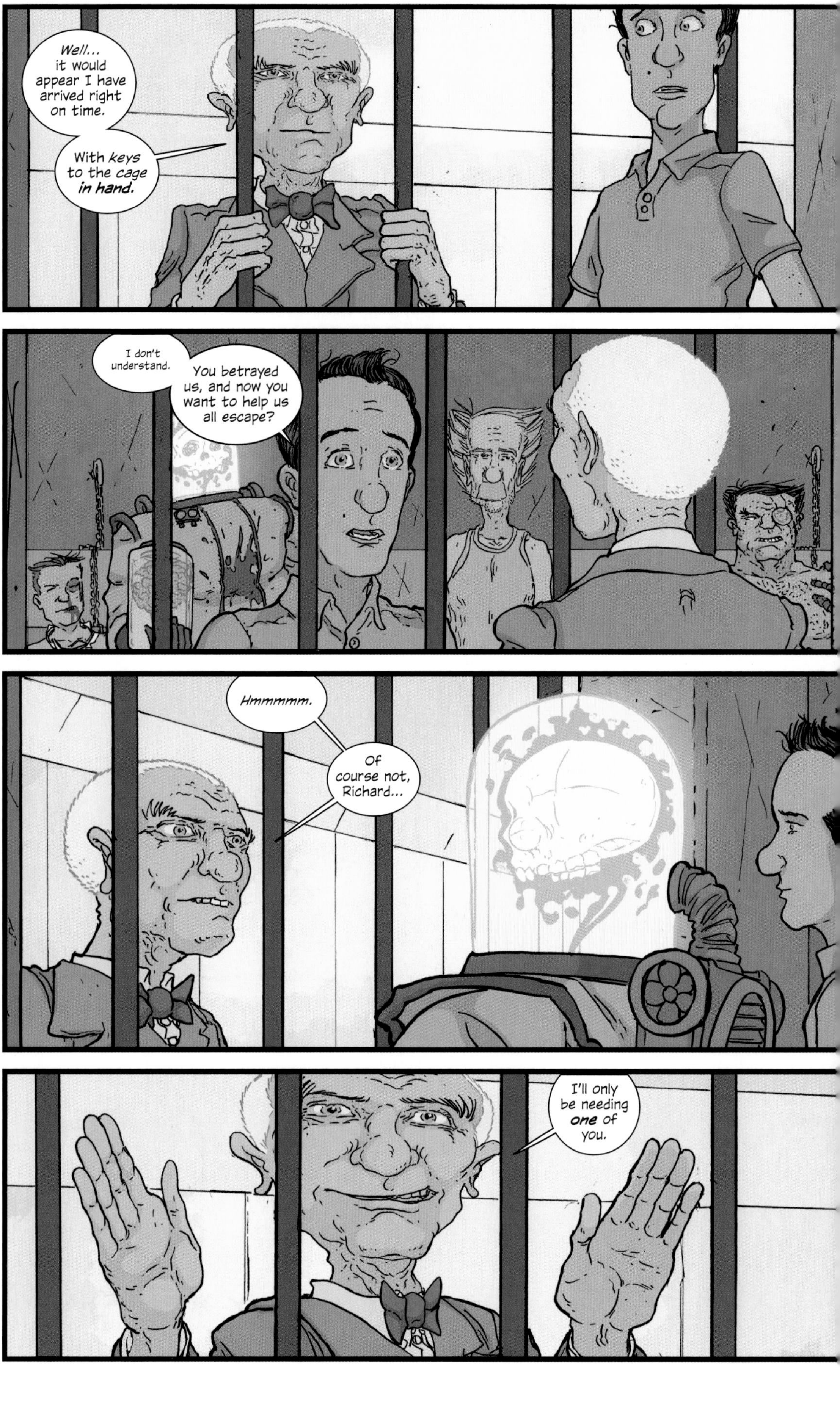
Well... it would appear I have arrived right on time.
With keys to the cage in hand.
I don't understand.
You betrayed us, and now you want to help us all escape?
Hmmmmm.
Of course not, Richard...
I'll only be needing one of you.

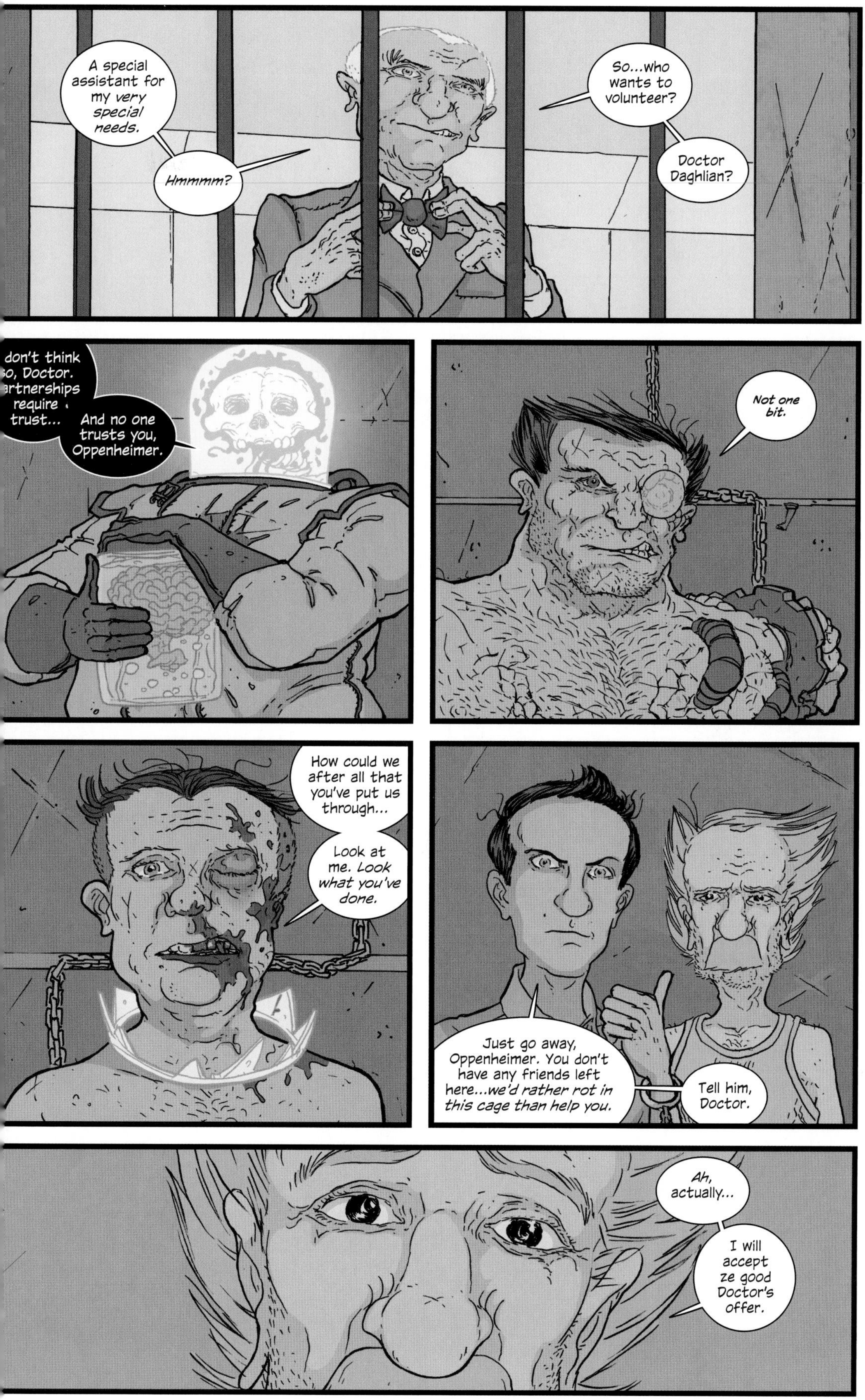

A special assistant for my *very special* needs.
Hmmmm?
So...who wants to volunteer?
Doctor Daghlian?
don't think so, Doctor. artnerships require trust...
And no one trusts you, Oppenheimer.
Not one bit.
How could we after all that you've put us through...
Look at me. *Look what you've done.*
Just go away, Oppenheimer. You don't have any friends left here...*we'd rather rot in this cage than help you.*
Tell him, Doctor.
Ah, actually...
I will accept ze good Doctor's offer.

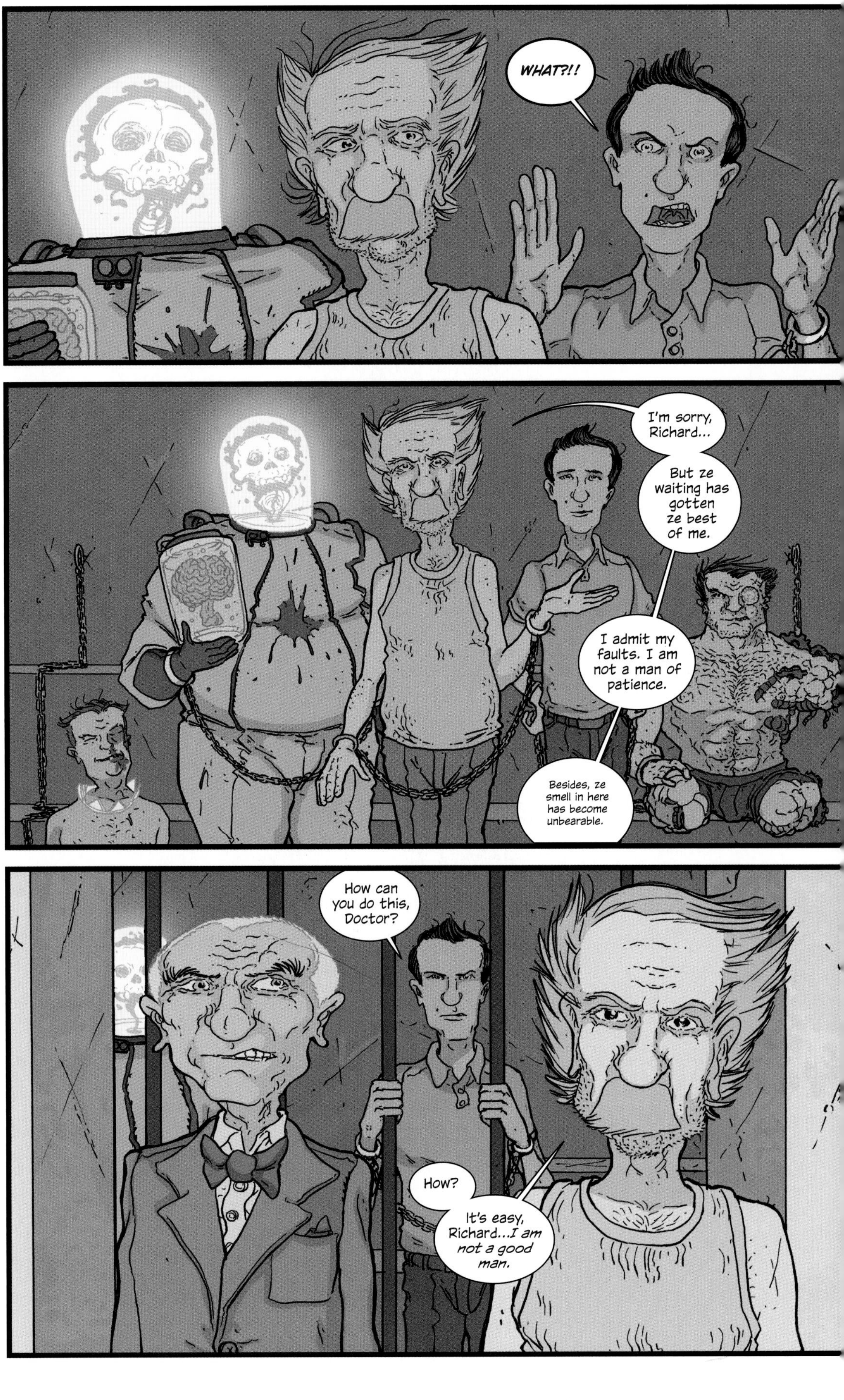
WHAT?!!
I'm sorry, Richard...
But ze waiting has gotten ze best of me.
I admit my faults. I am not a man of patience.
Besides, ze smell in here has become unbearable.
How can you do this, Doctor?
How?
It's easy, Richard...*I am not a good man.*

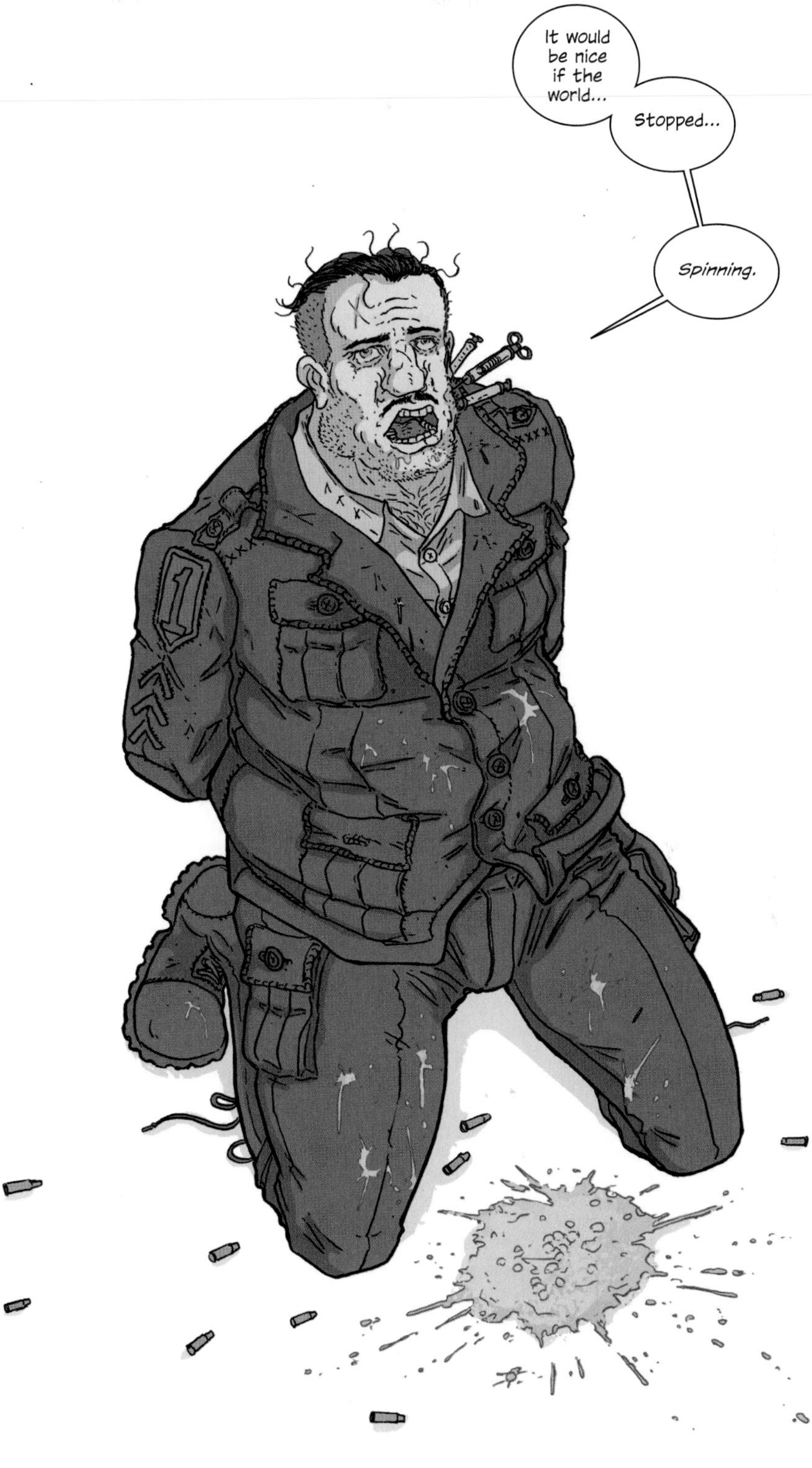
It would be nice if the world...
Stopped...
Spinning.

Well, would you look at this?

I have to be honest, Leslie...I am somewhat surprised to find you still alive.

There's a trail of bodies leading all the way here. How'd you manage to survive that monster?

I told the truth.

Is that a...*blue ear*?

It is indeed. Procured and processed this very day.

So, the truth, *huh*? Then I take it you're still pumped full of whatever serum Oppenheimer injected you with...

Maybe I should ask you a few questions of my own, would you like that?

No.

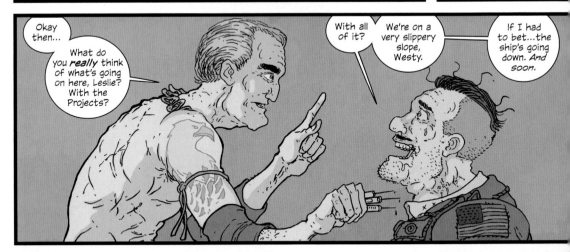

Okay then...

What do you *really* think of what's going on here, Leslie? With the Projects?

With all of it?

We're on a very slippery slope, Westy.

If I had to bet...the ship's going down. *And soon.*

But you still believe, right?

World's not what I once thought it was...

It's stranger. More dangerous. A good bit more wonderful.

Understood. At first I just wanted to carpet bomb the whole place. Now, after killin' that blue bastard with my bare hands, I'm thinkin' there's bigger, badder things out there.

Tell me the truth... would you be willin' to work with me to kill them before they kill us?

I would.

Well... all right then.

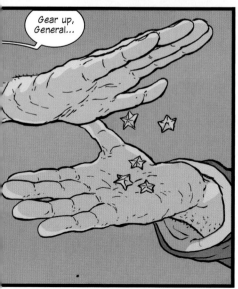

Gear up, General...

We've got a job to do.

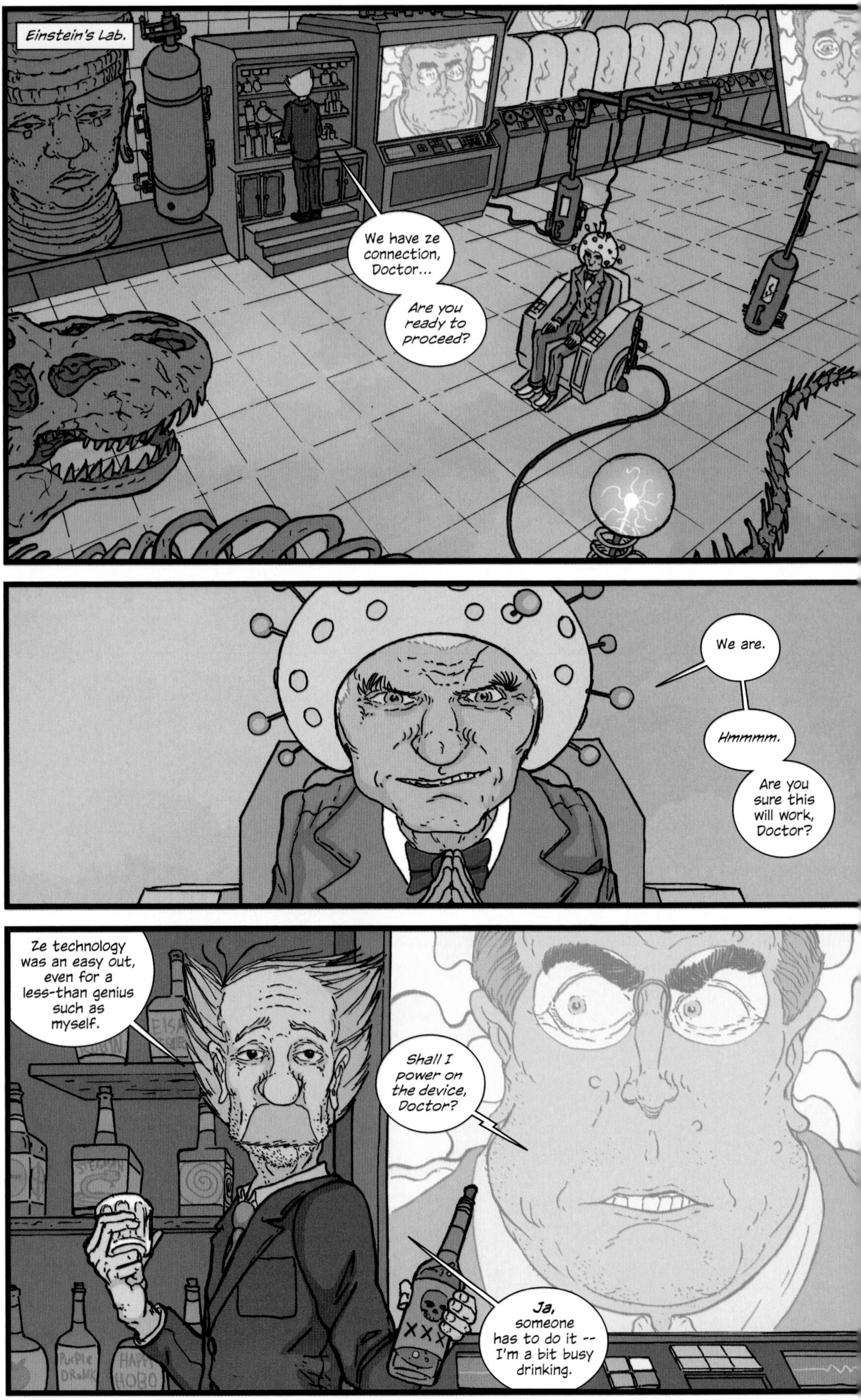
Einstein's Lab.
We have ze connection, Doctor...
Are you ready to proceed?
We are.
Hmmmm.
Are you sure this will work, Doctor?
Ze technology was an easy out, even for a less-than genius such as myself.
Shall I power on the device, Doctor?
Ja, someone has to do it -- I'm a bit busy drinking.
XXX
Purple Drank
Happy Hobo

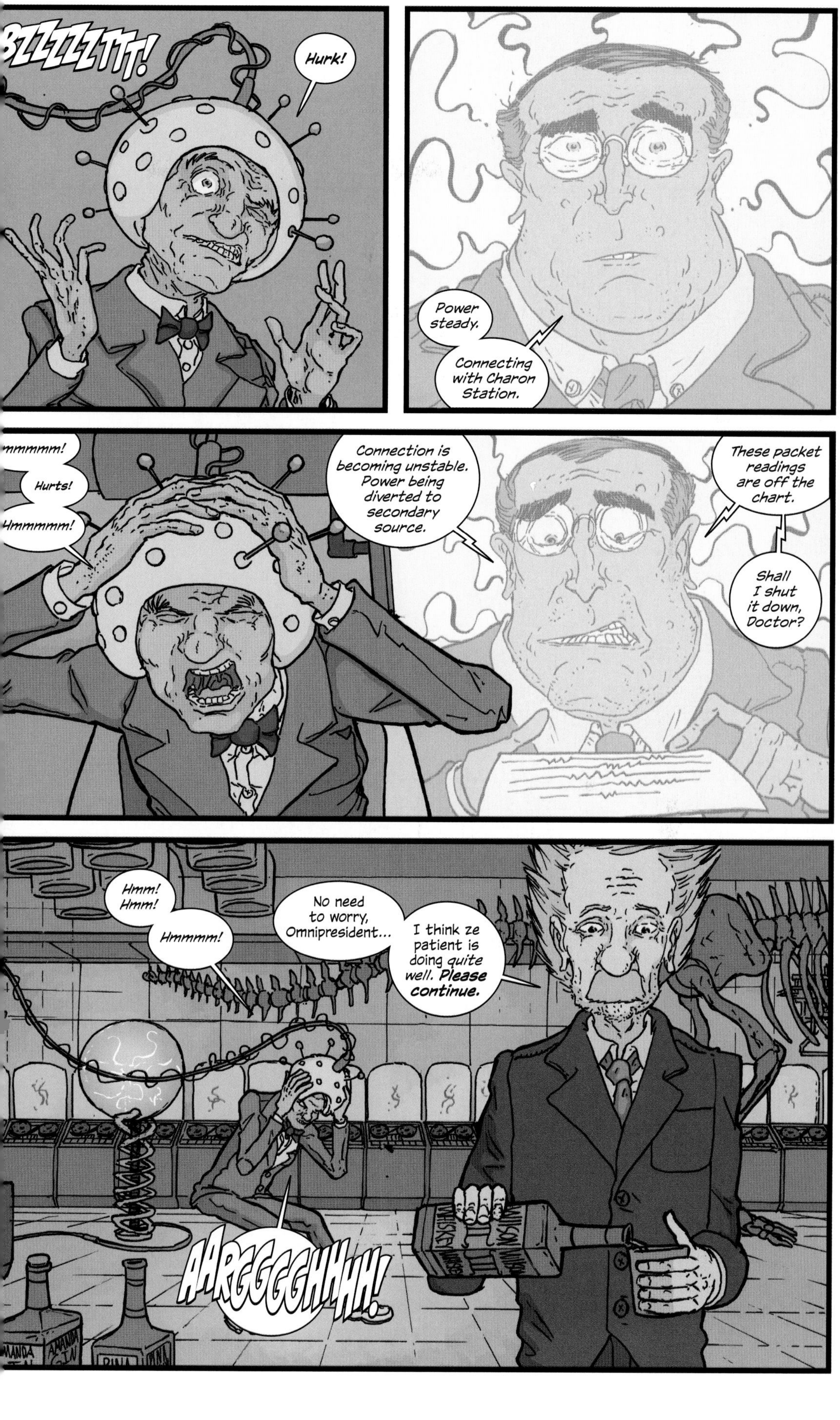

BZZZZZTTT!
Hurk!
Power steady.
Connecting with Charon Station.
mmmmmm!
Hurts!
Hmmmmm!
Connection is becoming unstable. Power being diverted to secondary source.
These packet readings are off the chart.
Shall I shut it down, Doctor?
Hmm! Hmm!
Hmmmm!
No need to worry, Omnipresident...
I think ze patient is doing *quite* well. **Please continue.**
AARGGGGHHHH!

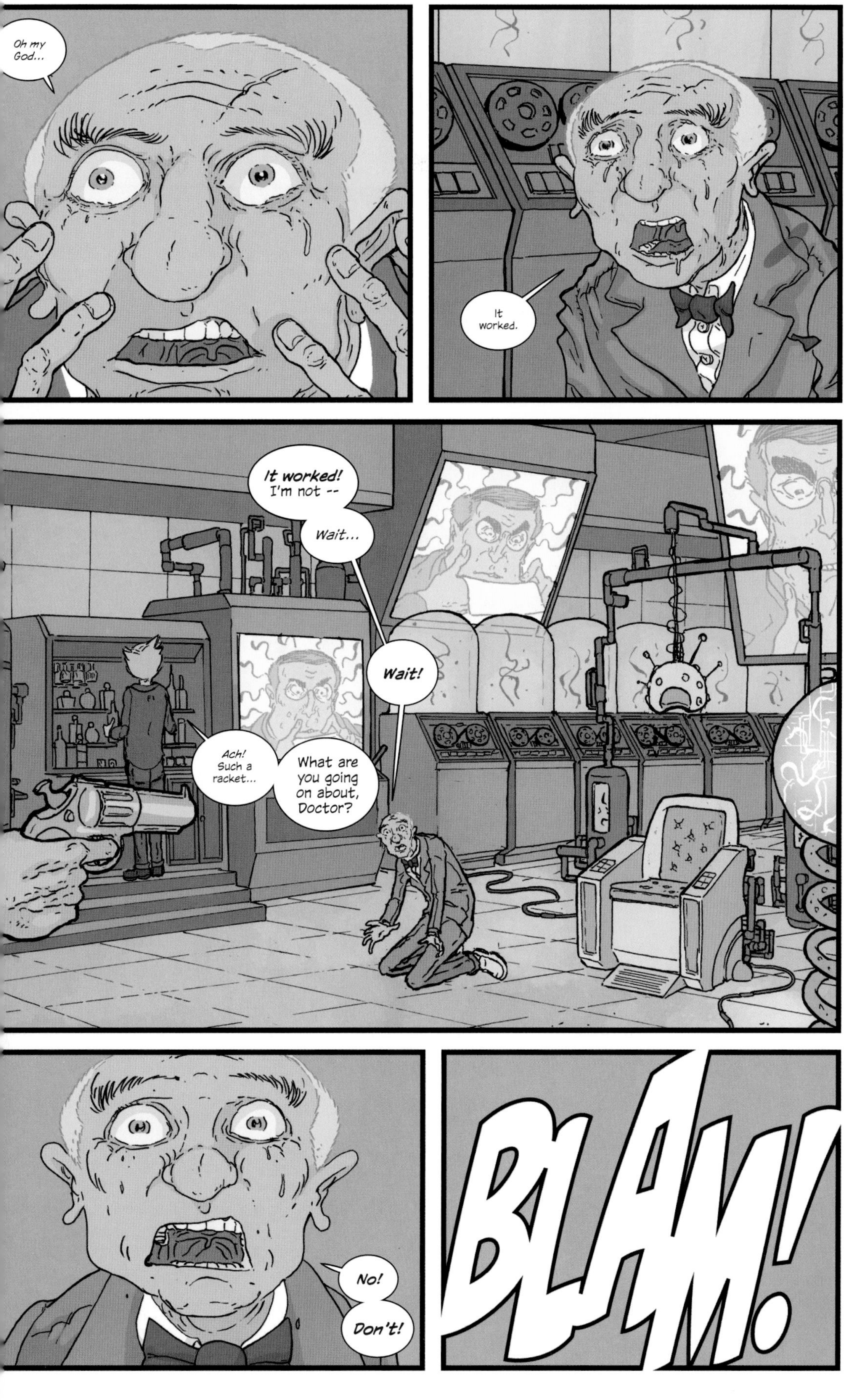
Oh my God...
It worked.
It worked! I'm not --
Wait...
Wait!
Ach! Such a racket...
What are you going on about, Doctor?
No!
Don't!
BLAM!

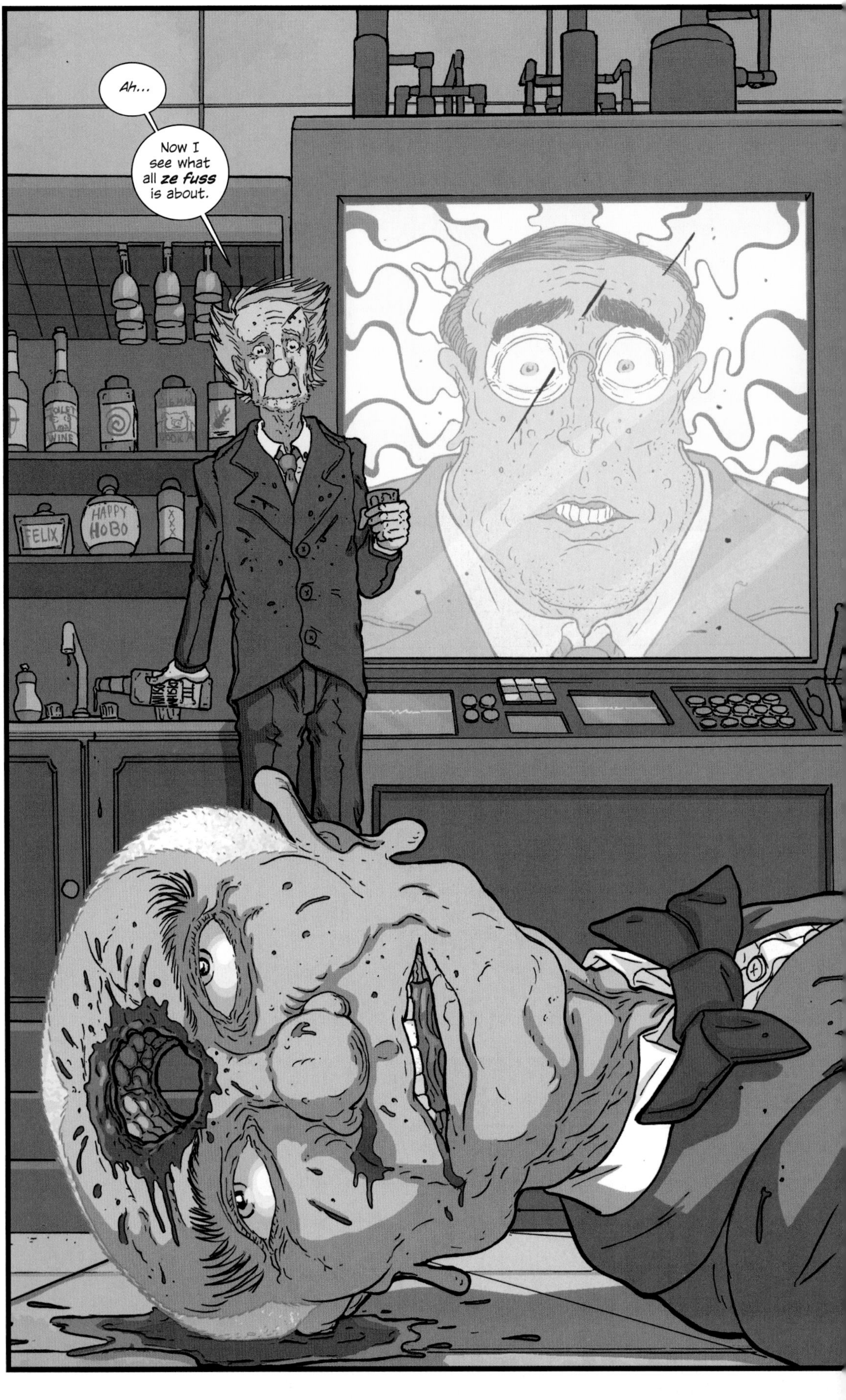

Ah...
Now I see what all ze fuss is about.
TOILET WINE
FELIX
HAPPY HOBO
XXX

"HMMM - - "

CLAVIS AUREA
THE RECORDED FEYNMAN | **VOL. 3**

AND THEN ONE DAY
HE WOKE UP

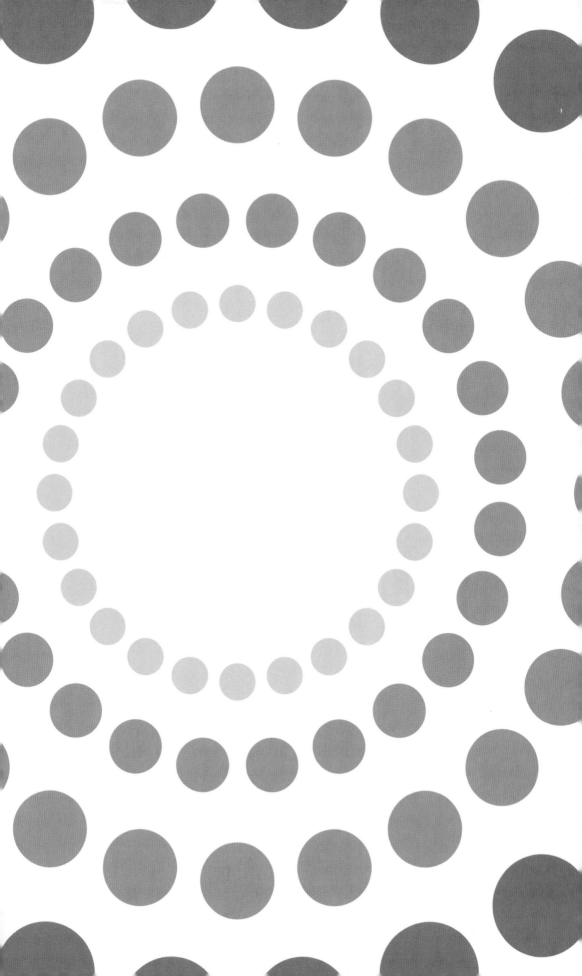

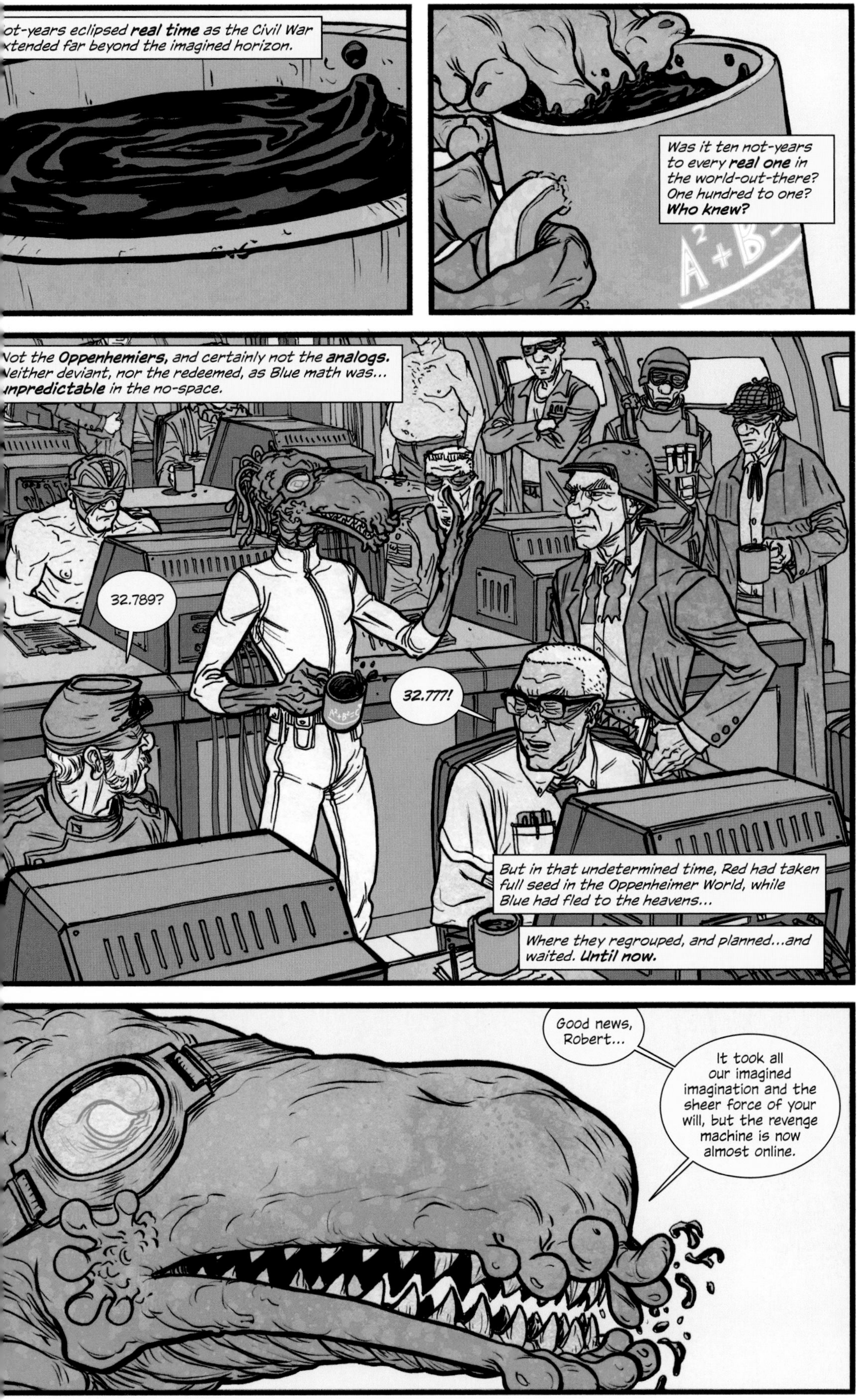
ot-years eclipsed real time as the Civil War xtended far beyond the imagined horizon.
Was it ten not-years to every real one in the world-out-there? One hundred to one? Who knew?
Not the Oppenhemiers, and certainly not the analogs. Neither deviant, nor the redeemed, as Blue math was... unpredictable in the no-space.
32.789?
32.777!
But in that undetermined time, Red had taken full seed in the Oppenheimer World, while Blue had fled to the heavens...
Where they regrouped, and planned...and waited. Until now.
Good news, Robert...
It took all our imagined imagination and the sheer force of your will, but the revenge machine is now almost online.

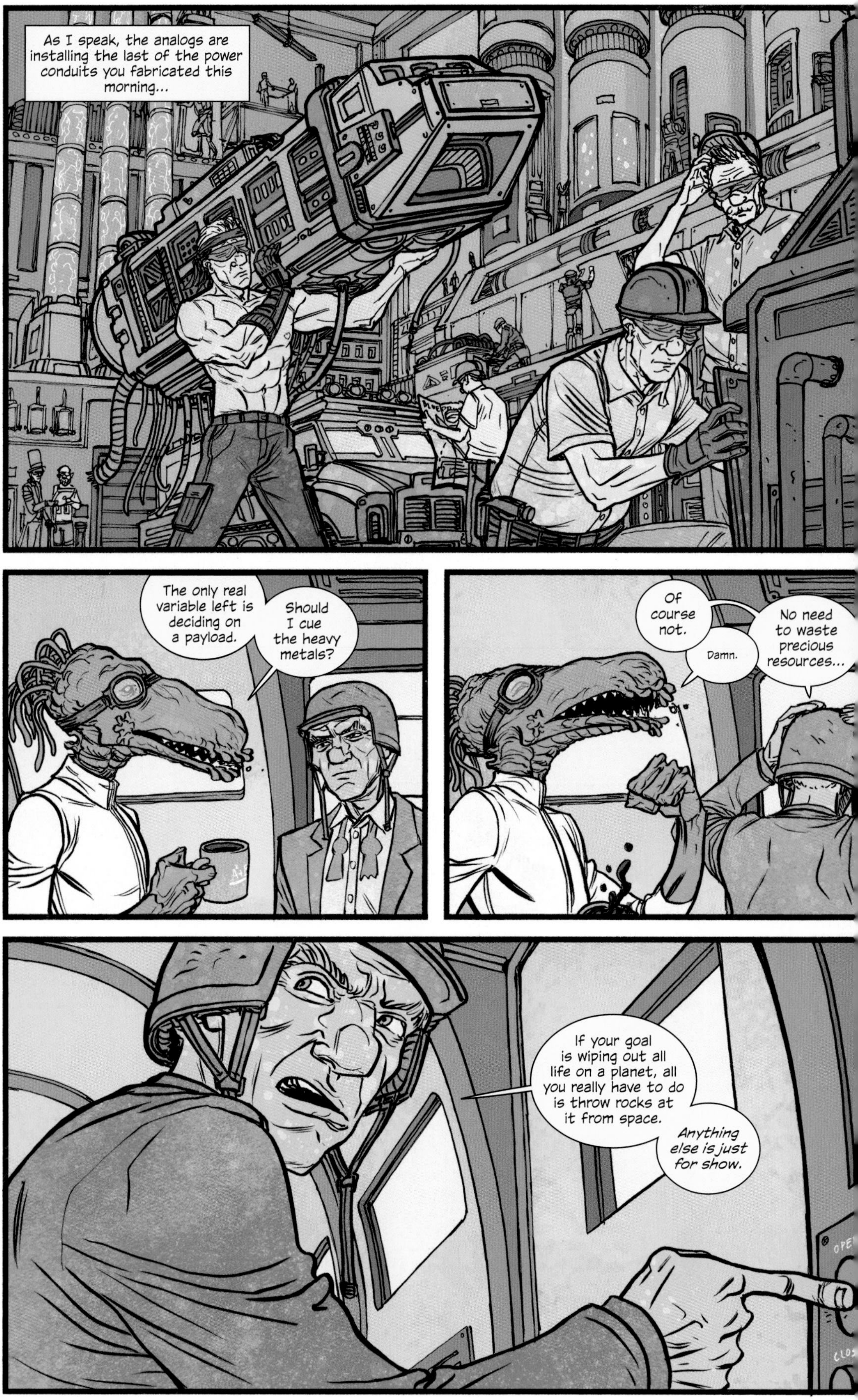
As I speak, the analogs are installing the last of the power conduits you fabricated this morning...
The only real variable left is deciding on a payload.
Should I cue the heavy metals?
Of course not.
Damn.
No need to waste precious resources...
If your goal is wiping out all life on a planet, all you really have to do is throw rocks at it from space.
Anything else is just for show.

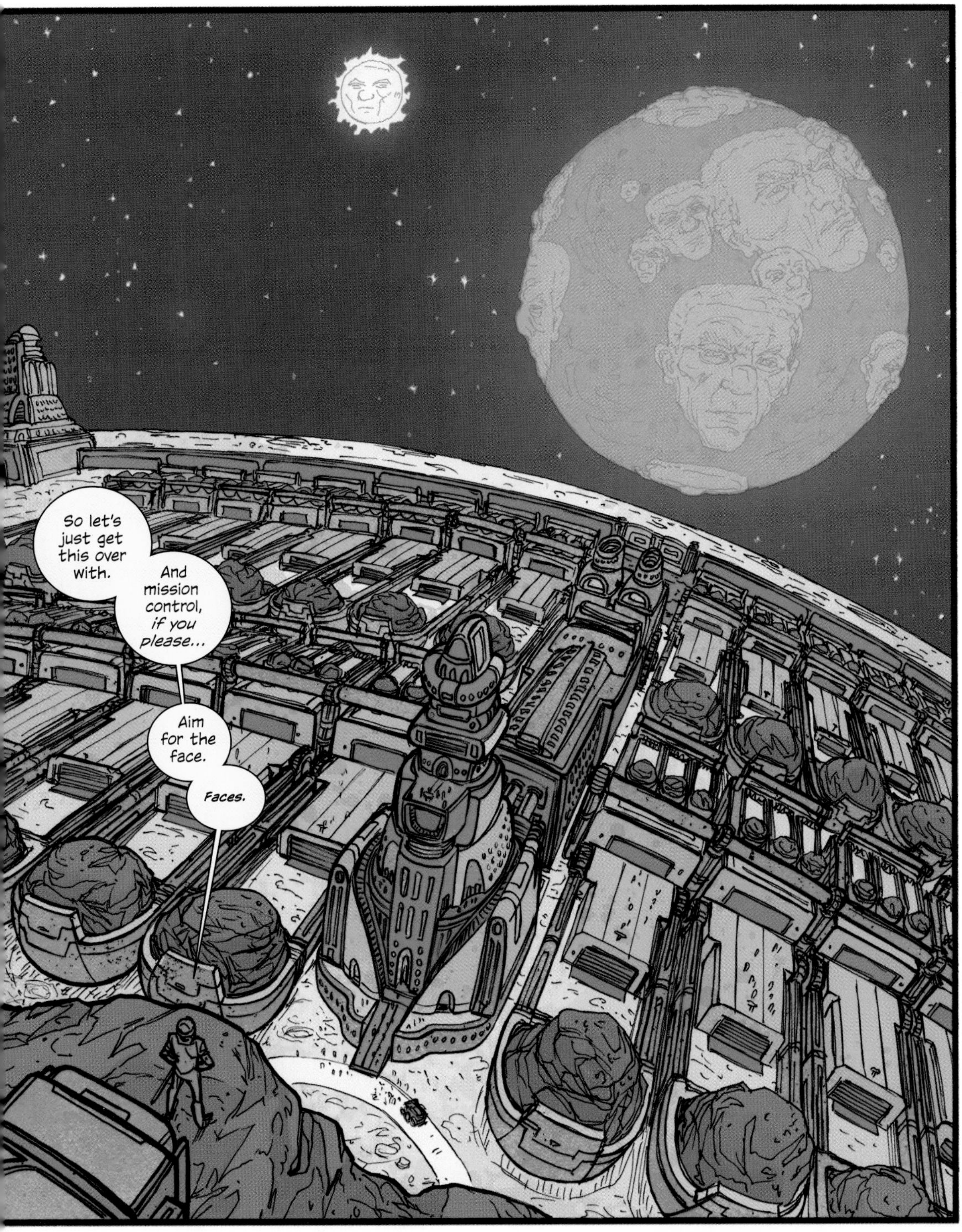
So let's just get this over with.
And mission control, *if you please...*
Aim for the face.
Faces.

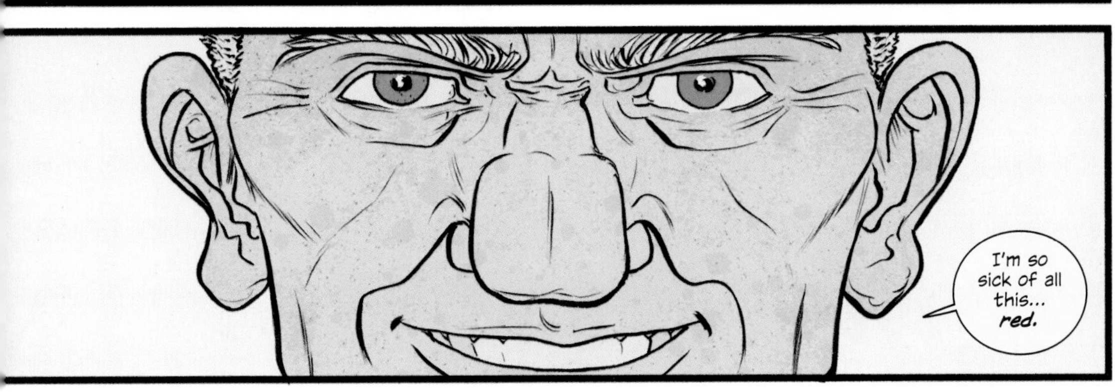
I'm so sick of all this... ***red.***

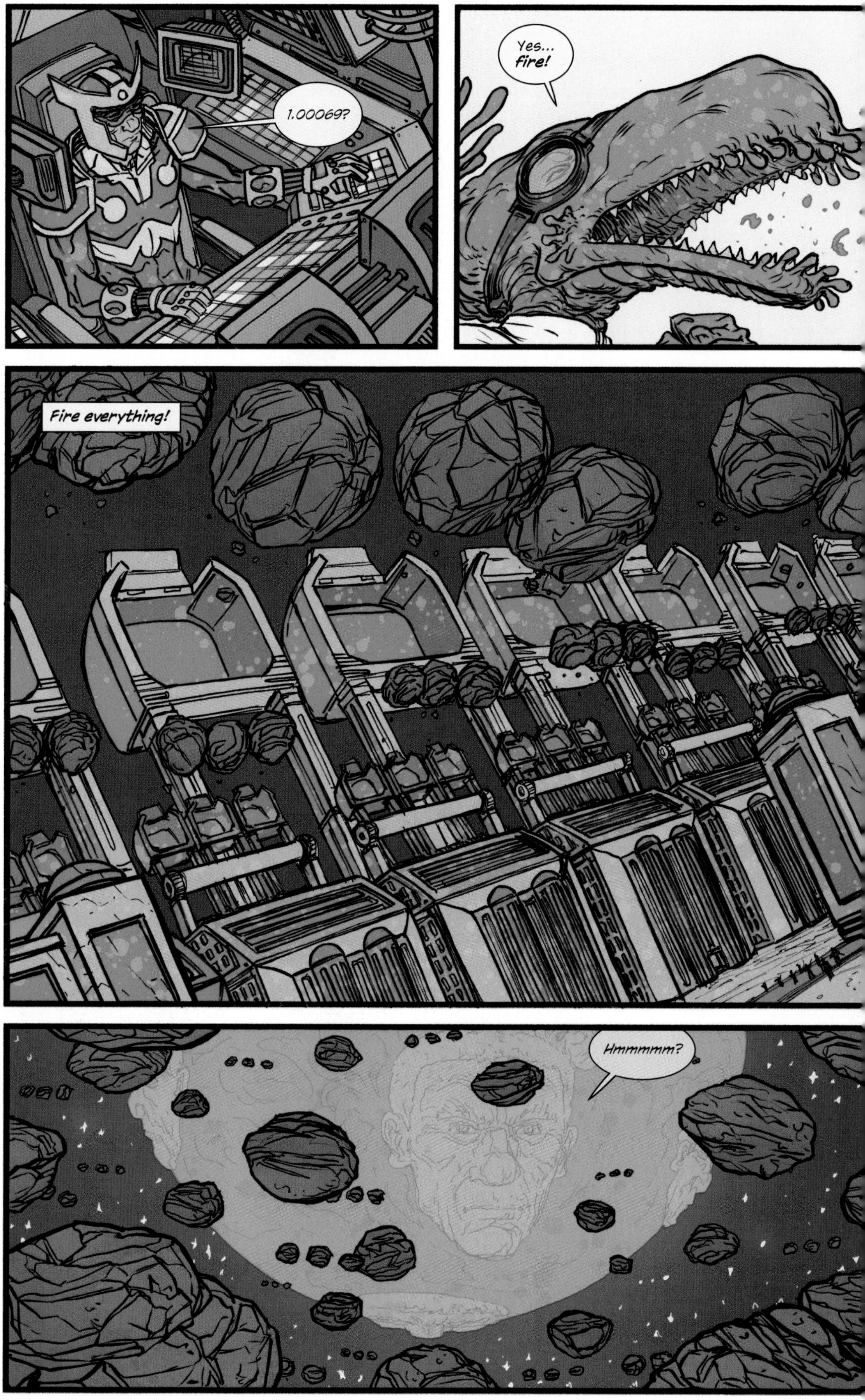
1.00069?
Yes... fire!
Fire everything!
Hmmmmm?

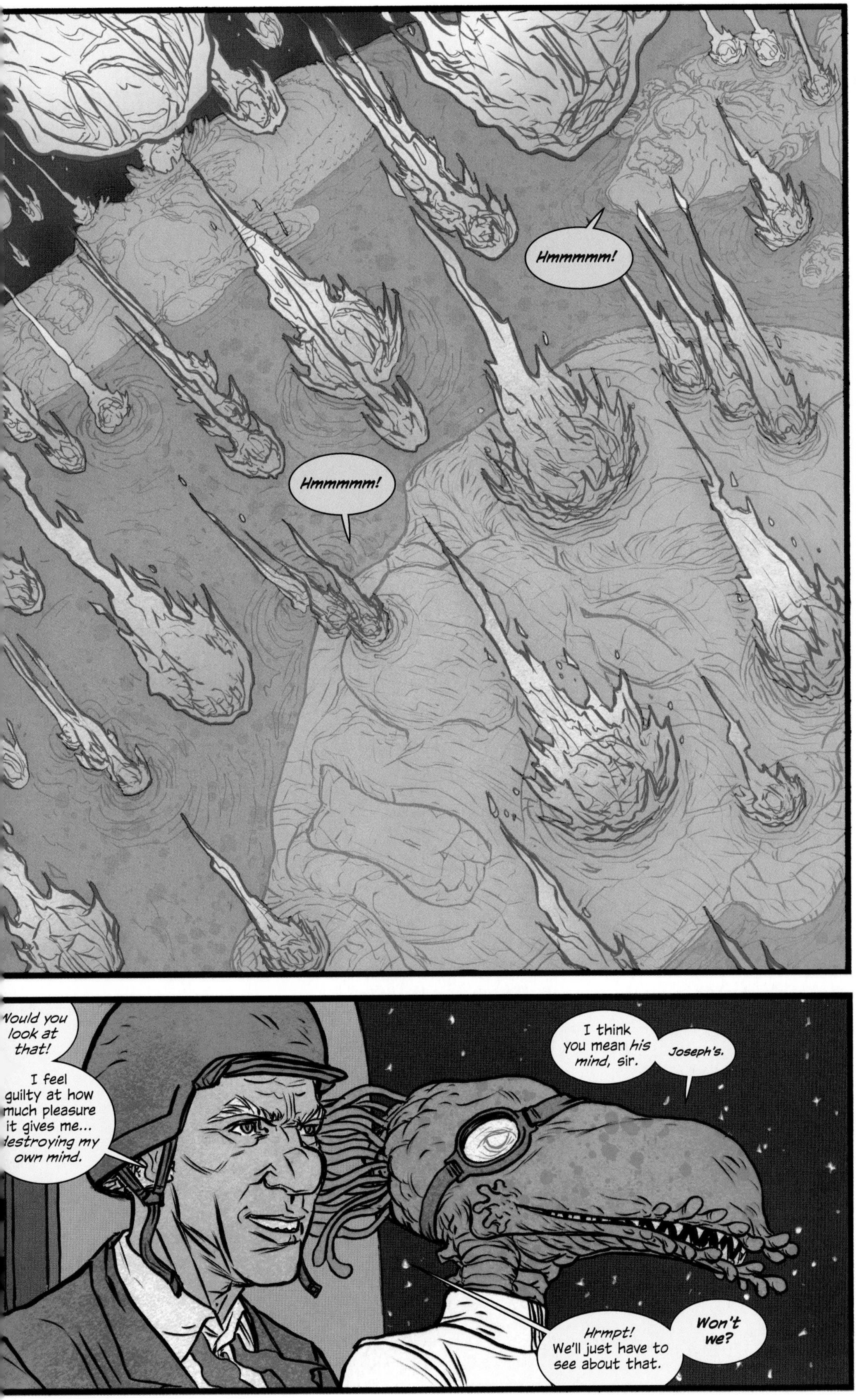
Hmmmmm!
Hmmmmm!
ould you look at that!
I feel guilty at how much pleasure it gives me... lestroying my own mind.
I think you mean his mind, sir.
Joseph's.
Hrmpt! We'll just have to see about that.
Won't we?

19

FINITE OPPENHEIMERS

"THE GREAT EYE OF JOSEPH WATCHED OVER THEM ALL UNTIL THE MEGAMID FELL.

THIS WAS THE APOCALYPSE."

- OPPENHEIMER

CLAVIS AUREA
THE RECORDED FEYNMAN

VOL. 3

No-rocks hurled from the fixed low-orbit blue moon reduced the analog population of Oppenworld from billions to thousands.

Only the inner Pyramid City -- too real in the not-real space -- survived the extinction event.

Hmmmmm!

Hmmmmm!

It was a sanctum built to withstand all but the super-ego. The Brain of Oppenheimer Prime -- the seat of conscience -- would have to be taken in person.

Right and wrong, you see, must be injected by hand.

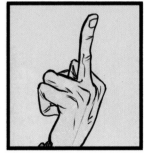

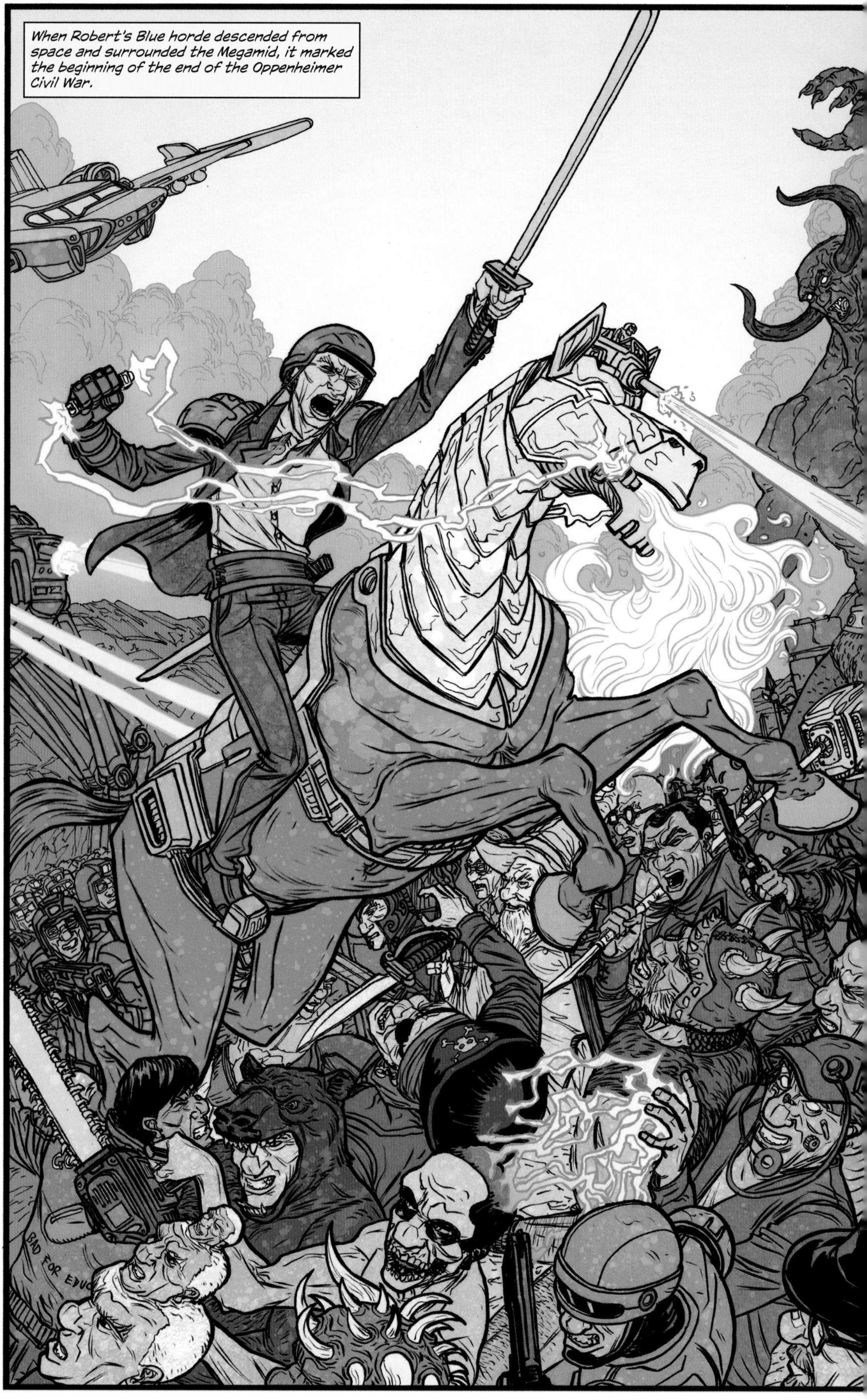
When Robert's Blue horde descended from space and surrounded the Megamid, it marked the beginning of the end of the Oppenheimer Civil War.

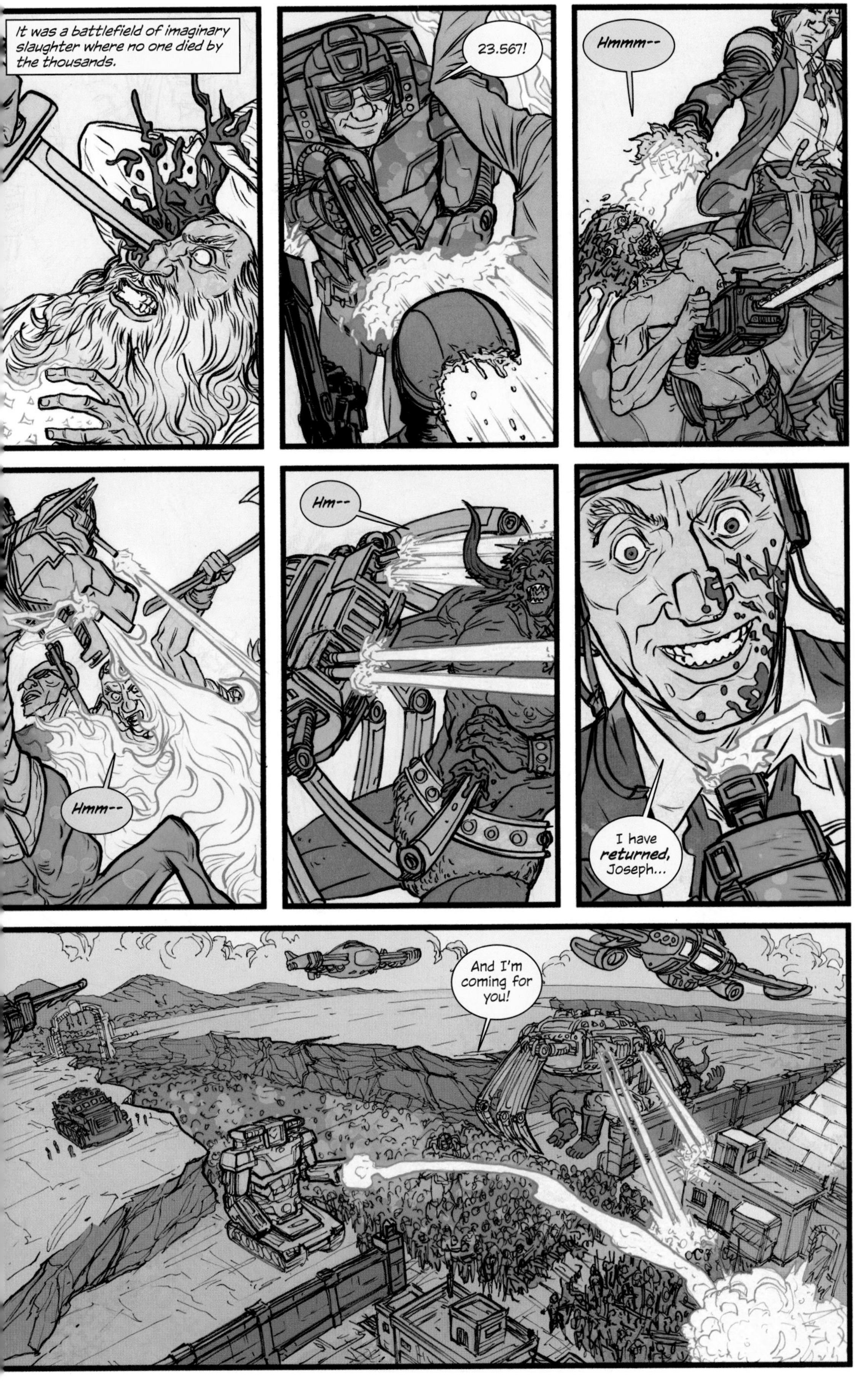
It was a battlefield of imaginary slaughter where no one died by the thousands.
23.567!
Hmmm--
Hmm--
Hm--
I have returned, Joseph...
And I'm coming for you!

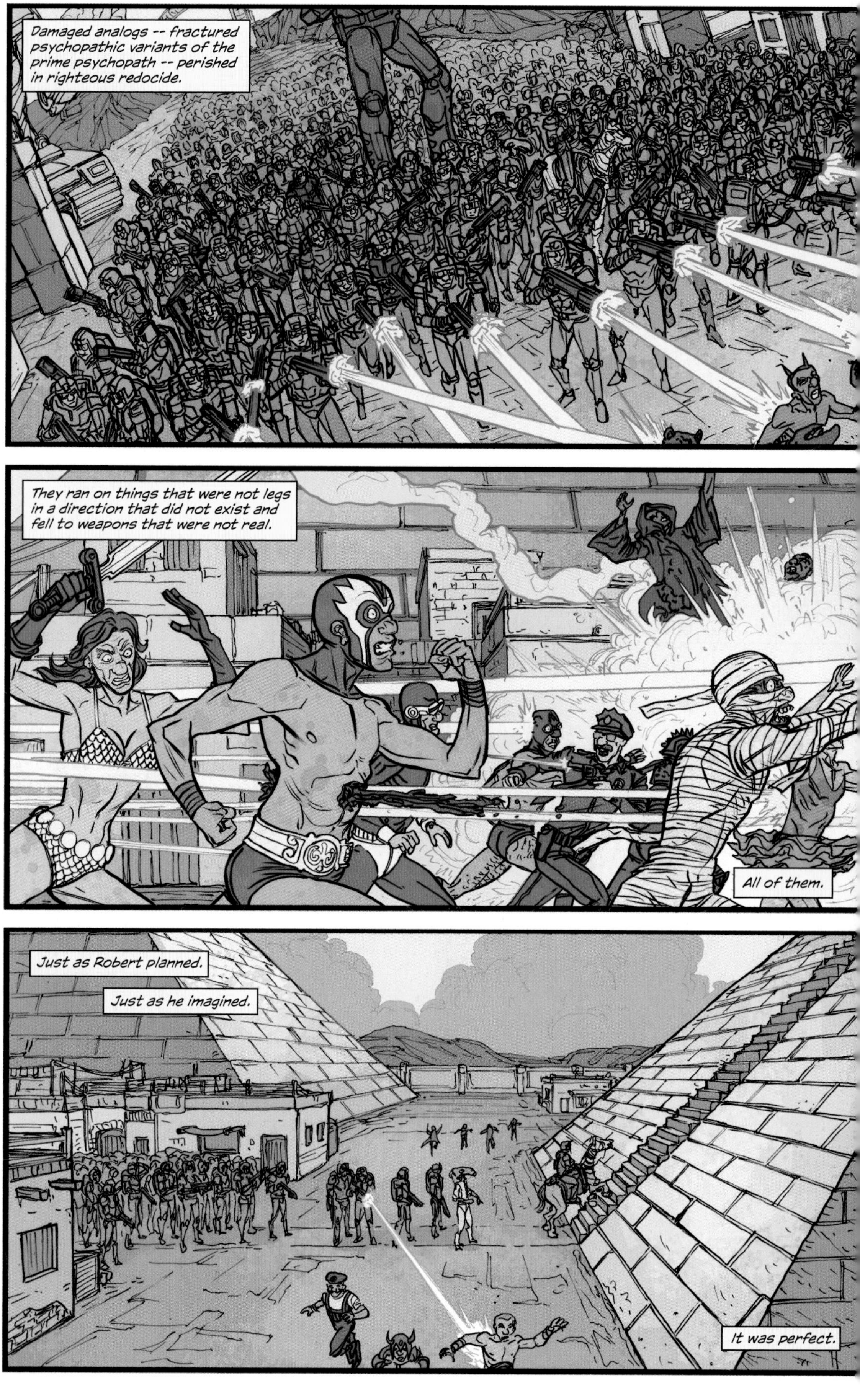
Damaged analogs -- fractured psychopathic variants of the prime psychopath -- perished in righteous redocide.
They ran on things that were not legs in a direction that did not exist and fell to weapons that were not real.
All of them.
Just as Robert planned.
Just as he imagined.
It was perfect.

I've spent quite a lot of no-time thinking about this...

How to replace your brain with mine, just like you replaced me in the real world.

And while a lobotomy might seem a mighty cruel fate for any mind as gifted as ours...you're a cancer, brother...

And the only solution here is to **start cutting.**

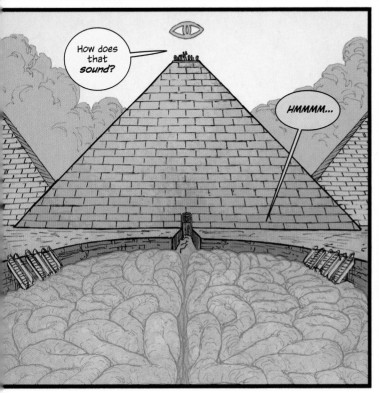

How does that **sound?**

HMMMM...

It began with something so simple...

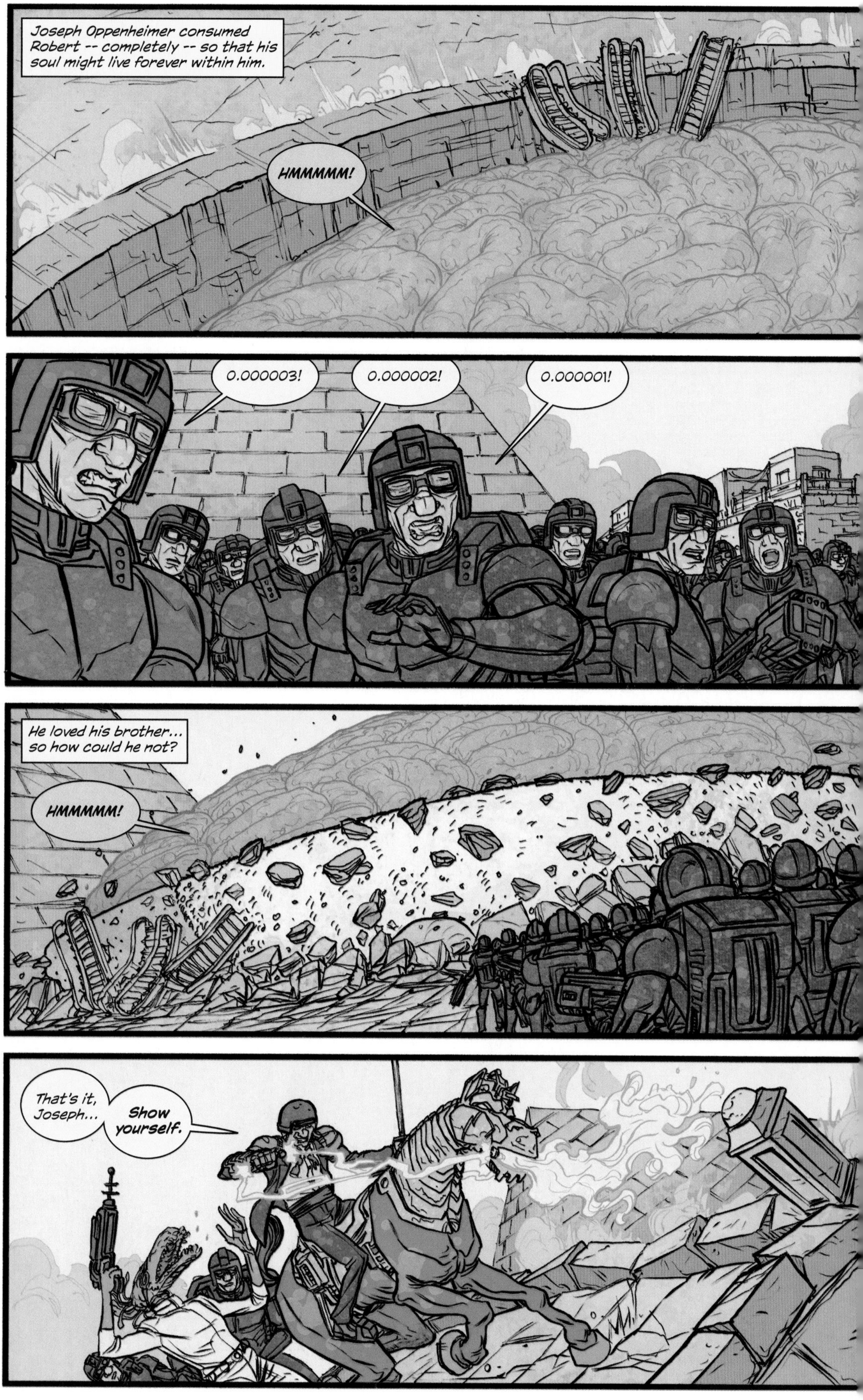

Joseph Oppenheimer consumed Robert -- completely -- so that his soul might live forever within him.
HMMMMM!
0.000003!
0.000002!
0.000001!
He loved his brother... so how could he not?
HMMMMM!
That's it, Joseph...
Show yourself.

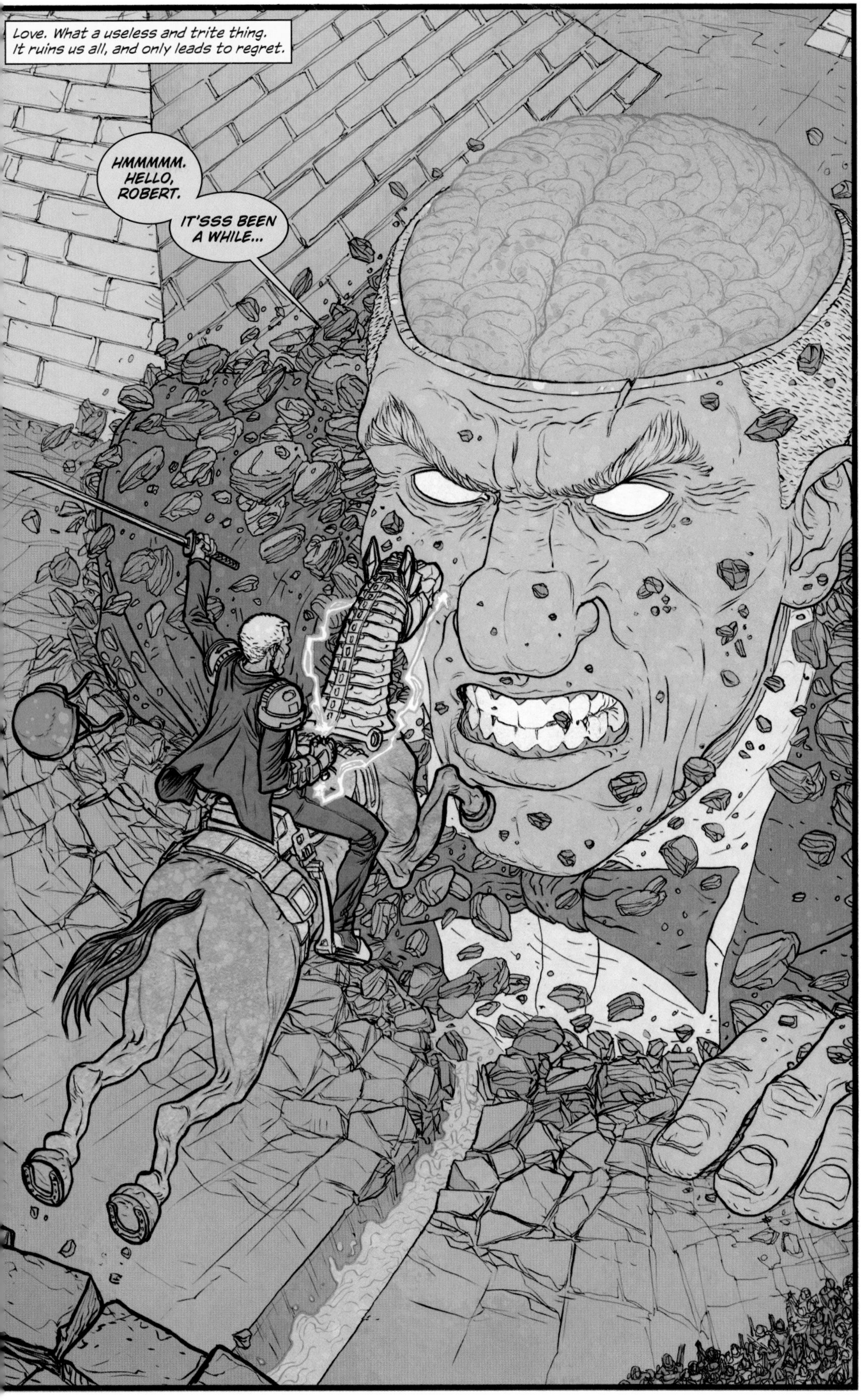
Love. What a useless and trite thing. It ruins us all, and only leads to regret.
HMMMMM. HELLO, ROBERT.
IT'SSS BEEN A WHILE...

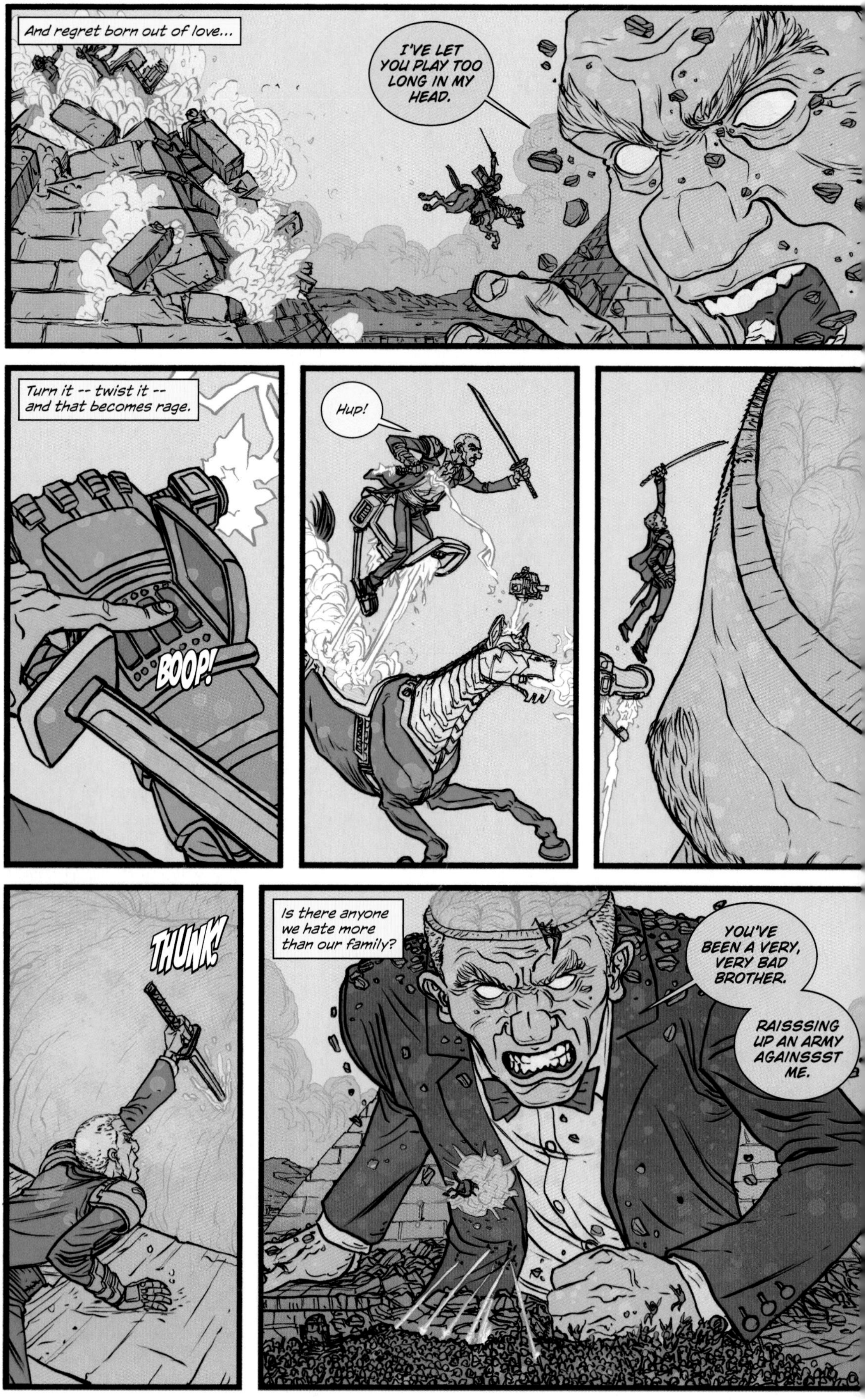
And regret born out of love...
I'VE LET YOU PLAY TOO LONG IN MY HEAD.
Turn it -- twist it -- and that becomes rage.
BOOP!
Hup!
THUNK!
Is there anyone we hate more than our family?
YOU'VE BEEN A VERY, VERY BAD BROTHER.
RAISSSING UP AN ARMY AGAINSSST ME.

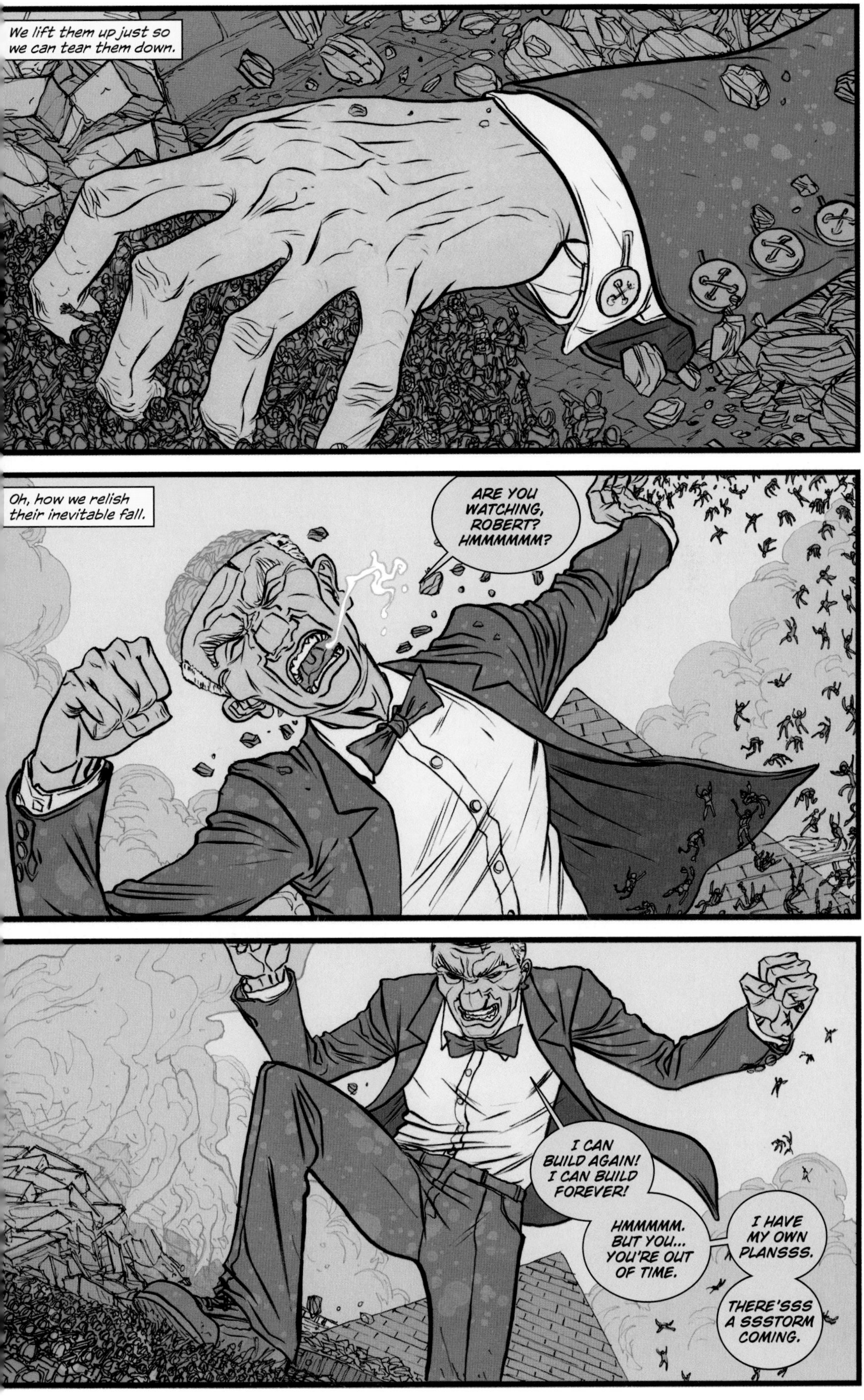

We lift them up just so we can tear them down.
Oh, how we relish their inevitable fall.
ARE YOU WATCHING, ROBERT? HMMMMMM?
I CAN BUILD AGAIN! I CAN BUILD FOREVER!
HMMMMM. BUT YOU... YOU'RE OUT OF TIME.
I HAVE MY OWN PLANSSS.
THERE'SSS A SSSTORM COMING.

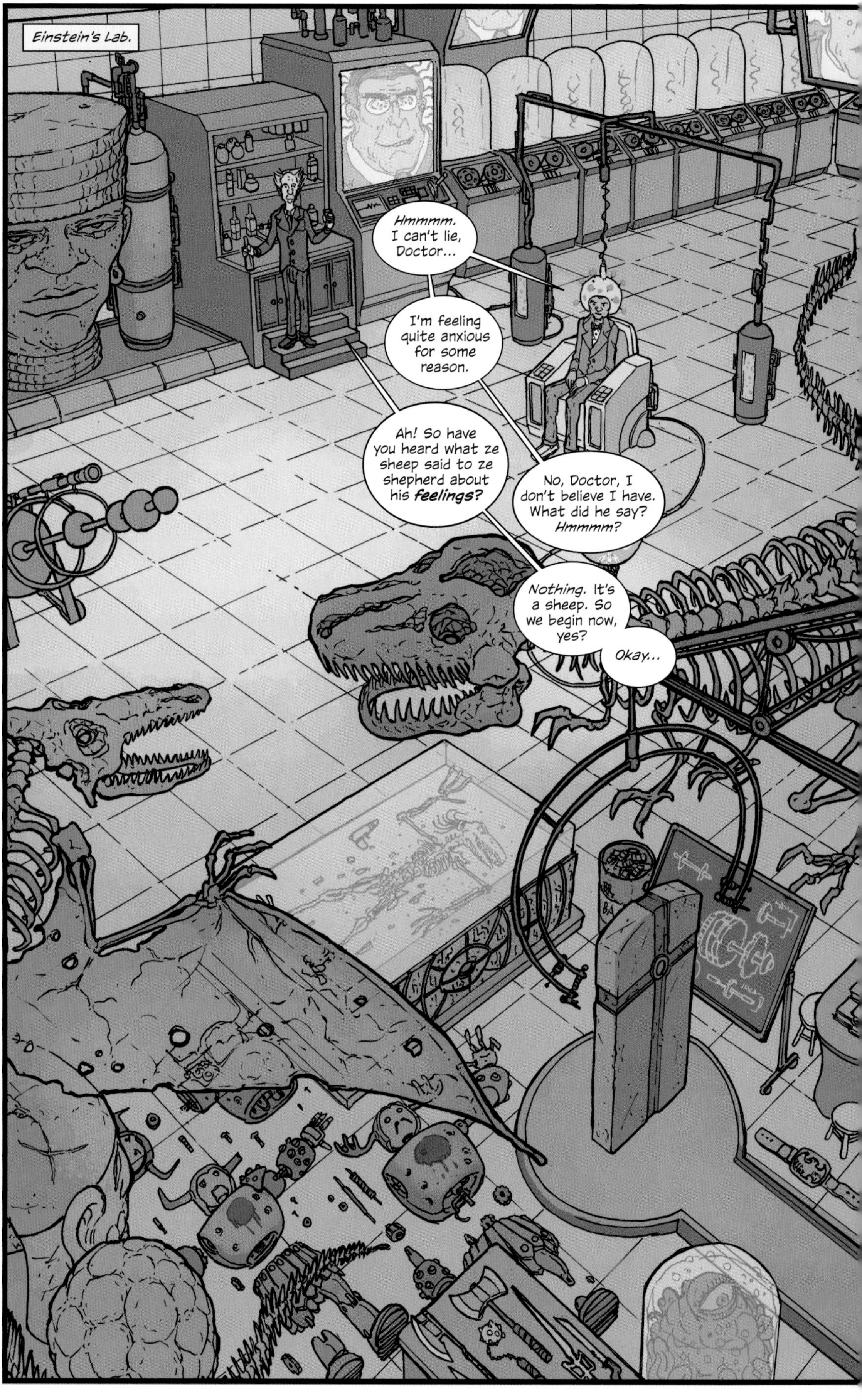

Einstein's Lab.
Hmmmm. I can't lie, Doctor...
I'm feeling quite anxious for some reason.
Ah! So have you heard what ze sheep said to ze shepherd about his feelings?
No, Doctor, I don't believe I have. What did he say? Hmmmm?
Nothing. It's a sheep. So we begin now, yes?
Okay...

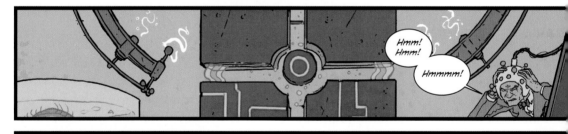

Please continue.

Odd.

Hyper-electric storms...

Must be a result of overcharged synaptic impulses.

You're throwing everything you have at me, Joseph...

But it's not going to stop me...

Try as hard as you want... you just don't have the *imagination* to see this coming.

SHUMP!

Prepare yourself for surgery, brother...

This might sting a bit!

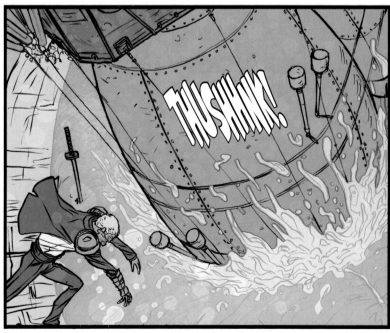

THUSHANK!

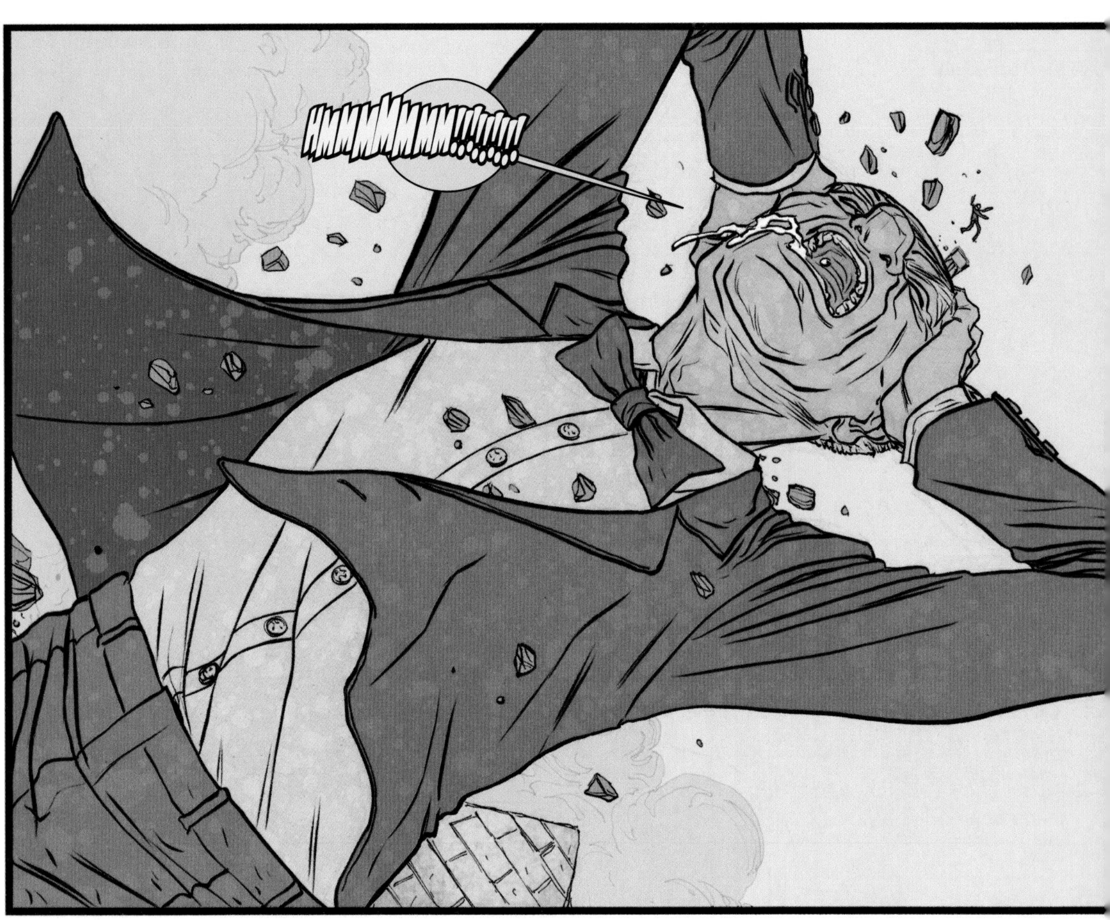
HMMMMMMM!!!!!!!!!!

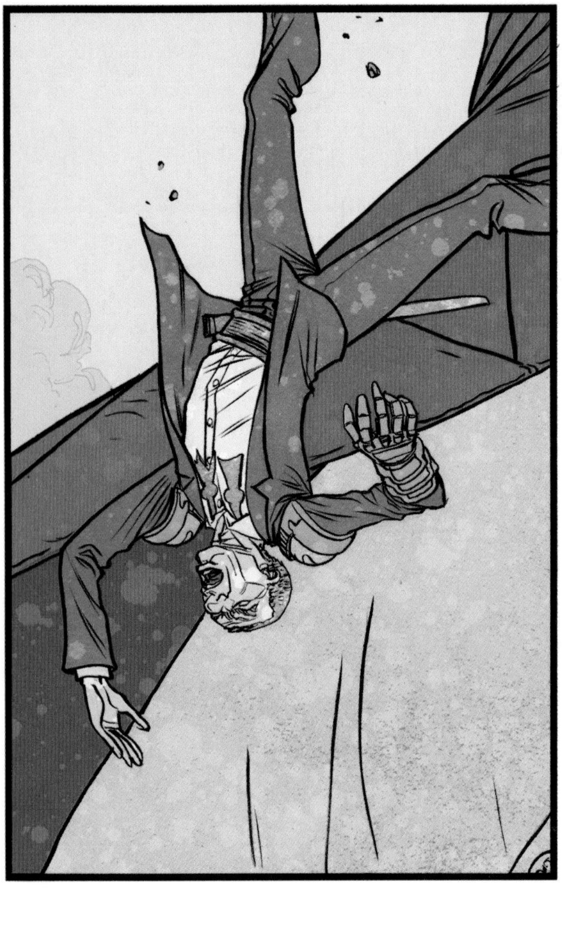

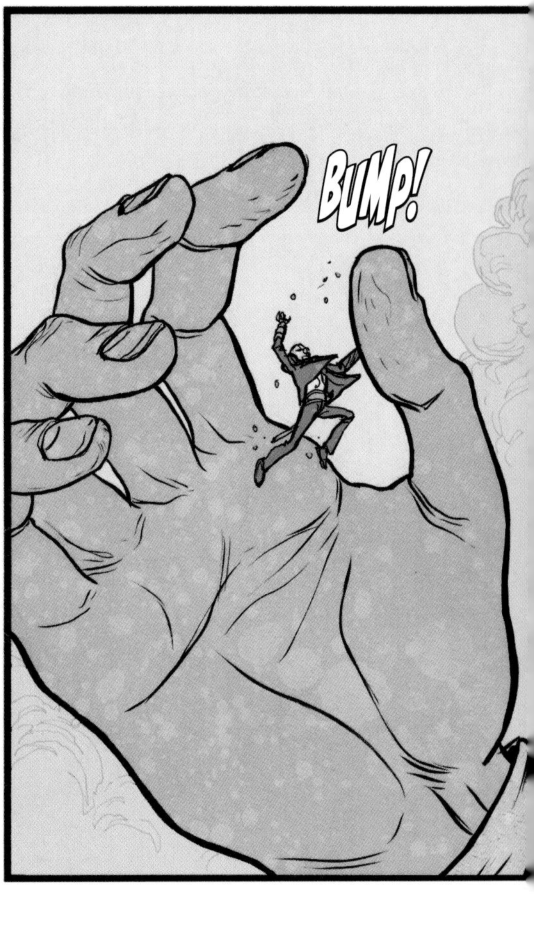
BUMP!

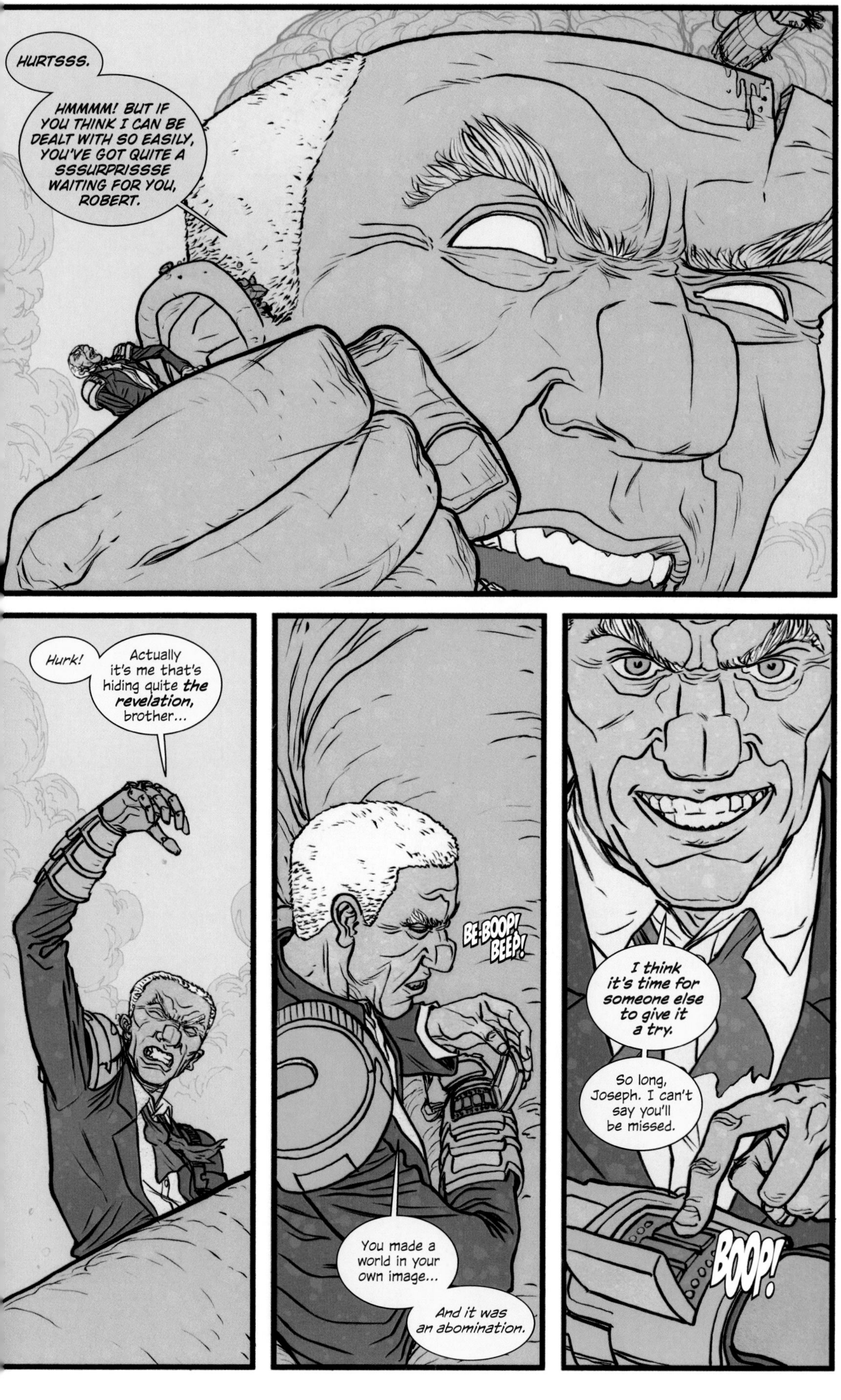
HURTSSS.
HMMMM! BUT IF YOU THINK I CAN BE DEALT WITH SO EASILY, YOU'VE GOT QUITE A SSSURPRISSSE WAITING FOR YOU, ROBERT.
Hurk!
Actually it's me that's hiding quite the revelation, brother...
BE-BOOP! BEEP!
You made a world in your own image...
And it was an abomination.
I think it's time for someone else to give it a try.
So long, Joseph. I can't say you'll be missed.
BOOP!

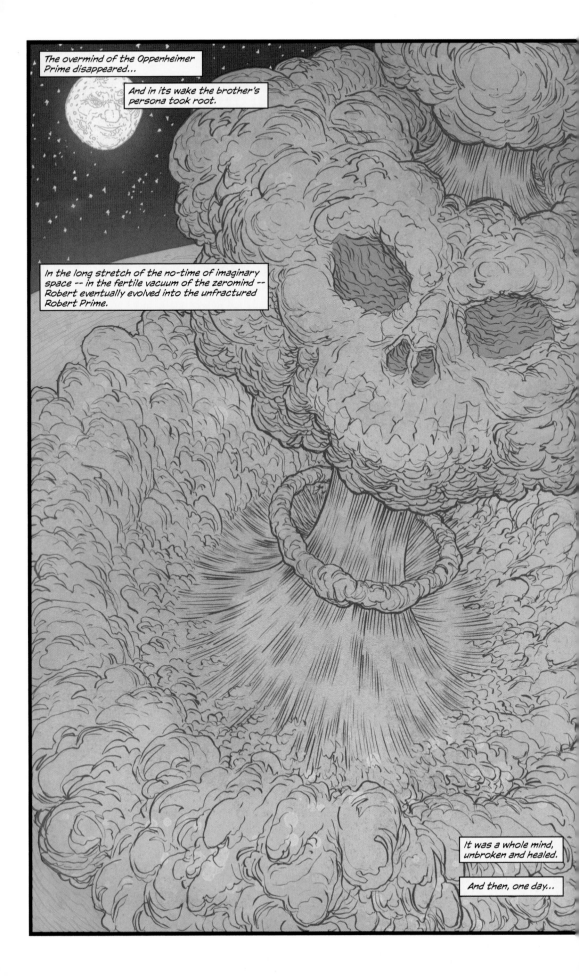

The overmind of the Oppenheimer Prime disappeared...

And in its wake the brother's persona took root.

In the long stretch of the no-time of imaginary space -- in the fertile vacuum of the zeromind -- Robert eventually evolved into the unfractured Robert Prime.

It was a whole mind, unbroken and healed.

And then, one day...

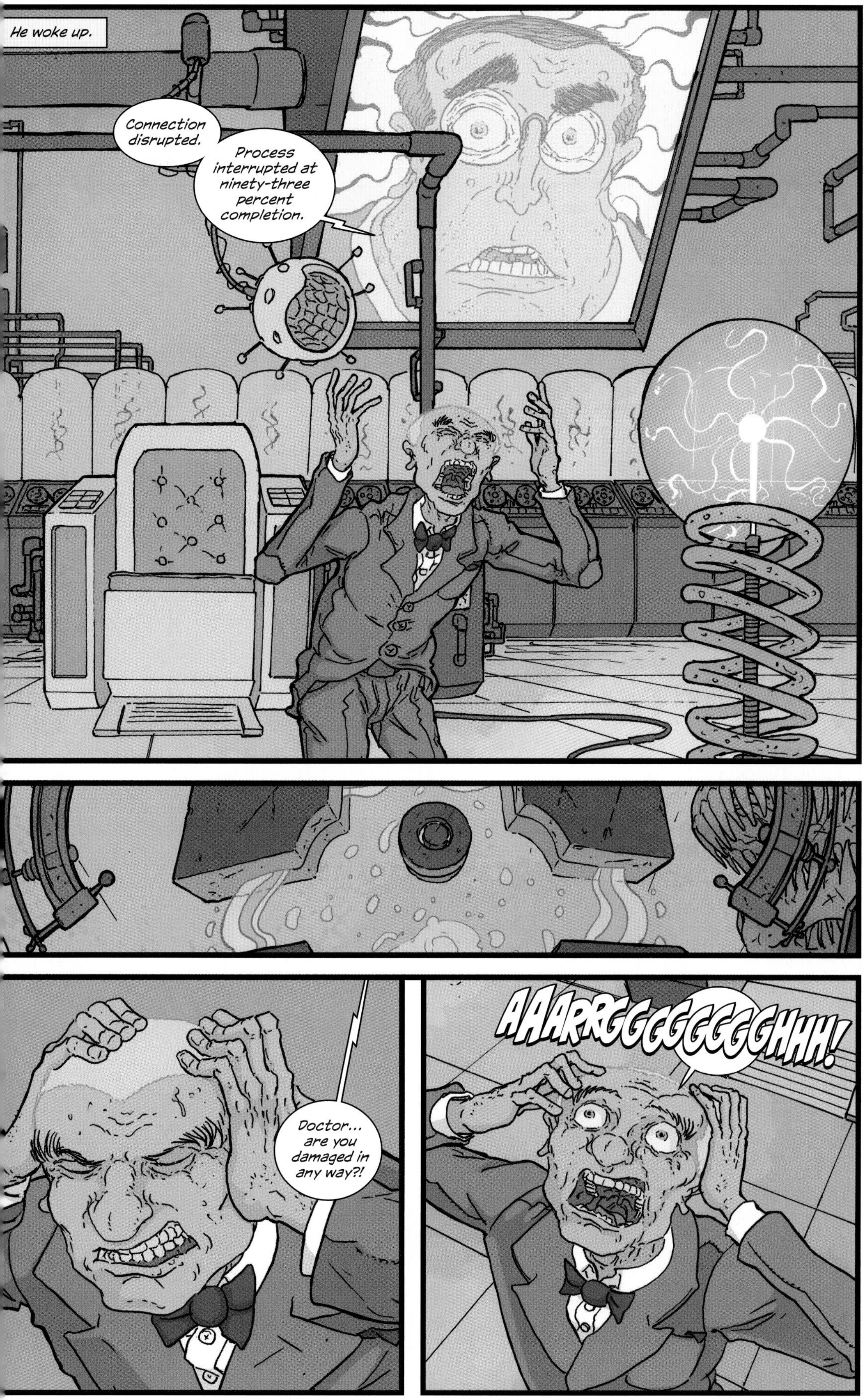
He woke up.
Connection disrupted.
Process interrupted at ninety-three percent completion.
Doctor... are you damaged in any way?!
AAARRGGGGGGGHHH!

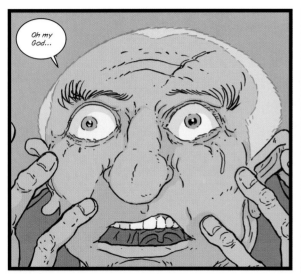

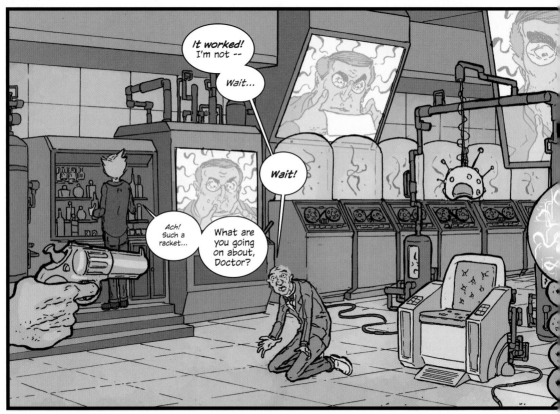

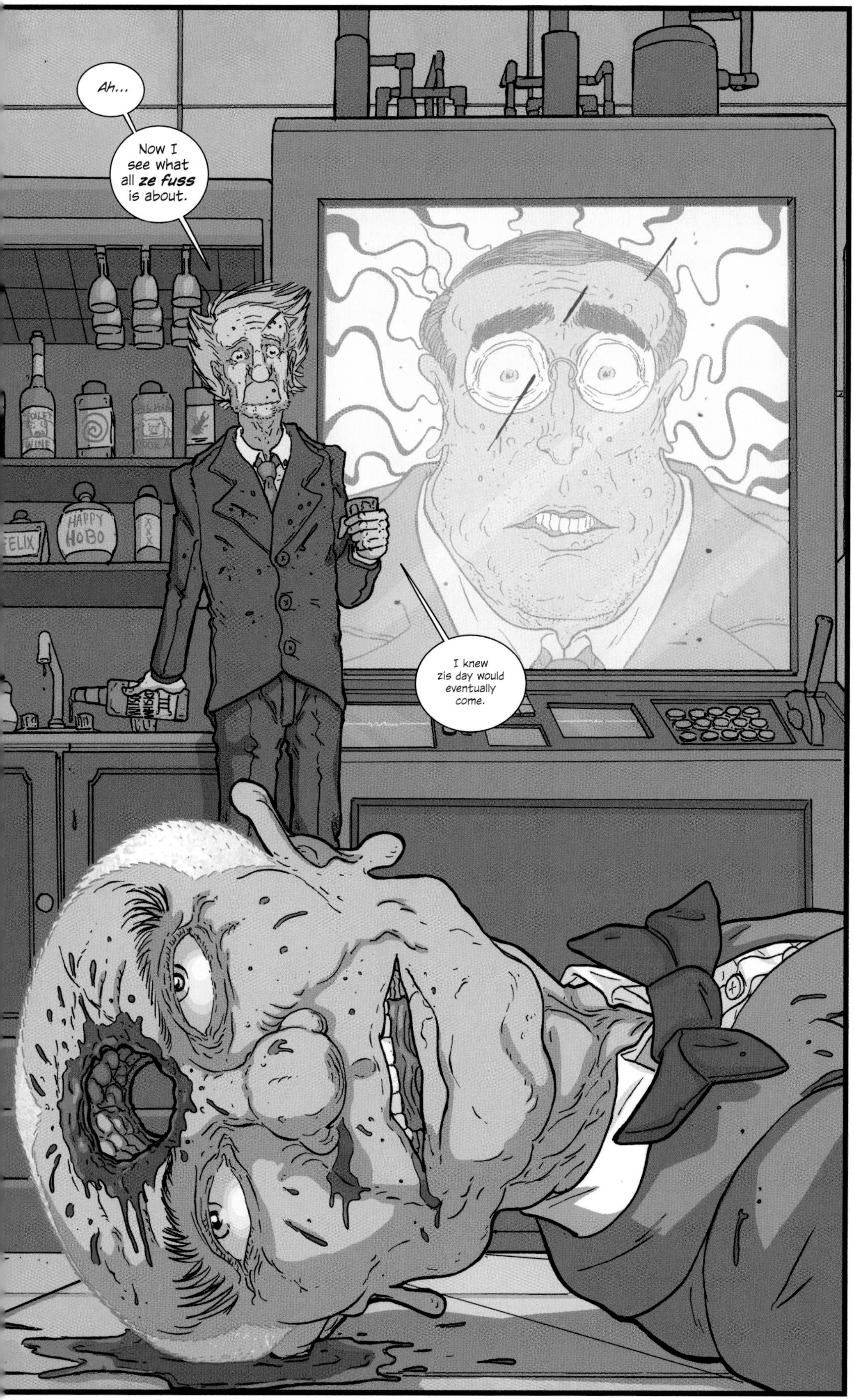
Ah...
Now I see what all ***ze fuss*** is about.
I knew zis day would eventually come.

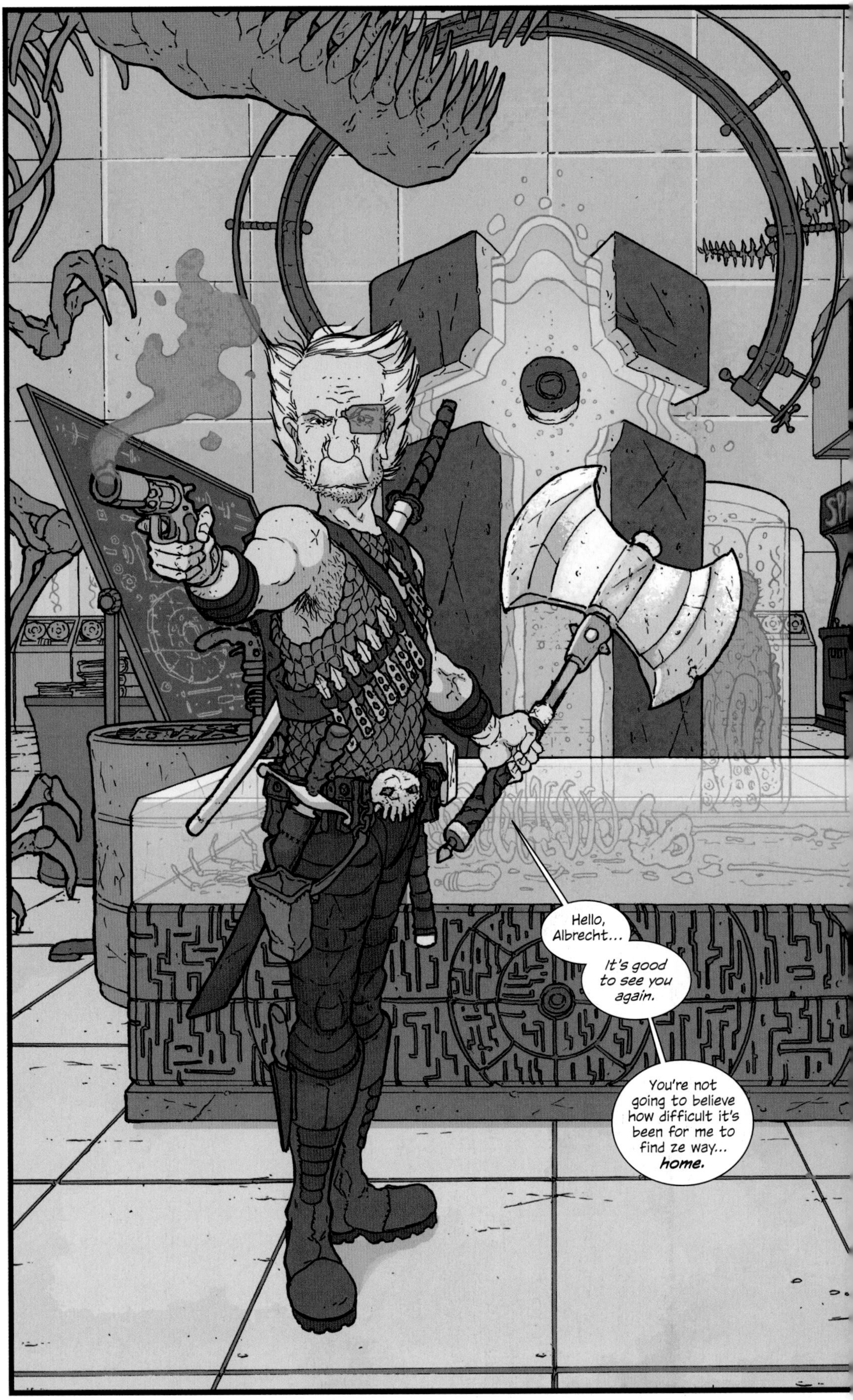

Hello, Albrecht...
It's good to see you again.
You're not going to believe how difficult it's been for me to find ze way... ***home.***

"THEY CAST OUT THE GREAT EYE OF JOSEPH, AND IN ITS PLACE LIFTED UP THEMSELVES.

ROBERT RECEIVED EXACTLY WHAT HE DESERVED."

- OPPENHEIMER

CLAVIS AUREA
THE RECORDED FEYNMAN | **VOL. 3**

WELCOME
WIZARD

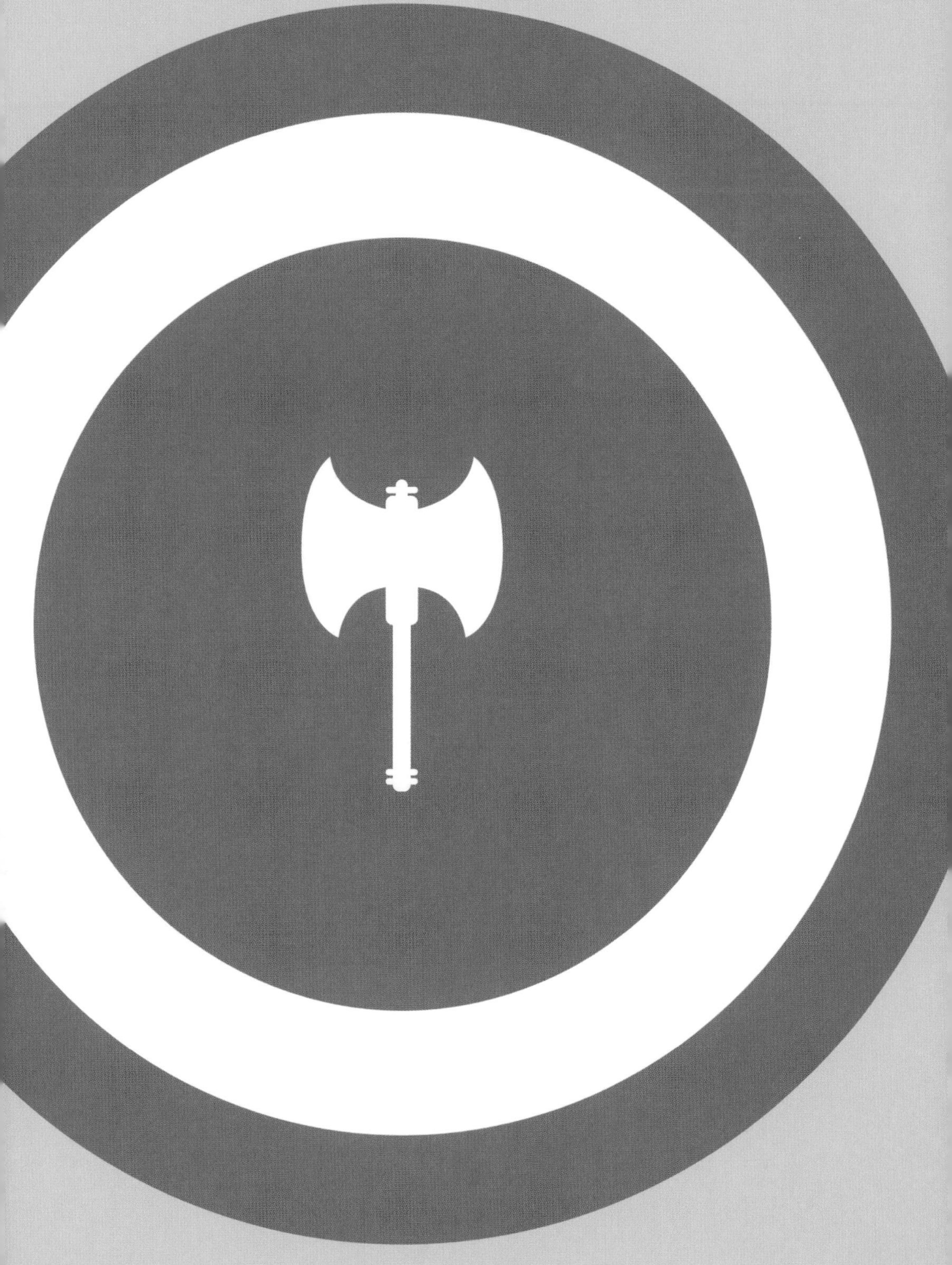

"WHAT IS THE GREATER PURPOSE OF AN EXPERIMENT?"

CLAVIS AUREA
THE RECORDED FEYNMAN

VOL. 4

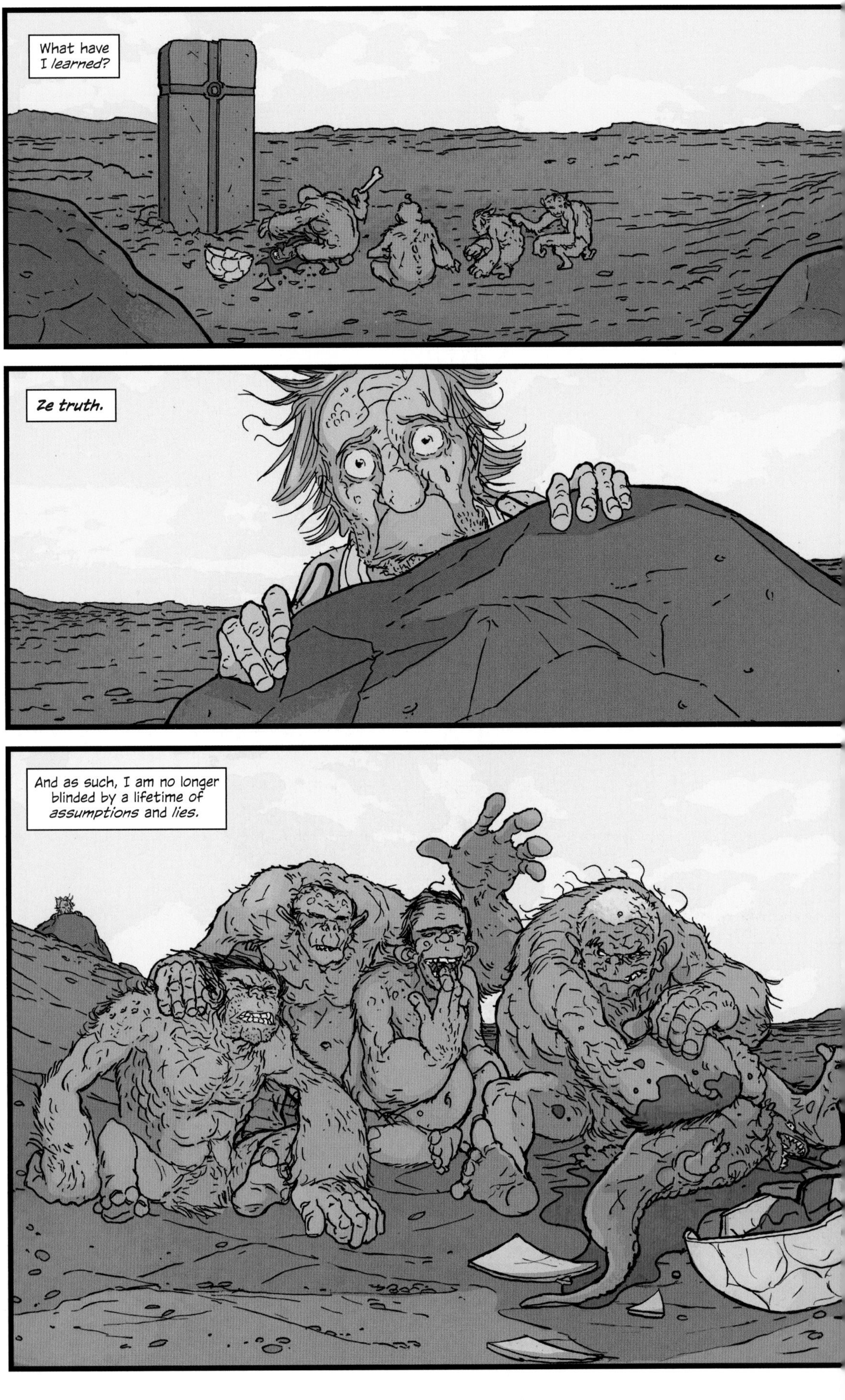
What have I *learned?*
Ze truth.
And as such, I am no longer blinded by a lifetime of *assumptions* and *lies.*

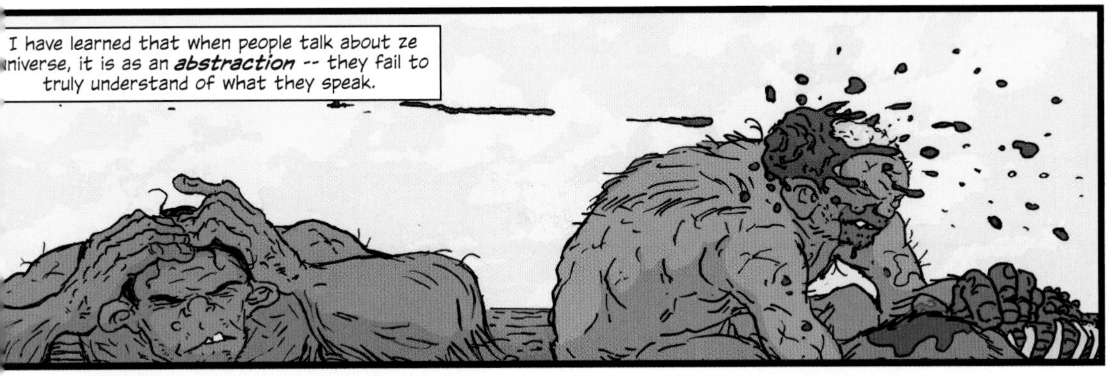
I have learned that when people talk about ze universe, it is as an ***abstraction*** -- they fail to truly understand of what they speak.

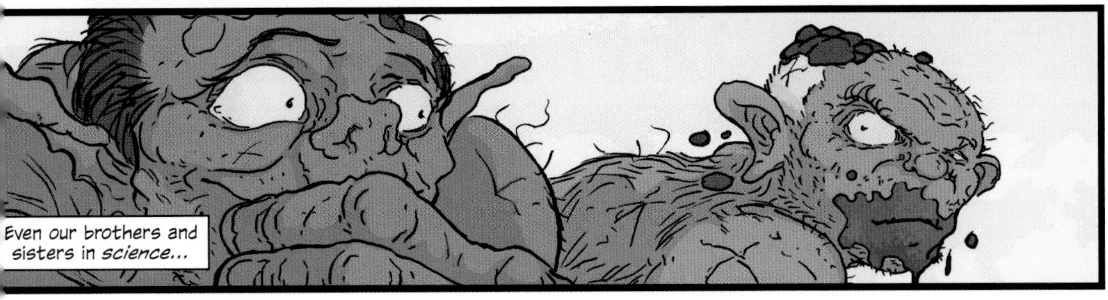
Even our brothers and sisters in *science*...

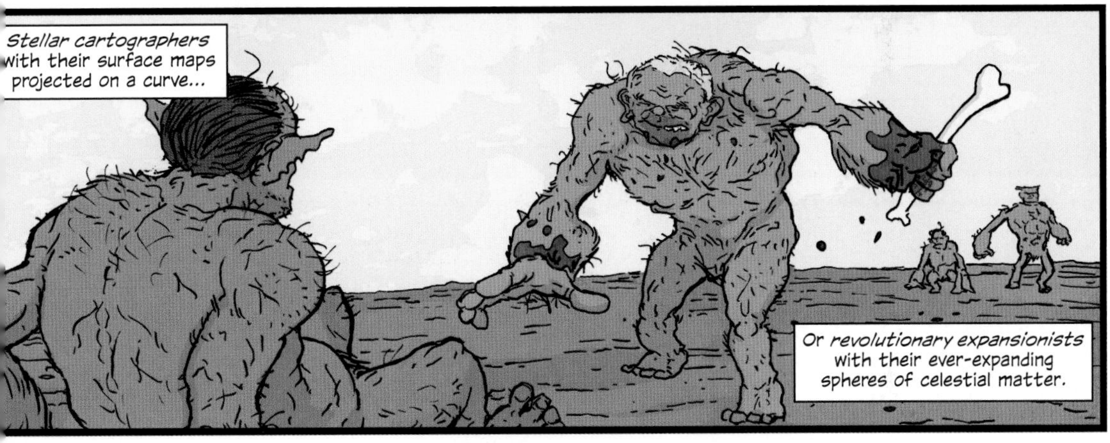
Stellar cartographers with their surface maps projected on a curve...
Or *revolutionary expansionists* with their ever-expanding spheres of celestial matter.

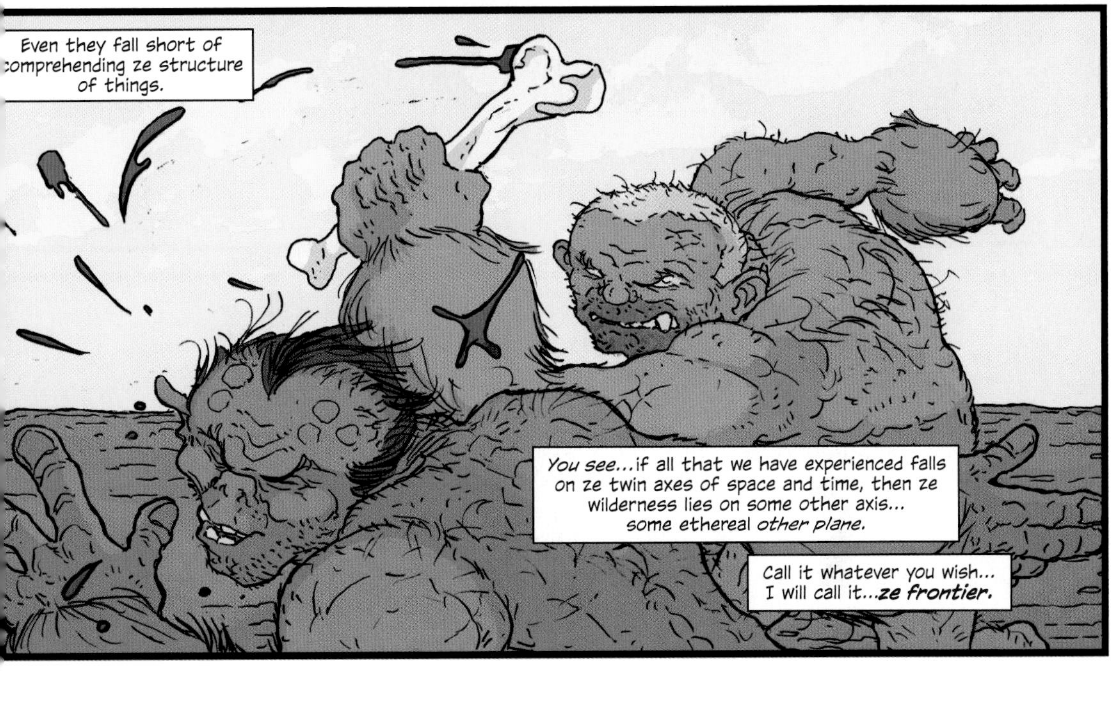
Even they fall short of comprehending ze structure of things.
You see...if all that we have experienced falls on ze twin axes of space and time, then ze wilderness lies on some other axis... some ethereal *other plane*.
Call it whatever you wish... I will call it...***ze frontier.***

And are there other things that I have learned? *There are many.* I am old, just as you, so some ideas escape me, but, *ah, yes...* there is one other thing that matters very much...

Nature.

I have learned that nature -- *true nature:* both that which we see and experience, and ze frontier that lies outside normal perception -- is a wild, brutal, and unforgiving place.

And ze ones who will explore it -- perhaps true explorers like you and I -- are prepared, and capable, of our own equal kind of violence: *discovery.*

We will change the world... simply by observing it with new eyes.

These are ze things I have **seen.**

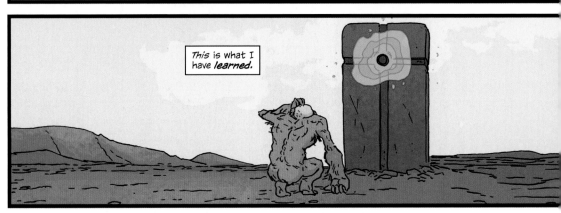

This is what I have **learned.**

"WHAT IS THE GREATER PURPOSE OF A LIFE?"

CLAVIS AUREA
THE RECORDED FEYNMAN

VOL. 4

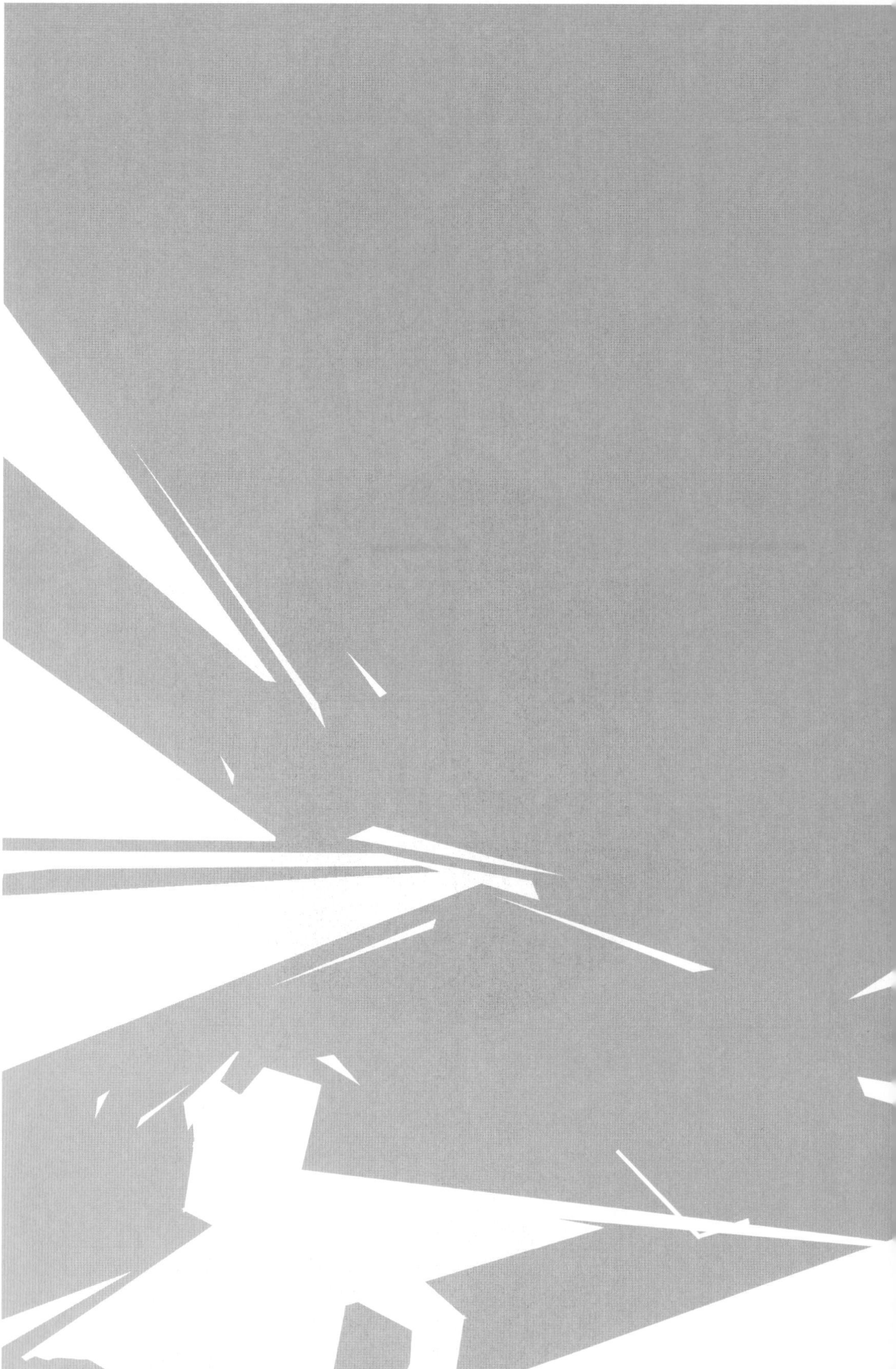

20

EINSTEIN THE BARBARIAN

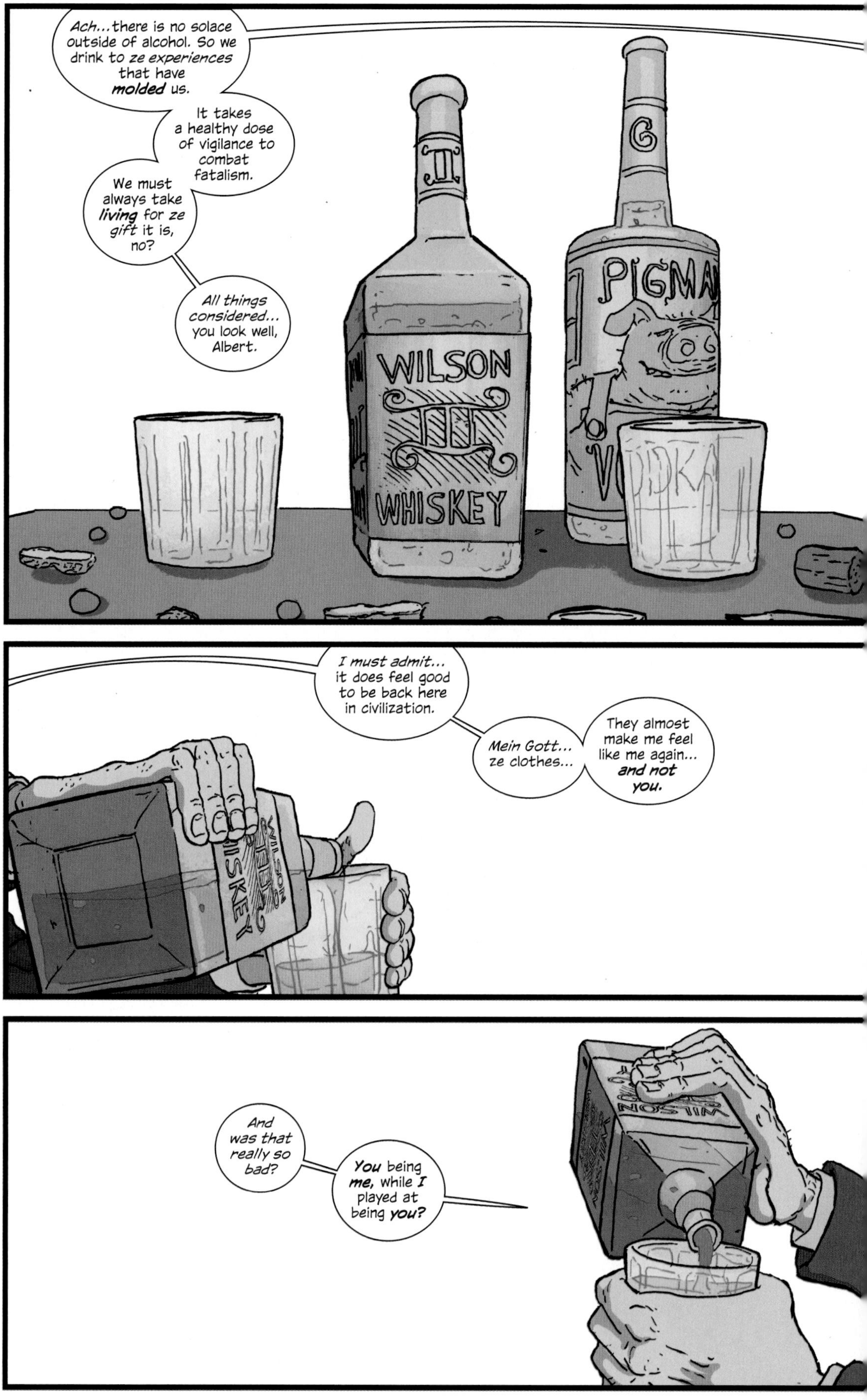

Ach... there is no solace outside of alcohol. So we drink to *ze experiences* that have ***molded*** us.
It takes a healthy dose of vigilance to combat fatalism.
We must always take ***living*** for *ze gift* it is, no?
All things considered... you look well, Albert.
WILSON
WHISKEY
I must admit... it does feel good to be back here in civilization.
Mein Gott... ze clothes...
They almost make me feel like me again... ***and not you.***
And was that really so bad?
You being ***me,*** while ***I*** played at being ***you?***

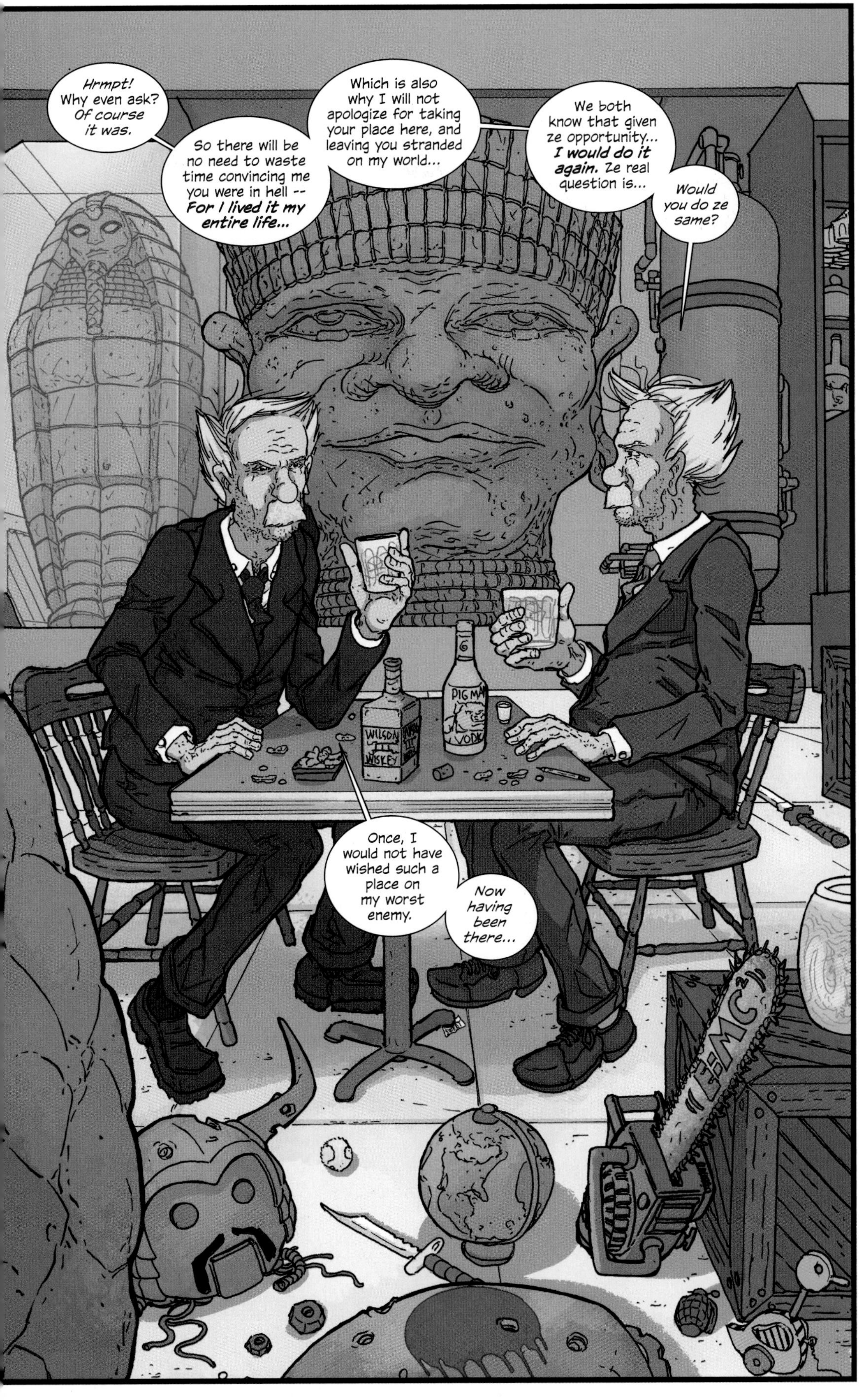
Hrmpt! Why even ask? Of course it was.
So there will be no need to waste time convincing me you were in hell -- For I lived it my entire life...
Which is also why I will not apologize for taking your place here, and leaving you stranded on my world...
We both know that given ze opportunity... I would do it again. Ze real question is...
Would you do ze same?
Once, I would not have wished such a place on my worst enemy.
Now having been there...

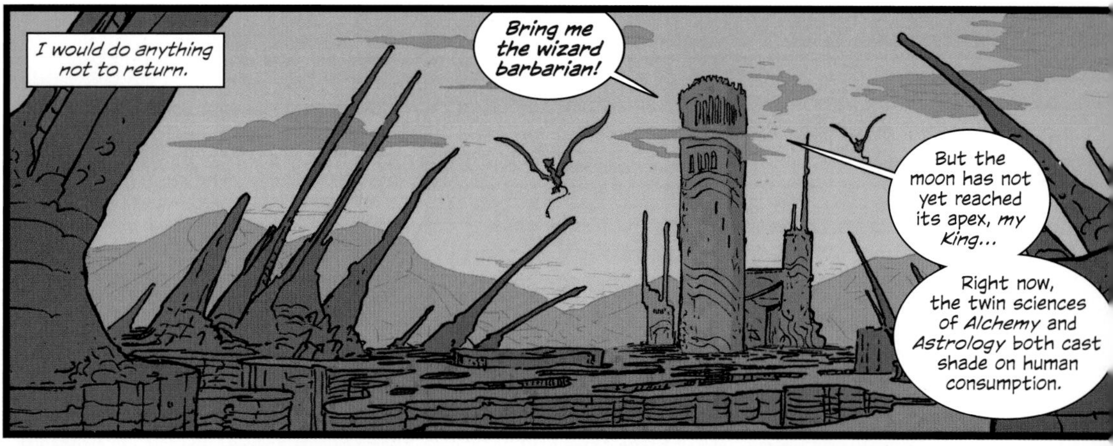
I would do anything not to return.
Bring me the wizard barbarian!
But the moon has not yet reached its apex, *my King*...
Right now, the twin sciences of *Alchemy* and *Astrology* both cast shade on human consumption.

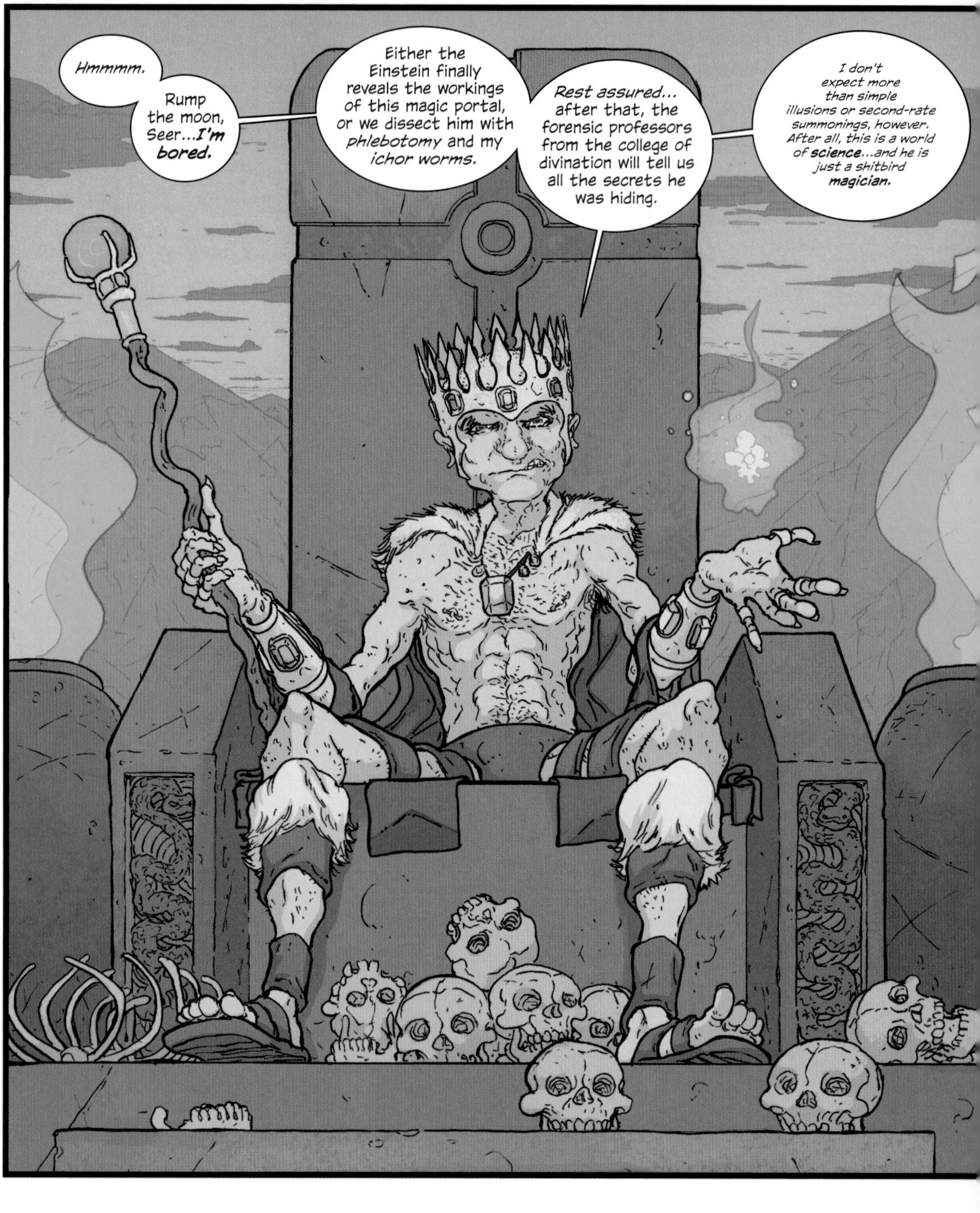
Hmmmm.
Rump the moon, Seer...***I'm bored.***
Either the Einstein finally reveals the workings of this magic portal, or we dissect him with *phlebotomy* and my *ichor worms.*
Rest assured... after that, the forensic professors from the college of divination will tell us all the secrets he was hiding.
I don't expect more than simple illusions or second-rate summonings, however. After all, this is a world of ***science****...and he is just a shitbird* ***magician.***

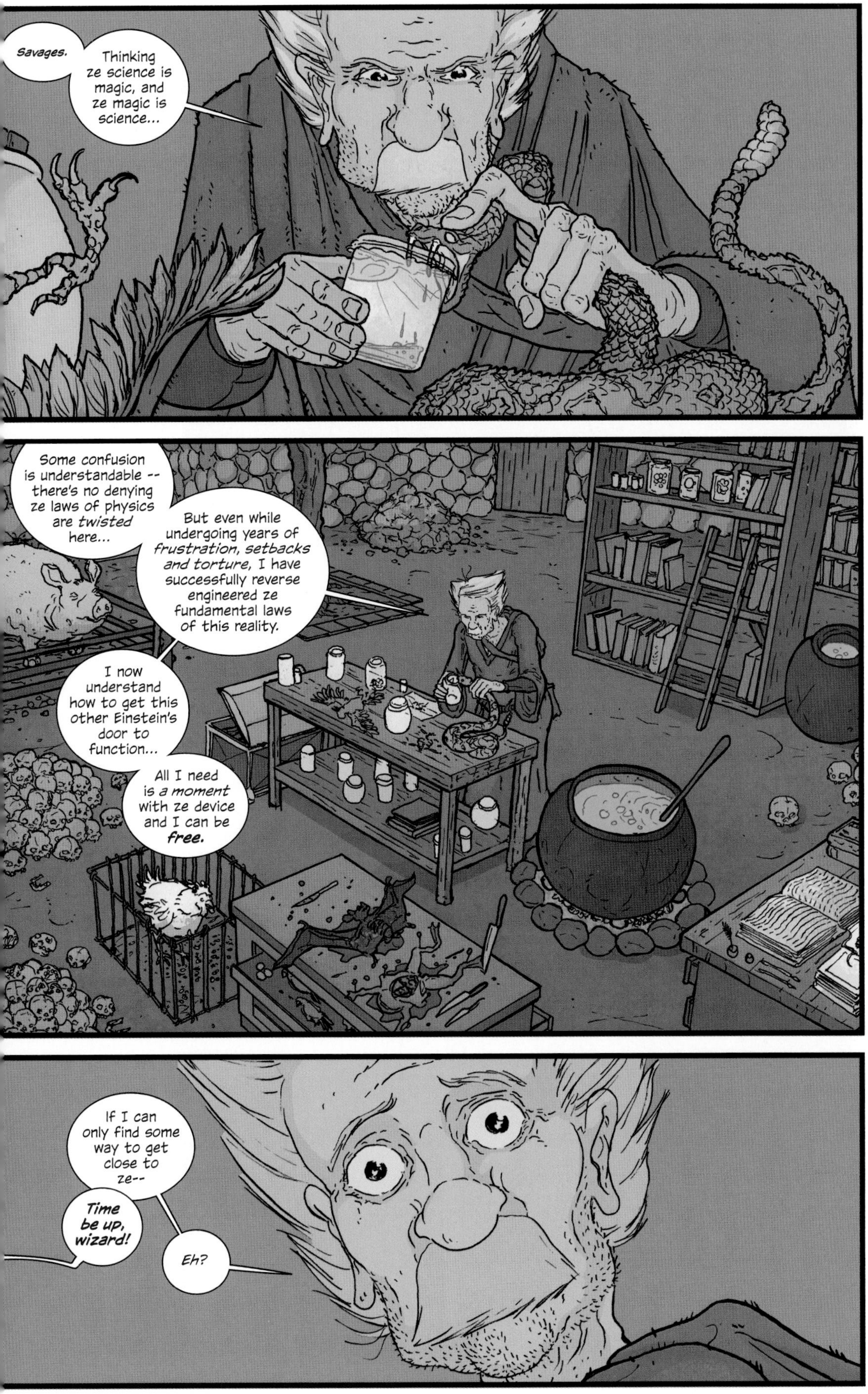
Savages.
Thinking ze science is magic, and ze magic is science...
Some confusion is understandable -- there's no denying ze laws of physics are *twisted* here...
But even while undergoing years of *frustration, setbacks and torture,* I have successfully reverse engineered ze fundamental laws of this reality.
I now understand how to get this other Einstein's door to function...
All I need is *a moment* with ze device and I can be **free.**
If I can only find some way to get close to ze--
Time be up, wizard!
Eh?

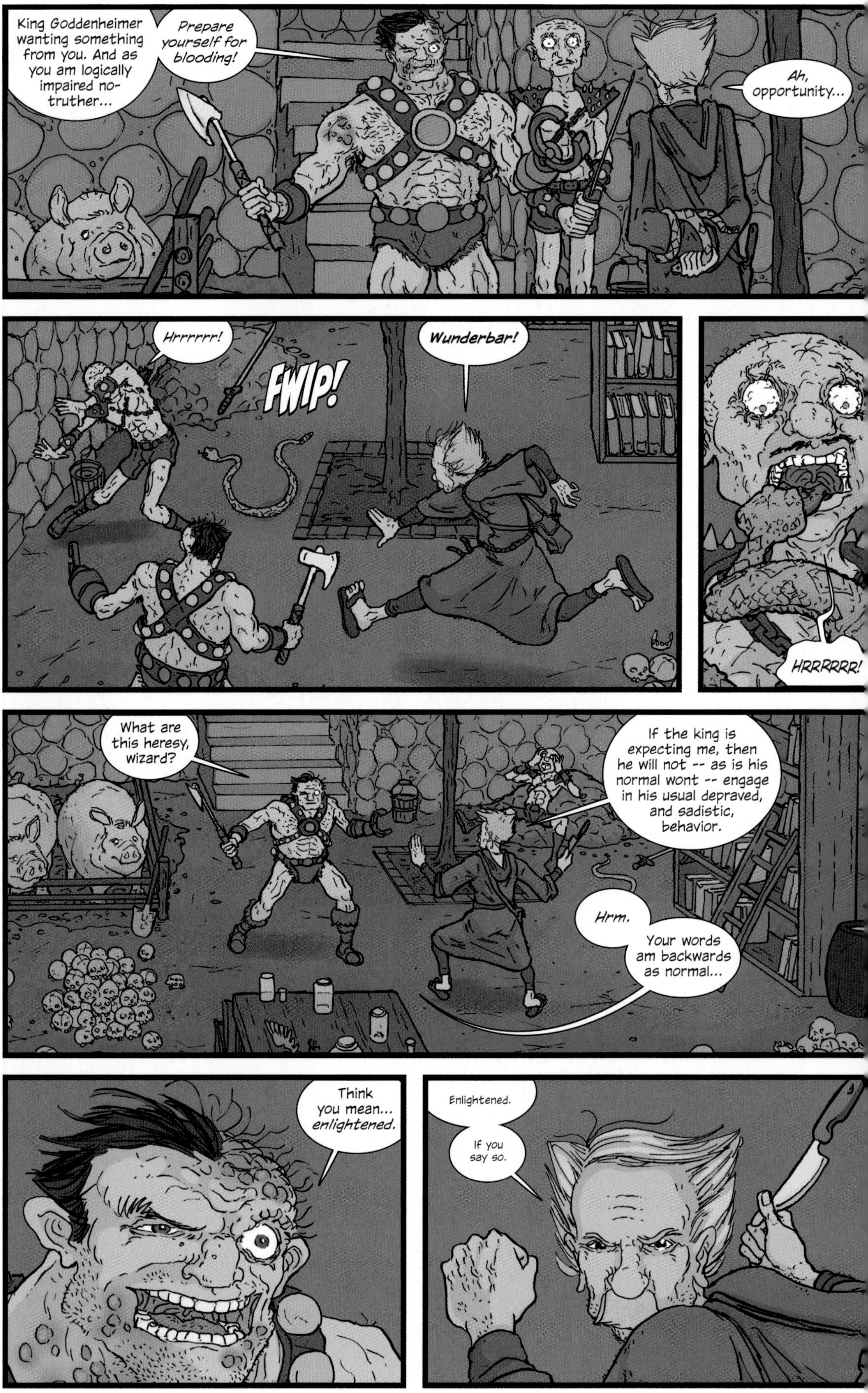
King Goddenheimer wanting something from you. And as you am logically impaired no-truther...
Prepare yourself for blooding!
Ah, opportunity...
Hrrrrrr!
FWIP!
Wunderbar!
HRRRRRR!
What are this heresy, wizard?
If the king is expecting me, then he will not -- as is his normal wont -- engage in his usual depraved, and sadistic, behavior.
Hrm.
Your words am backwards as normal...
Think you mean... enlightened.
Enlightened.
If you say so.

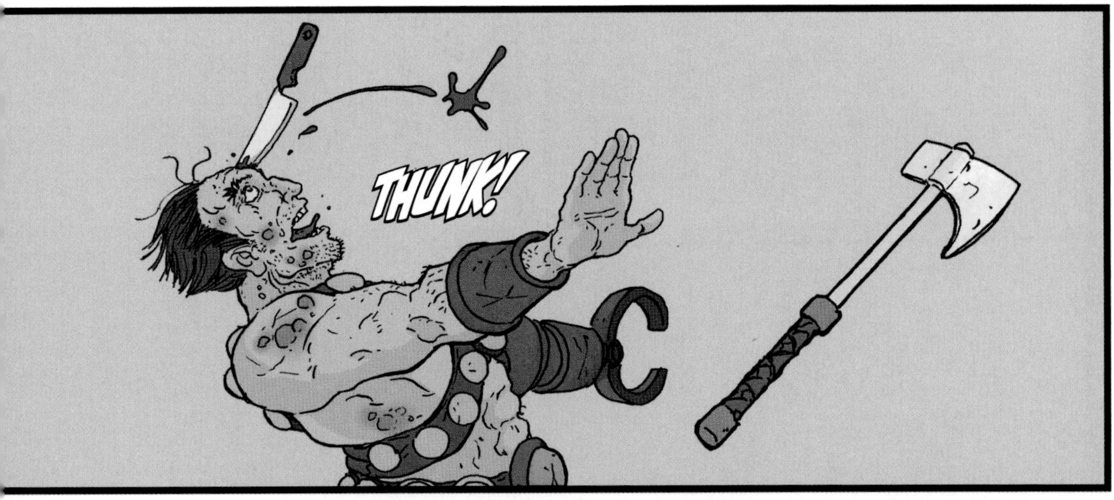
THUNK!

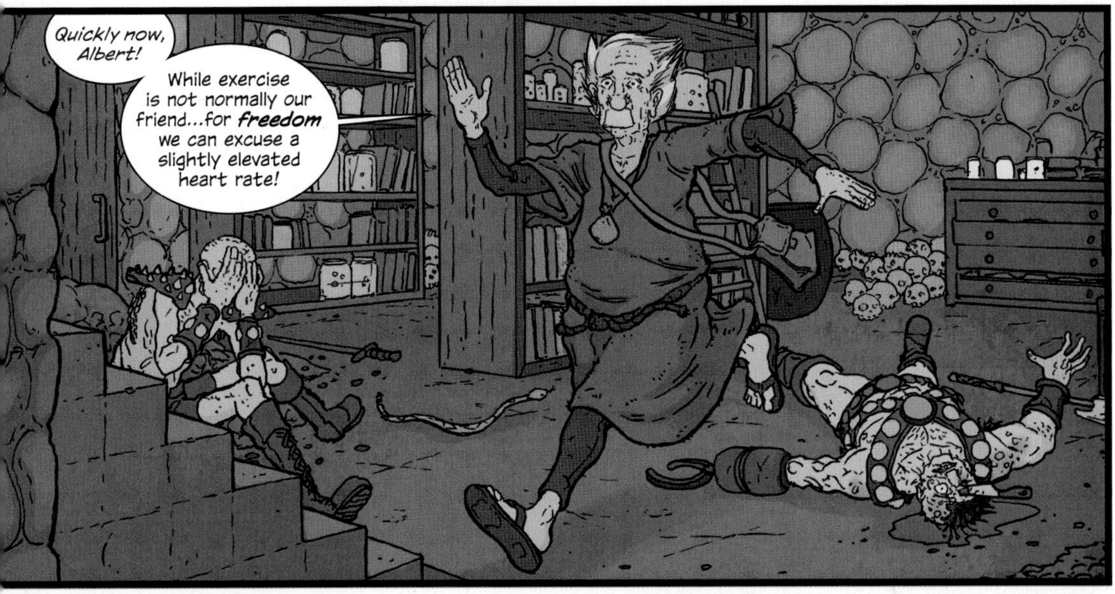
Quickly now, Albert!
While exercise is not normally our friend...for *freedom* we can excuse a slightly elevated heart rate!

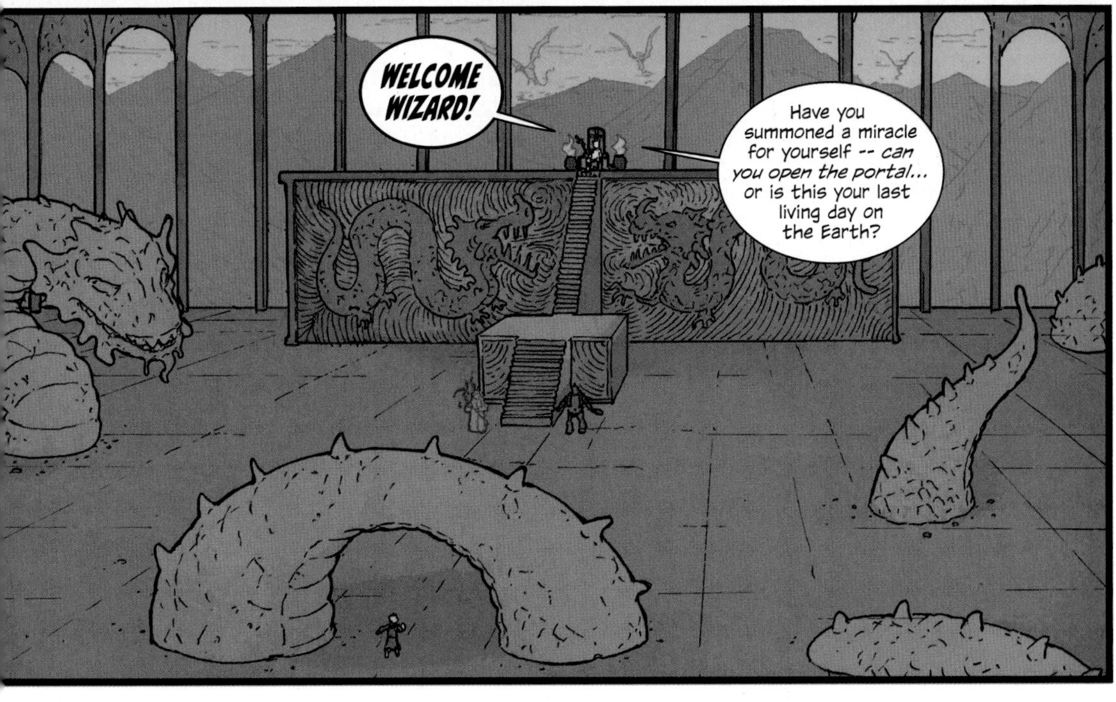
WELCOME WIZARD!
Have you summoned a miracle for yourself -- *can you open the portal...* or is this your last living day on the Earth?

Executioner. Seer.

I believe the King desires an audience.

Ansssswer hisss quesssstion first, heretic.

Yes. *I can.*

Ohhhhh. Tinkle. Tinkle.

I see my death.

Science damn you, Wizard!

What is the meaning of this?

I'm going home, you bastard.

Tinkle. Tinkle. Slippery steps.

You're going to do no such thing, Wizard.

Haven't you learned by now...*I won't allow it.*

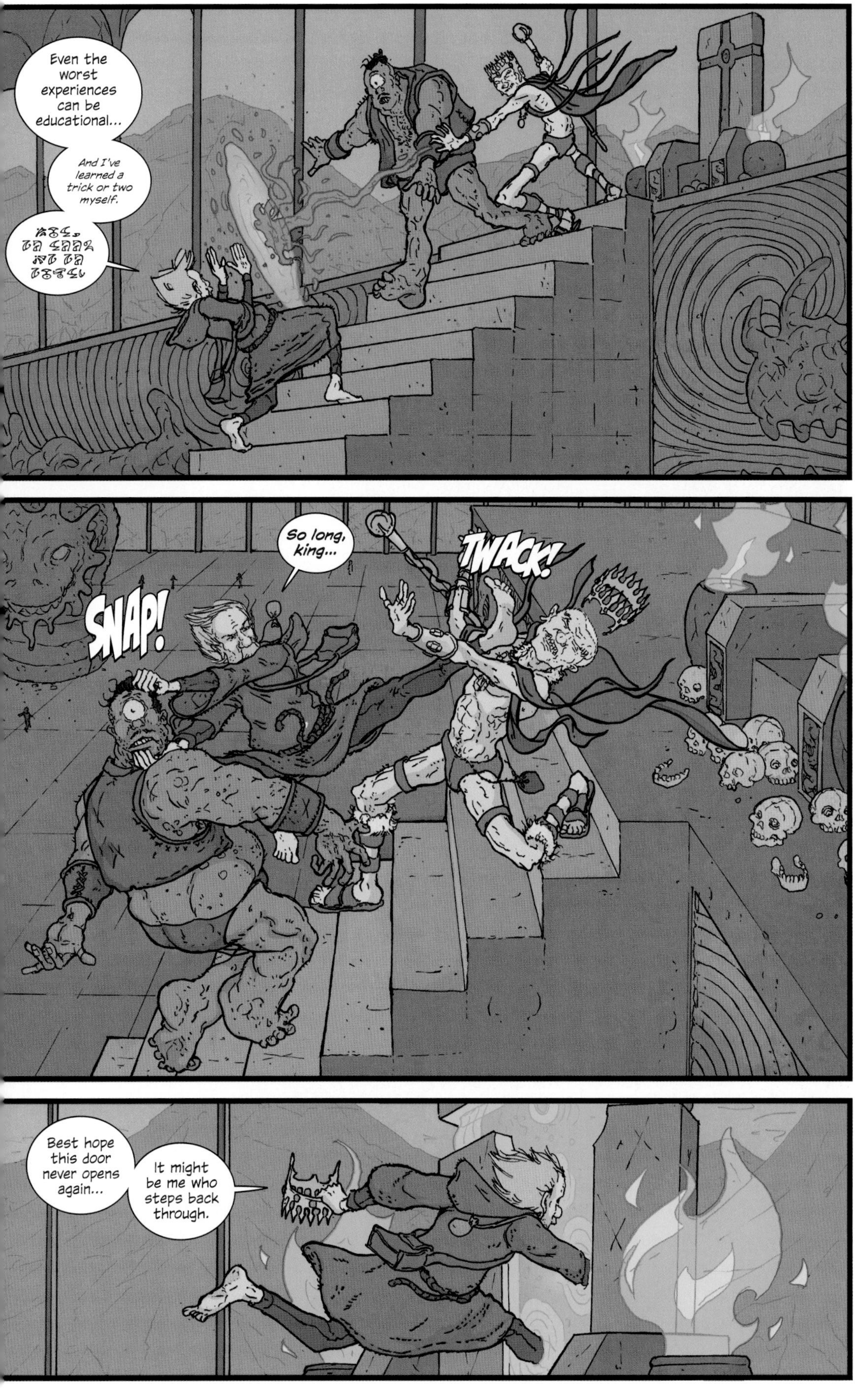
Even the worst experiences can be educational...
And I've learned a trick or two myself.
So long, king...
SNAP!
TWACK!
Best hope this door never opens again...
It might be me who steps back through.

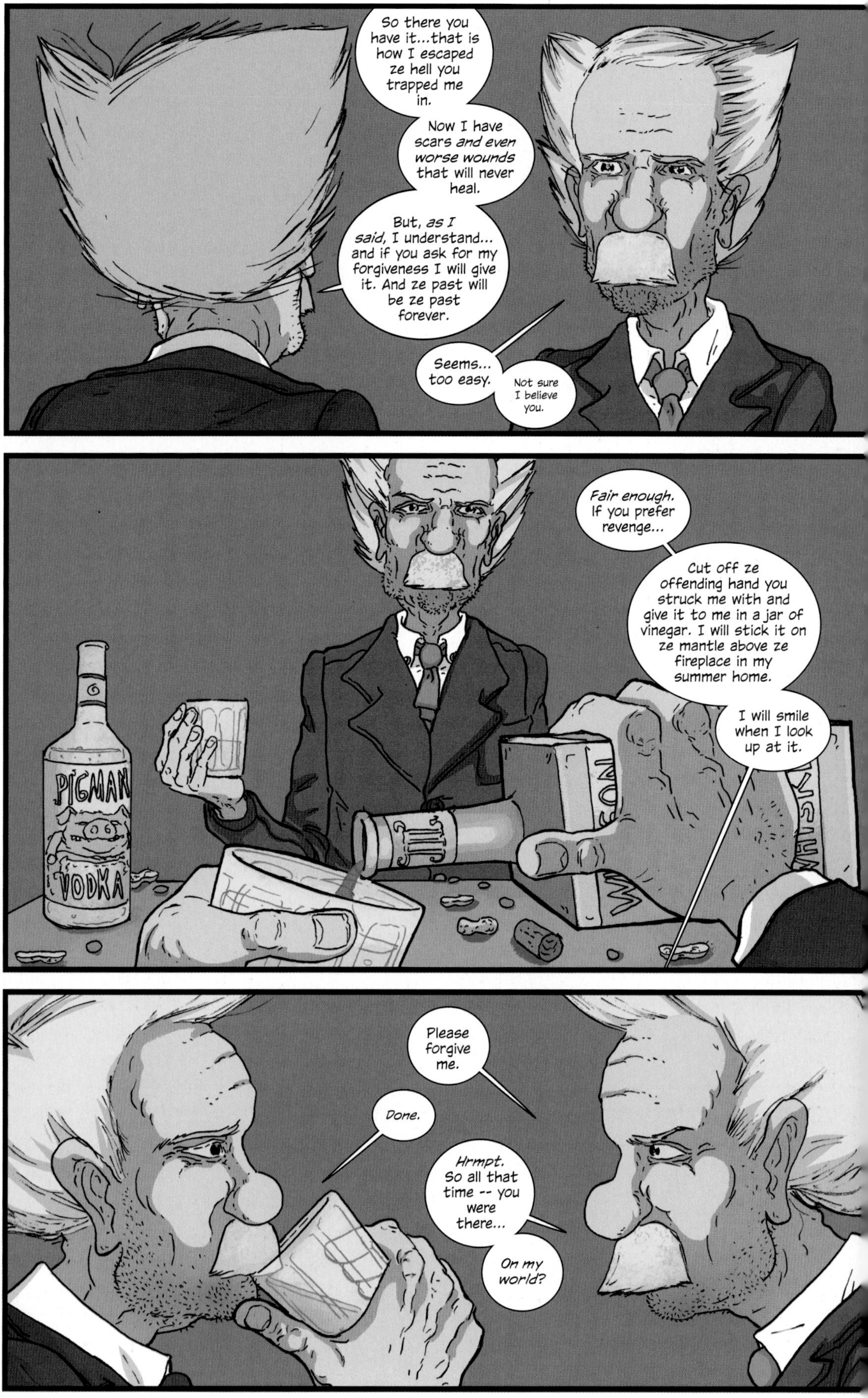
So there you have it...that is how I escaped ze hell you trapped me in.
Now I have scars *and even worse wounds* that will never heal.
But, *as I said,* I understand... and if you ask for my forgiveness I will give it. And ze past will be ze past forever.
Seems... too easy.
Not sure I believe you.
Fair enough. If you prefer revenge...
Cut off ze offending hand you struck me with and give it to me in a jar of vinegar. I will stick it on ze mantle above ze fireplace in my summer home.
I will smile when I look up at it.
PIGMAN VODKA
Please forgive me.
Done.
Hrmpt. So all that time -- you were there...
On my world?

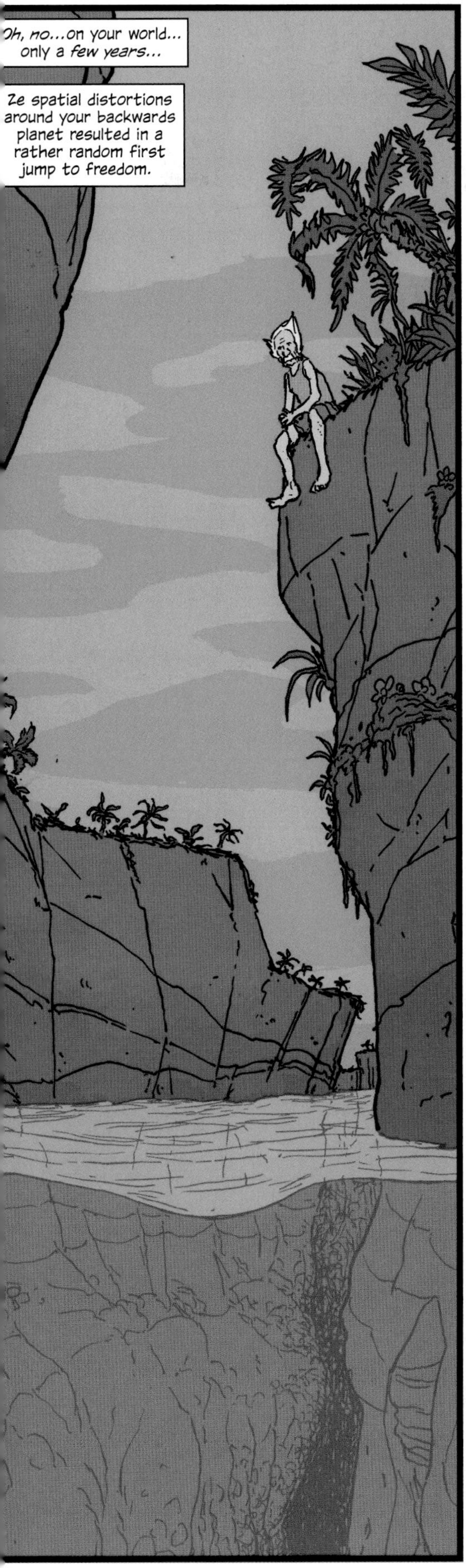
Oh, no...on your world... only a *few years...*
Ze spatial distortions around your backwards planet resulted in a rather random first jump to freedom.

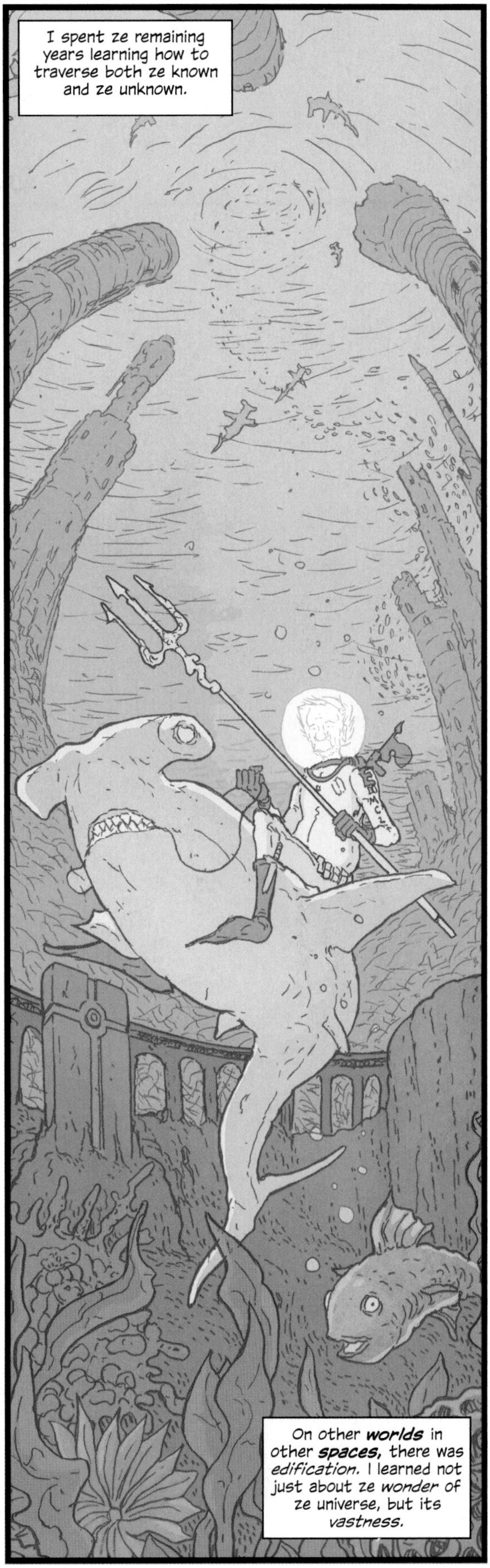
I spent ze remaining years learning how to traverse both ze known and ze unknown.
On other ***worlds*** in other ***spaces,*** there was *edification.* I learned not just about ze *wonder* of ze universe, but its *vastness.*

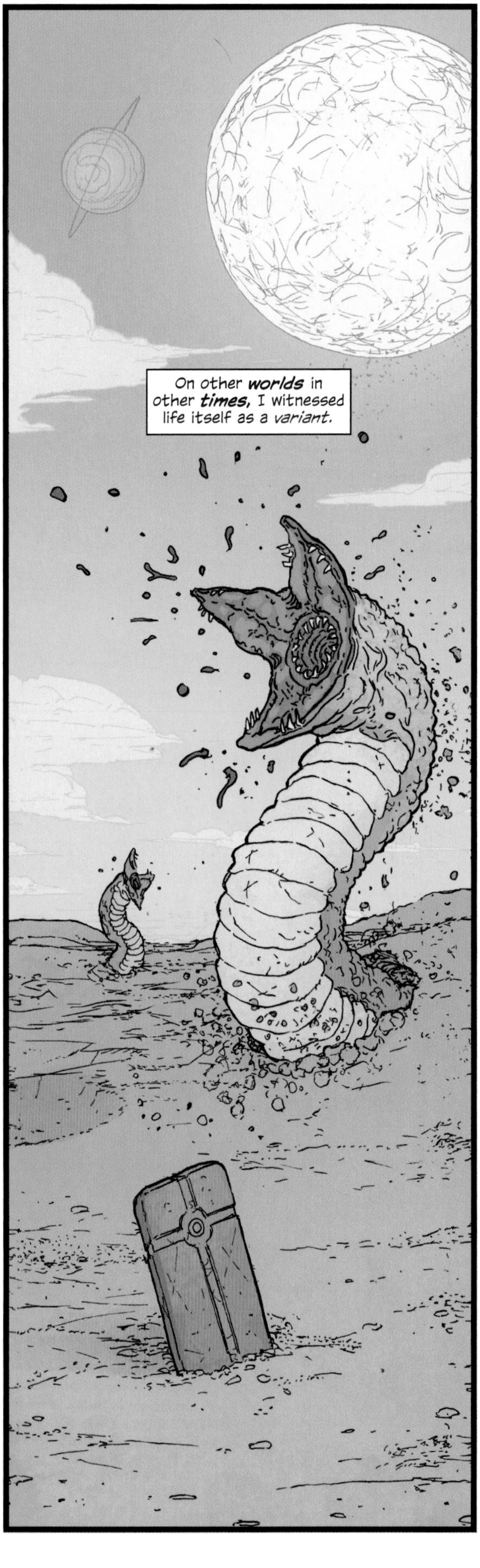
On other *worlds* in other *times,* I witnessed life itself as a *variant.*

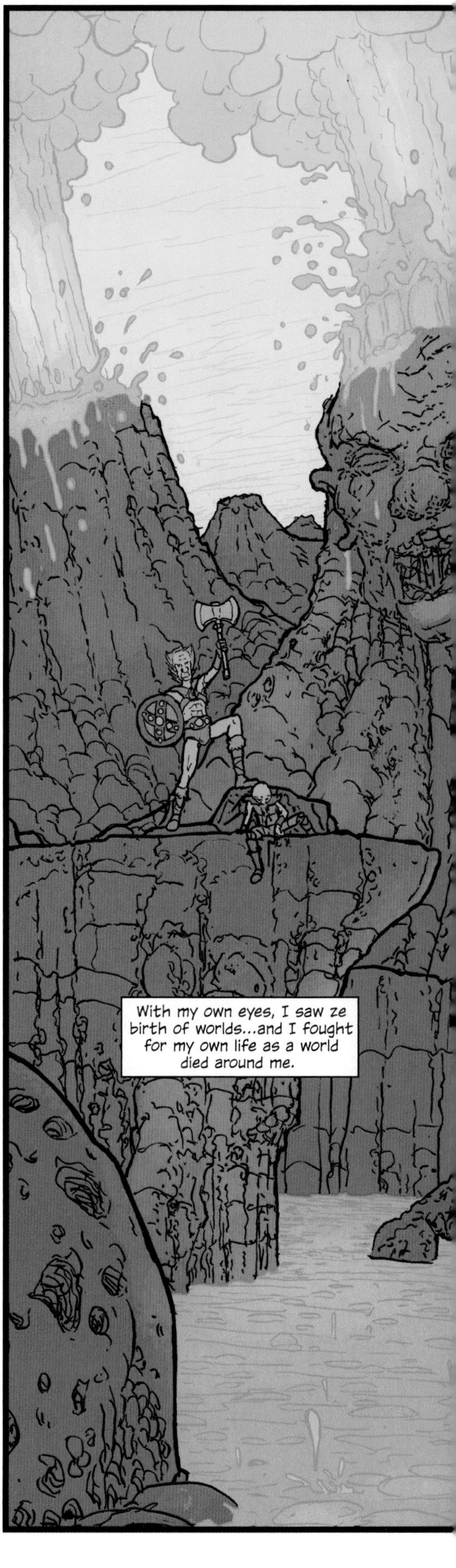
With my own eyes, I saw ze birth of worlds...and I fought for my own life as a world died around me.

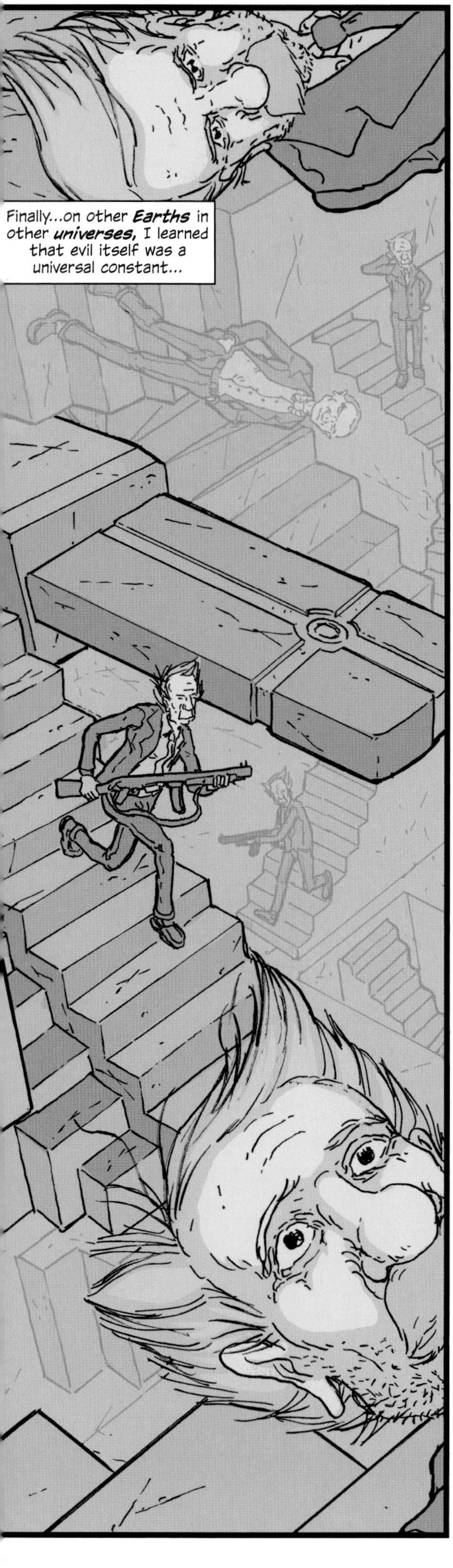
Finally...on other *Earths* in other *universes,* I learned that evil itself was a universal constant...

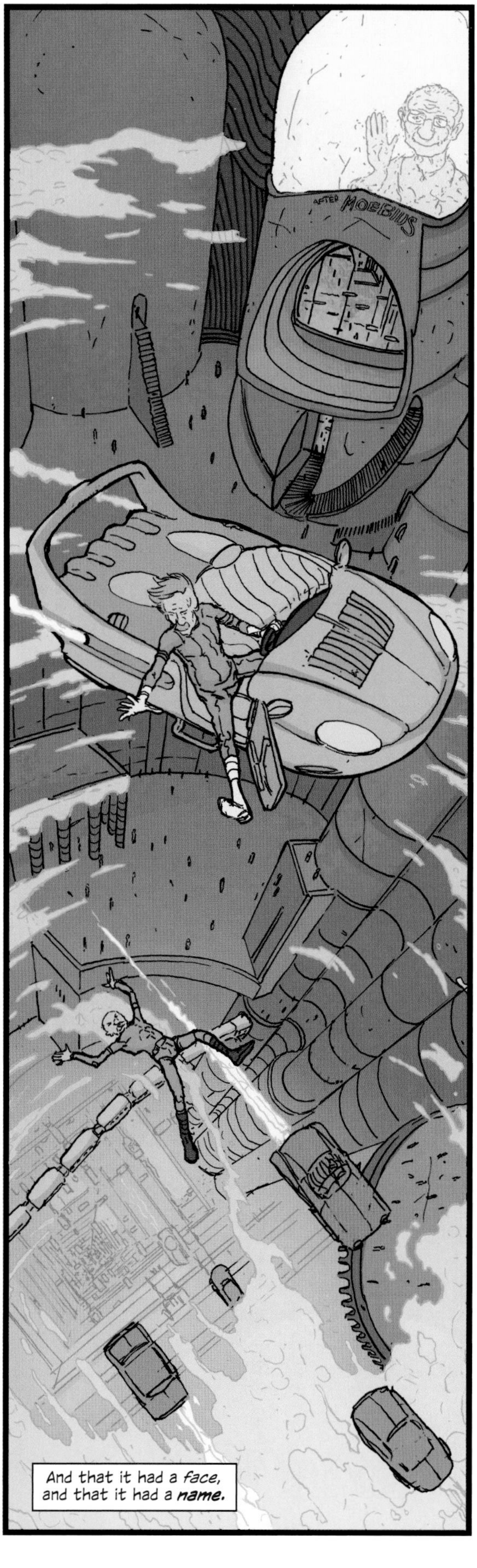
AFTER MOEBIUS
And that it had a *face,* and that it had a *name.*

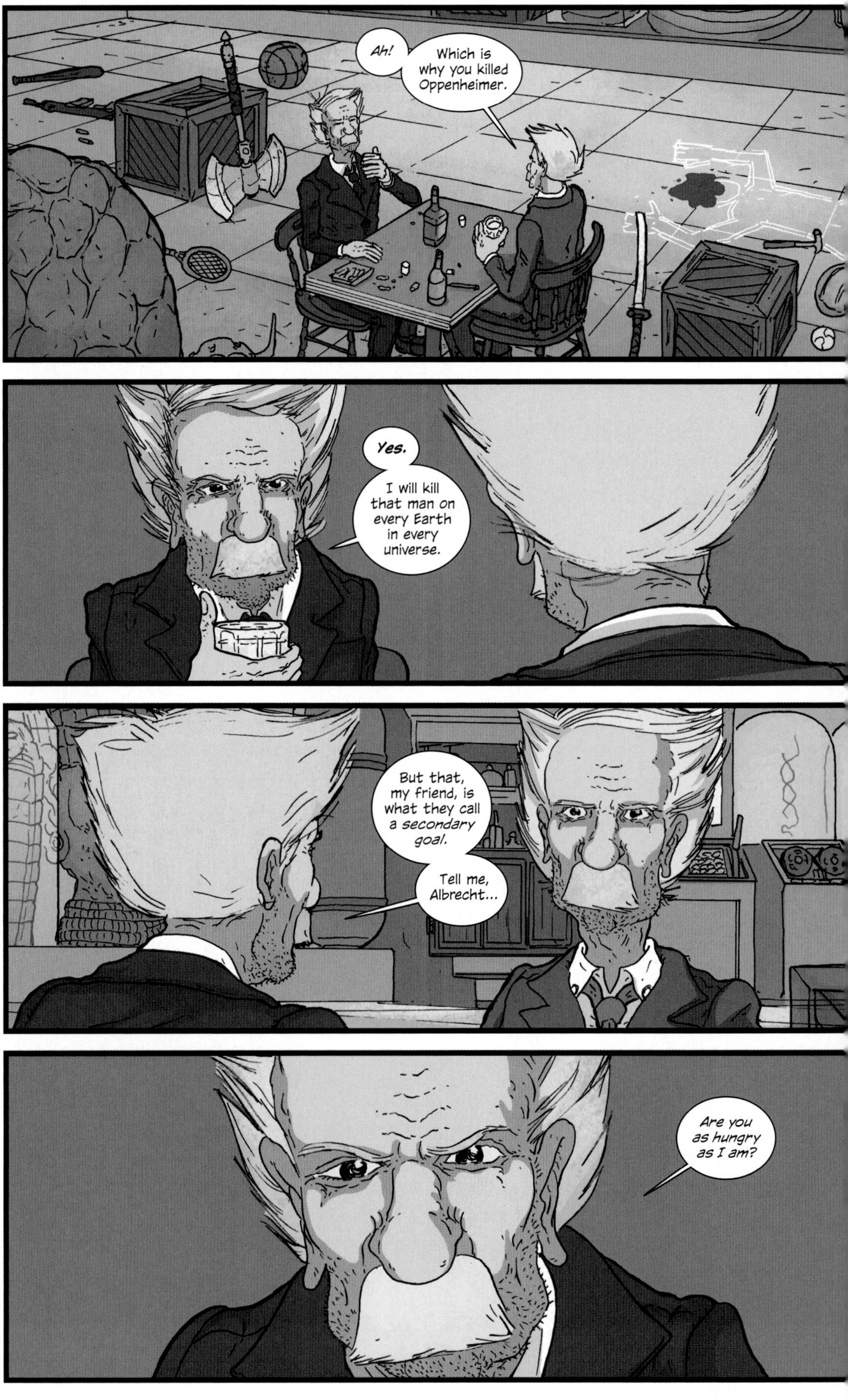
Ah!
Which is why you killed Oppenheimer.
Yes.
I will kill that man on every Earth in every universe.
But that, my friend, is what they call a *secondary* goal.
Tell me, Albrecht...
Are you as hungry as I am?

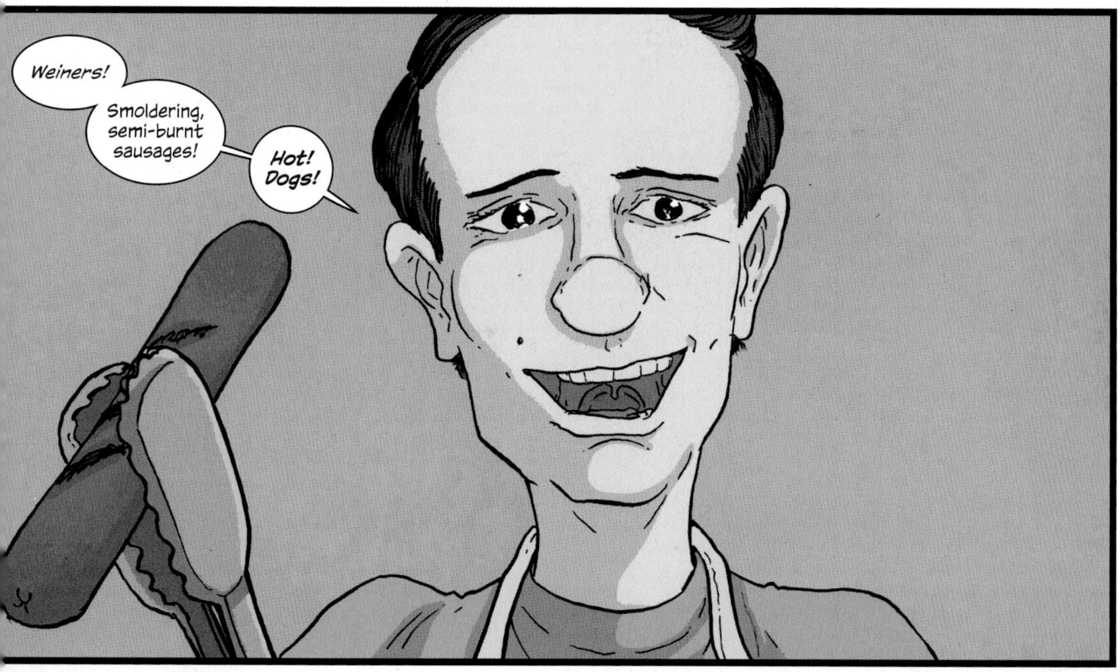
Weiners!
Smoldering, semi-burnt sausages!
Hot! Dogs!

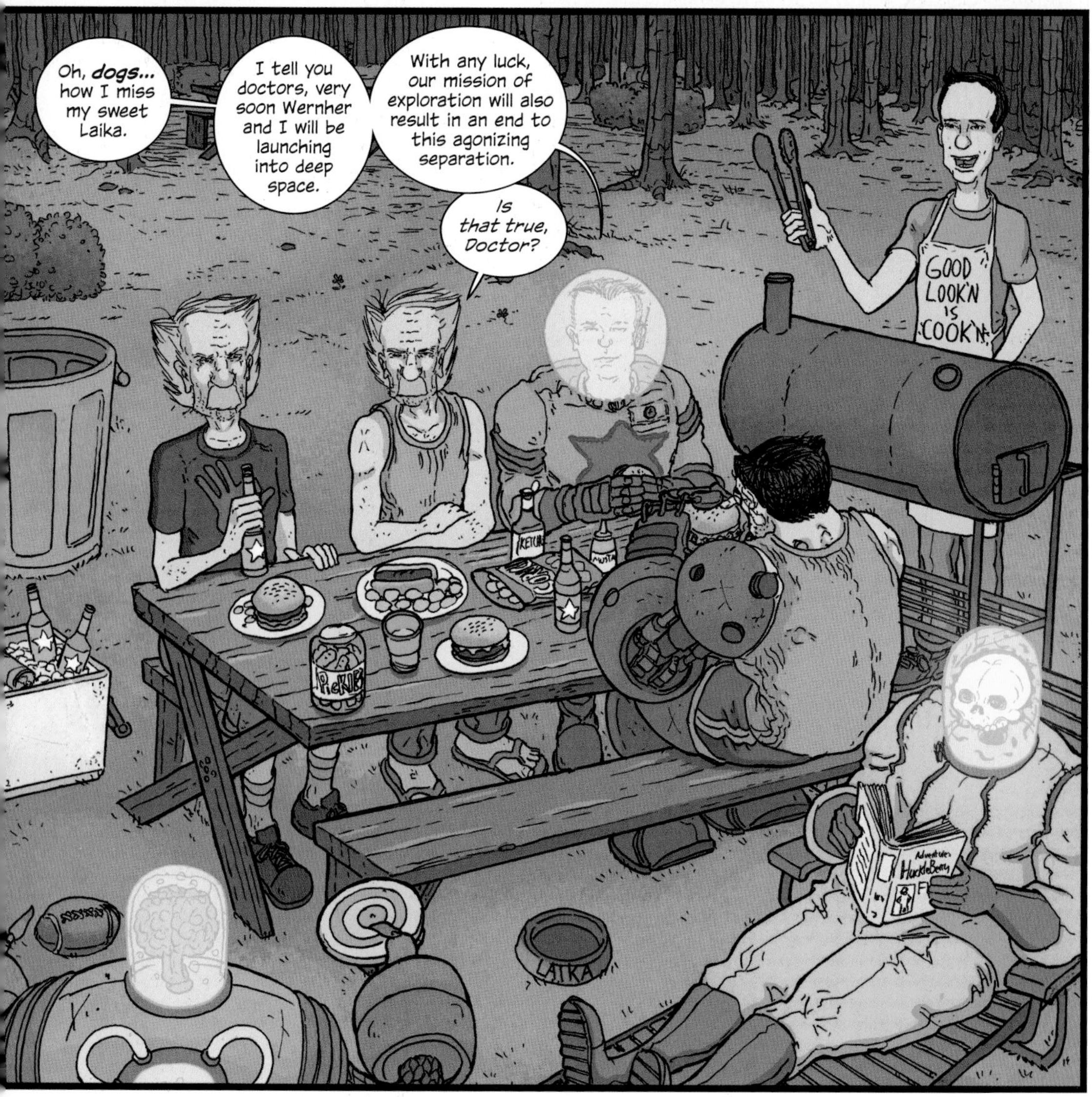
Oh, dogs... how I miss my sweet Laika.
I tell you doctors, very soon Wernher and I will be launching into deep space.
With any luck, our mission of exploration will also result in an end to this agonizing separation.
Is that true, Doctor?
GOOD LOOK'N IS COOK'N
LAIKA

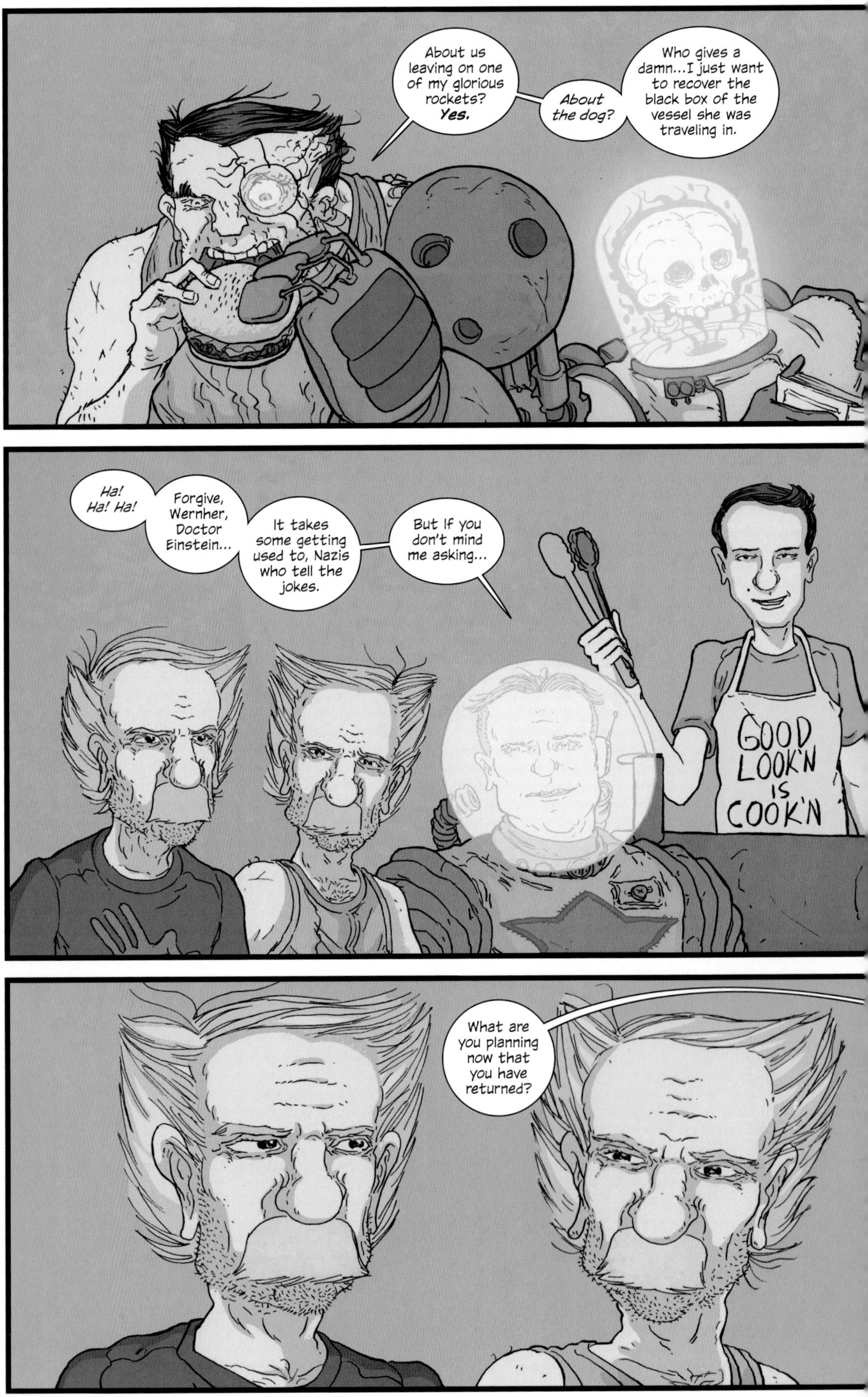

About us leaving on one of my glorious rockets? *Yes.*
About the dog?
Who gives a damn...I just want to recover the black box of the vessel she was traveling in.
Ha! Ha! Ha!
Forgive, Wernher, Doctor Einstein...
It takes some getting used to, Nazis who tell the jokes.
But If you don't mind me asking...
GOOD LOOK'N IS COOK'N
What are you planning now that you have returned?

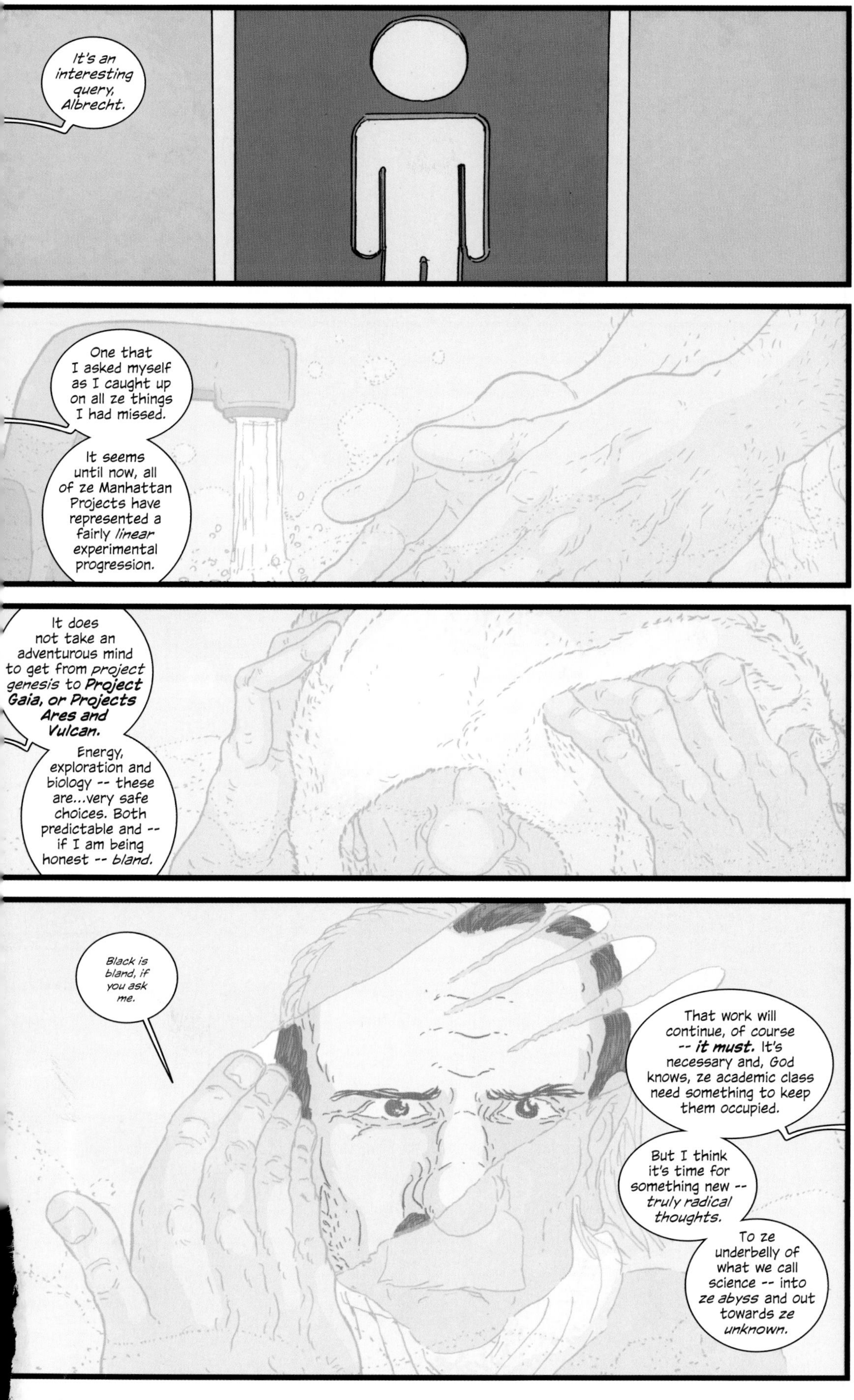
It's an interesting query, Albrecht.
One that I asked myself as I caught up on all ze things I had missed.
It seems until now, all of ze Manhattan Projects have represented a fairly *linear* experimental progression.
It does not take an adventurous mind to get from *project genesis* to ***Project Gaia, or Projects Ares and Vulcan.***
Energy, exploration and biology -- these are...very safe choices. Both predictable and -- if I am being honest -- *bland.*
Black is bland, if you ask me.
That work will continue, of course -- ***it must.*** It's necessary and, God knows, ze academic class need something to keep them occupied.
But I think it's time for something new -- *truly radical thoughts.*
To ze underbelly of what we call science -- into *ze abyss* and out towards ze *unknown.*

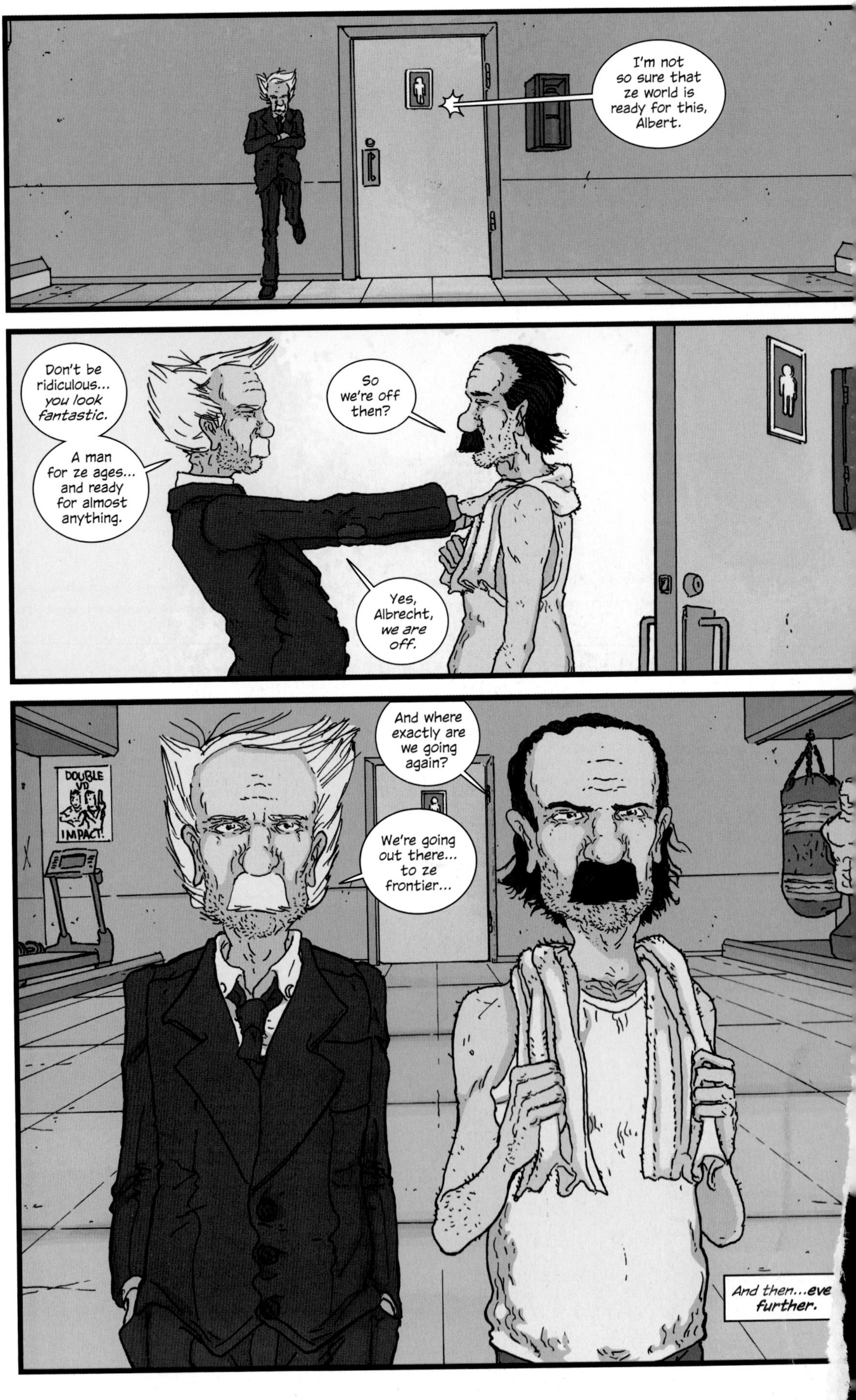
I'm not so sure that ze world is ready for this, Albert.
Don't be ridiculous... *you look fantastic.*
So we're off then?
A man for ze ages... and ready for almost anything.
Yes, Albrecht, *we are off.*
DOUBLE VD IMPACT!
And where exactly are we going again?
We're going out there... to ze frontier...
And then...eve ***further.***